ALSO BY ZACHARY KARABELL

Peace Be Upon You: The Story of Muslim, Christian, and Jewish Coexistence

Chester Alan Arthur

Parting the Desert: The Creation of the Suez Canal

Kennedy, Johnson, and the Quest for Justice: The Civil Rights Tapes (with Jonathan Rosenberg)

The Generation of Trust: Public Confidence in the U.S. Military since Vietnam (with David King)

A Visionary Nation: Four Centuries of American Dreams and What Lies Ahead

The Last Campaign: How Harry Truman Won the 1948 Election

Architects of Intervention: The United States, the Third World, and the Cold War

What's College For? The Struggle to Define American Higher Education

Super

How China and America Became

One Economy and Why the World's

Prosperity Depends on It

fusion

~

Zachary Karabell

Simon & Schuster

NEW YORK   LONDON   TORONTO   SYDNEY

Simon & Schuster
1230 Avenue of the Americas
New York, NY 10020

First Simon & Schuster hardcover edition October 2009

SIMON & SCHUSTER and colophon are registered trademarks
of Simon & Schuster, Inc.

For information about special discounts for bulk purchases,
please contact Simon & Schuster Special Sales at
1-866-506-1949 or business@simonandschuster.com.

The Simon & Schuster Speakers Bureau can bring authors to your
live event. For more information or to book an event contact the
Simon & Schuster Speakers Bureau at 1-866-248-3049
or visit our website at www.simonspeakers.com.

Designed by Paul Dippolito

Manufactured in the United States of America

10 9 8 7 6 5 4 3 2

Library of Congress Cataloging-in-Publication Data
Karabell, Zachary.
Superfusion : how China and America became one economy and why the
world's prosperity depends on it / Zachary Karabell.
    p. cm.
    Includes bibliographic references.
1. United States—Foreign economic relations—China. 2. China—Foreign
economic relations—United States. 3. International economic relations.
I. Title.
HF1456.5.C6K37   2009
337.73051—dc22   2009023717

ISBN 978-1-4165-8370-7
ISBN 978-1-4165-8404-9 (ebook)

Contents

Superfusion

Introduction: Superfusion

THIS IS A BOOK about how two countries became one
economy. It is about how the fusion of the two most powerful economies in the world today is upending conventional
wisdom and reshaping the global system. In the wake of the financial crisis that erupted in 2008, the fusion of China and the
United States has become even more vital to the prosperity not
just of hundreds of millions of Americans and more than a billion Chinese but for everyone everywhere. As the world emerges
from that crisis and turns to the future, how China and the
United States manage their relationship will determine whether
the coming decades hold increased global prosperity or fractious,
unstable growth with sharp divides between winners and losers.

In the first months of 2009, the U.S. government authorized
more than $1 trillion of spending and tax cuts in order to jump-
start a moribund economy. The spending attracted considerable
attention, but the funding did not. Also in those first months,
the U.S. Treasury auctioned off hundreds of billions of dollars of
new bonds in order to underwrite the various stimulus bills. Like
all such auctions, they took place quietly, barely rating a notice
in the media. But the absence of attention did not make what
happened any less important. The primary buyer was not Americans; U.S. corporations were cash strapped, and consumers were
too busy paying down their own debts to lend the government
money. No, the most important buyer in 2009 was the same as

the primary buyer in 2008, when the global credit system began to implode, and in 2007, when clouds were gathering but the storm seemed distant. That buyer, of course, was China.

In the aftermath of the near-meltdown of the global financial system that shook the world in 2008 and reverberated into 2009, the unique relationship between China and the United States has become the axis of the world economy. It is a relationship that has seen China become the largest creditor of a United States in acute need of funds to repair the damage from the credit and housing bubble. But the relationship is more complex and layered than that. China's lending and the United States' spending make up one facet of a kaleidoscopic interaction that has allowed American companies to reinvent themselves selling to Chinese consumers; has led U.S. factories to thrive because of demand from Chinese buyers; and has shaped everything from interest rates to inflation to the global balance of power in unexpected and unpredictable ways.

Today's economic upheavals, as severe as they are, would have been much worse were it not for the interdependence of the Chinese and U.S. economies. For all the concern about the imbalances of trade, when the Wall Street implosion threatened to bring down the financial system, the presence of trillions of surplus dollars in China provided a vital bulwark. There have been many meltdowns at various points in history; there have been economic disruptions in the United States at regular intervals since the founding of the country. But the present is marked by the symbiosis of the world's two most important economies. They are the superpowers of the global economic system, and their fusion is therefore a superfusion. Understanding that is essential to gauging not just what lies ahead but how to navigate the present.

For much of the first decade of the new millennium, the United States focused on the challenge posed by terrorism, on the wars in Iraq and Afghanistan, and on the rumbling tensions between parts of the Muslim world and the West. The emergence of China as an economic force was certainly noticed, but not with the level of urgency commensurate with its importance. Yet the rise of China—and how that is managed—is the fulcrum of the future, not just for China and the United States but for the global system. While terrorism may continue to be a challenge to societies everywhere, the relationship between China and the United States is the crucial issue for the twenty-first century. The stakes are dollars and cents rather than blood and guts, but that relationship will likely shape the lives of the average worker in Ohio or Shenzhen more than what happens to al-Qaeda in the mountains of Pakistan.

Recent economic travails have triggered intensive questioning of the financial system that was created by the United States and warped by Wall Street. That has led many to reconsider America's place in the world and wonder whether this is indeed the twilight of American power. Yet what remains largely unchallenged is the assumption that the world remains a collection of nations, markets, and companies. For much of the twentieth century, that made sense. No longer. What is perceived as the rise of China is actually much more than that. The most important story is one that has yet to be explicitly told, largely because most don't yet recognize what has taken place. In short, over the past two decades, China and the United States have become one intertwined, integrated hypereconomy: *Chimerica*.[1]

There is little precedence for this system. The only thing comparable is the European Union (EU). The difference is that the European Union was the result of the deliberate efforts of generations of leaders. Chimerica, however, has developed without anyone ever deciding on it. It has happened not because of, but in spite of, the policies of both the Chinese and American governments, and judging from public attitudes in both countries, it has occurred against the wishes of many millions whose lives are being reshaped by it. In short, Chimerica is hiding in plain sight, unrecognized, unacknowledged, and unwanted.

Whether desired or not, the economic fusion of China and America is transforming the landscape. Little of what has happened economically in the past decade makes much sense; expected outcomes have not materialized; and almost no one can claim to have accurately gauged what is going on. The financial carnage of 2008 led many to take a hard look at the forecasting tools and models that allowed for the credit bubble, but it wasn't just quantitative models that were wrong; so too were basic tenets of how we think our economic system functions. And yet, governments—especially governments of powerful and prosperous countries—continue to behave as if they have sovereignty over their domestic economies even as the measures they take are increasingly dependent on forces beyond their control. The United States could not have unrolled a multitrillion-dollar stimulus package without China's willingness to fund those outlays. China in turn would not have a surplus had it not sold so heavily to American consumers and learned so much from American and multinational companies doing business in China over the past 20 years.

This book will trace how Chimerica came to be. It will chart how two diametrically opposed countries became enmeshed in the 1990s and then fused in the first decade of the twenty-first century. It is a story that began almost exactly 20 years ago, with an event that seemed like an end but was actually a beginning: Tiananmen Square, Beijing, 1989. One million people, many of them students, had camped out in the central square of Beijing. Zhao Ziyang was then the general secretary of the Communist Party. Just before dawn on May 19, he went out to the protestors of Tiananmen, accompanied by his chief of staff, Wen Jiabao, who was to become premier in 2003. He was greeted with respect and enthusiasm, but he didn't succeed in convincing the students to disband. "You have good intentions," Zhao told them. "You want our country to become better. The problems you have raised will eventually be resolved. But things are complicated, and there must be a process to resolve these problems."

Within days, Zhao was purged and placed under house arrest. Hard-liners declared martial law and moved troops from the provinces into the heart of the capital. Finally, on June 4, the army moved to clear the vast square. The result was violent, and the end was quick. Thousands were killed, and many more arrested, wounded, and exiled. One image came to define that day: a static, poetic, haunting picture of a lone man, standing in front of a tank, holding up his hands, asking why and imploring it to stop. The image of the "Tank Man" was hailed as a heroic symbol of defiance and courage. But it was only one story from that day, and ultimately less important than what happened behind the scenes, in the shrouded corridors of power, where the octogenarian chain-smoker Deng Xiaoping and the elders of the Chinese Communist Party turned the Tiananmen movement into a gossamer thread: bright, shiny, and then gone.

Deng and others were willing to break the protestors, and they did. The excoriations of the international community must have been irritating, but they were just words. Countless foreign eulogies pronounced the death of reform in China and the end of a brief experiment in openness to new ideas and to the world outside that had characterized much of Deng's decade in power. In the words of the *Times* of London, "this weekend's vicious massacre has earned China's leadership the fear and contempt of its own people and pariah status in the world." But while Tiananmen seemed like the end of something, things were not as they seemed. After 1989, Deng was more determined than ever to accelerate the modernization of the Chinese economy. His message to the country was simple: you can have economic prosperity, but do not challenge the primacy of the Chinese Communist Party. He believed that political openness would create either a Soviet scenario of collapse, or, worse, a repeat of the chaos that had plagued China during the first half of the twentieth century. He saw in economic development a perfect path, a middle way between moribund Maoism and unchecked liberal democracy.

The image of the Tank Man may have left an indelible impression outside of China, but inside China, the image that came to matter more was banal, even crass. It wasn't the picture of a lone soul standing against oppression. It was, of all things, the image of Colonel Sanders, the benevolent, smiling face of Kentucky Fried Chicken.

In the immediate aftermath of the iron-fisted suppression of the movement, the stores around Tiananmen Square were shuttered. There was one exception: the vast Kentucky Fried Chicken outlet at the southern end of the square near Mao's tomb. Within a week, KFC was open for business. The restaurant that had done a booming business among the students a few weeks before now catered to soldiers. Having just crushed a Western-leaning democracy movement, the soldiers happily sat down under the shadow of the Colonel and enjoyed the fruits of Western capitalism and democracy.

In the two decades between 1989 and 2009, Colonel Sanders shaped China more than the Tank Man. Kentucky Fried Chicken arrived in China in the late 1980s and quickly became one of the most popular and widely recognized brands in the country. It wasn't really about the food. It was about aspiration and dreams. American fried chicken came to represent for millions of Chinese the embrace of the market and the global economy, a finger-licking promise of wealth and prosperity. The end of the protest movement in the blood of Tiananmen meant that political reform and economic reform, so intimately entwined in Western history and consciousness, would be decoupled in China. It meant that the future of China would be determined by economic openness, not political participation, and that dollars and not democracy would shape society.

Companies like Kentucky Fried Chicken did more than remake themselves in China; they also transformed Chinese society and the global economic system. That is the unwritten story of the past 20 years. Multinationals and the Communist Party of China should have been strange bedfellows, but much of history is the product of odd and unexpected alliances. As companies such as Procter & Gamble, Kentucky Fried Chicken, Avon, Nike, General Electric, Siemens, and IBM went to China in the late 1980s and 1990s, they constructed a new international system of trade, production, and capital flows. Yes, China produced cheap retail goods, and the United States and Europe consumed them. Less noticed but equally important was that China itself became a voracious consumer not only of imported goods and services but above all, knowledge.

Everywhere, there is deep discomfort with what this system has done to the world. In the United States and Europe, China has been blamed as the cause of job loss. Then the implosion of the U.S. economy in 2008 and into 2009 cast into sharp relief just how much America's economic sovereignty had been eroded and how much China's economic power had increased. In China itself, attitudes are more optimistic, yet the events of the past two years also shook China's leadership and led to questions about the wisdom of closer integration with the West and with the United States.

Even as they speak of interdependence as a fact, Chinese and Americans continue to see themselves locked in a great power rivalry. Chinese leaders in 2009 did not disguise their blame of

Wall Street as the cause of the economic crisis, yet they rarely took full responsibility for their role in shaping the global economy. American leaders have their own blind spots. In its annual assessment of global threats, the U.S. intelligence community in 2008 emphasized China's rising power and its potential to use its economic leverage for political aims, and the Pentagon in early 2009 warned that China was seeking new weapons to counter the U.S. military in the Pacific Rim.

These old ways of approaching the world—these us-versus-them dyads—are not just benign anachronisms. Clinging to them can and will have serious consequences, most of them negative. The current global economic system is unlike anything the world has known before. National economic data do not capture the mutual interdependence and exaggerate the quaint, and false, idea that each country is its own economic island. The longer we cling to old theories and past precedents, the longer it will take to grasp what is going on. The fusion of China and America is more important to divining what the future holds than most of the economic and political theories that have guided governments, academics, and business leaders over the past century.

The path ahead offers at least two possibilities. Either America—and to some extent Europe as well—works with China to refine and develop this system to our mutual benefit, or we fall back on old binary concepts that see every gain for "them" as a decline for "us." For the United States, if we choose to embrace our interdependence with China, we stand a chance of not only working through our current challenges and retaining our prosperity but enhancing it meaningfully in the decades ahead. While that may mean a shift in the relative position of the United States in the world, the benefits will far outweigh the costs.

As of now, however, the United States has a "China problem."

It is not, as commonly assumed, a problem with the challenges of China as a rising economy. It is a problem with the very fact of China as a force to be reckoned with. For a half century, the United States fought for the creation of a global capitalist system. Now that one exists, however, Americans seem to have forgotten one little thing: capitalism means risk and sometimes chaos, and the global position of the United States is not a birthright.

The fundamental question for the United States is whether to accept or resist the fusion with China and all that it entails. While the election of Barack Obama signifies a return of a more pragmatic approach to the world and a wiser recognition of the limits of both economic and military power, many Americans remain locked in a mentality that sees the United States as a nation that can remain powerful only by being more powerful than everyone else. The likely outcome? Rather than recognizing that this old framework is flawed, Americans remain wedded to it, and contest the rise of China every step of the way. The outcome will not be good. Rather than hobbling China, the United States may end up hobbling itself. In response, China will forge partnerships with others in the world who are more willing, including—oddly enough—U.S. corporations that will then become even less tied to the United States and in time become American only in name, and perhaps not even that. In trying to prevent China from assuming its place at the table, we instead evict ourselves.

Because companies have been the most obvious beneficiaries of this superfusion, it has been easy to portray this emerging system as simply one more example of the way that capitalism and corporations satisfy the interests of the few and fail to enrich the many. Witness the populist anger at Wall Street and avaricious companies that generated obscene, and illusory, profits while the vast majority of everyday people saw their incomes pressured and their purchasing power eroded. Then, to add to the insult, these companies proved to be not just venal but incompetent, and placed the entire financial system in jeopardy.

There can be no argument that U.S. companies reaped extraordinary profits from the growth of China. For more than five years, I ran an investment fund that focused on American, Chinese, and multinational companies whose growth was being fueled by China. And for nearly seven years, I helped run an asset management firm in New York. Before that, I spent many years as an academic, writing, studying, and teaching about international relations, and my perspective stems as much from that experience as from my years on Wall Street. Whether or not the rise of China is desirable, it is a fact. How that is managed, by the Chinese themselves, by the United States, and by other vital actors in the international system, will determine the arc of this century.

It is tempting to impute to Chinese leaders an unusual degree of wisdom and foresight. They seem to have absorbed the lessons of thousands of years of ups and downs, and distilled those experiences into a pragmatic realism that respects the status quo as a necessary barrier against chaos yet admits the necessity of change as the only guarantee of ultimate stability. It is true that Chinese leaders have learned from their past, and from the collapse of the Soviet Union and other Communist nations after 1989. They have been trying to steer an unwieldy society of 1.3 billion souls and to date have succeeded beyond imagining. That success does not negate the substantial challenges, nor should it be an excuse for autocratic abuses and environmental damage. But China has moved hundreds of millions out of poverty, raised living standards, and built, almost from nothing, an industrial economy in the space of a few decades. That is a fact, much like the dawn and human mortality, whether we like it or not.

Yet China is just as prone to view its development in nationalist terms, and to assume some sort of congruence between its national boundaries and its economy. In that sense, it can just as easily fall victim to a prison of old concepts. The Chinese have a fetish for sovereignty and are susceptible to delusions of national grandeur and to an unrealistic sense of their own limitless potential. Their rigid stance on Tibet is one glaring example. The desire for control makes China no different than the Americans, the British, the Romans, and any number of nations past and present. But its rise is occurring in dramatically different circumstances.

Just as the United States will need to recognize that the us-them framework is no longer applicable, so will China need to revise how it sees itself in the world. It cannot rest in its self-conception of being a poor country that is only beginning to join the ranks of the world's leading nations. It is more central to the global system than the statements of its leaders often suggest. China is what it is today because it is part of the hybrid economy of Chimerica. In the spring of 2009, Chinese leaders indicated that they wanted to be less reliant on the U.S. dollar. Fair enough. But they also continued to buy U.S. bonds and to lend America money. The desire for autonomy is at odds with the reality of mutual dependence. The reality of Chimerica has altered China even more than it has changed the United States and the rest of the world. If Chinese leaders do not fully realize that, they too will make unnecessary and perhaps critical mistakes.

Finally, while China and the United States are the primary components of this new system, they are not the only actors. Many European companies are playing their parts in shaping it, and many companies from resource-rich parts of the world—from Latin America to Australia to Russia—have also had their impact. Chimerica is anchored by its two largest elements, but it is a global phenomenon with tentacles everywhere. India has also been charting a unique path that may eventually have as significant an impact on the world as Chimerica currently does, but not yet.

This 20-year period between Tiananmen and the present has given us Chimerica. The question now is: where do we go from here? Already the rumblings of America's decline and China's rise are reaching a certain pitch, as is speculation about the sunset of the West and the dawn of the East. China is capital rich, with $2 trillion in reserves, and the U.S. is capital poor, with mounting debt as it attempts to spend its way out of its self-dug hole. But while the sun may have set on the British Empire, and Rome certainly rose and then fell, the prognosis for the United States or for China is not fated. China's supposed march toward global hegemony may prove much less predictable and the path less straight than history would dictate. If Chimerica has already exploded the familiar, then it would be unwise not to allow that the future will hold a fair share of surprises.

What does seem clear, however, is that standing in the way of change is a fool's errand. America's role in the world, and its place in the global firmament, is shifting—for better, for worse, no one knows—but it is changing. That China is becoming a central actor—well, that too can brook no argument. But the idea that one must fall so that another will rise, or that the future will invariably be one of nation-states with national economies, those are less certain. To the contrary, it would be astonishing if the world in the middle of the twenty-first century looks at all like the world in the middle of the twentieth century, and equally surprising if the frameworks to understand that world are not significantly different.

If someone tried to impose the basic concepts of sixteenth-century European society, with its wars of reformation, the debates over the divine right of kings, and its questions about whether the earth was spherical or flat, on the late twentieth century, the results would be a combination of tragic, absurd, and hilarious. The world we are creating, with change accelerated by technology and occurring at a dizzying pace, will likely be just as different, just as new, and just as surprising. Time and again, people fall victim to the same fallacy of believing that the future will offer similar challenges to the present. We all tend to fight the last war and fail to anticipate the new. Whether this is called the prison of old concepts, the danger of black swans, or simply human inability to grapple with the unknown, it is an ongoing challenge.

Understanding the unique fusion of China and the United States is essential to grasping our world today. How we manage that relationship will determine whether the growth and prosperity of the past 20 years continues or grinds to a halt and whether the interdependence that produced affluence for hundreds of millions of Americans and Chinese and billions of people throughout the world will evolve and generate even more gains in the future. The stakes could not be higher, and if we are to navigate through the challenges of our present, we need a clearer sense of the currents that brought us here. The Chimerica phenomenon isn't old, but it didn't begin yesterday. Before we go forward, we need to take a look back and see where this all began.

CHAPTER 1

Black Cat, White Cat

T HE CONVERGENCE OF CHINA and the United States
began when the two were worlds apart. There was nothing inevitable about what took place. It didn't have to happen,
yet it did.

At the end of the 1970s, few societies were more distinct and
distant. China was a predominantly agricultural nation mired
in poverty and cut off from the world after the excesses of the
dictatorship of Chairman Mao. By the 1970s, trade accounted
for only 5 percent of China's gross domestic product, an astonishing low figure for a country of China's size and scale. In
fact, China in the waning years of Mao had become significantly
more isolated and detached from the international system than
it had been either before the Communist victory in 1949 or
during the initial years of the revolution in the 1950s.

The United States, by contrast, was the dominant power
in the world in the late 1970s, even though its self-perception
was mired in malaise and doubt. The experience of the Vietnam War, the stagflation of the domestic economy, the Water-
gate imbroglio, and a sense that it was no longer perceived as
a champion of freedom all contributed to a crisis of confidence
and self-image. The 1970s also saw the beginning of a long and
permanent decline in U.S. manufacturing employment, as other
parts of world began to produce an ever-larger share of con-

sumer goods for sale in U.S. and European markets. But in both military and economic terms, the United States remained the central force on the globe, even factoring in the military challenge of the Soviet Union and the growing economic strength of Japan and West Germany.

The United States and China had a dramatic and surprising rekindling of relations in 1972, when Richard Nixon traveled to Beijing to meet with Mao in the Great Hall of the People off of Tiananmen Square. It was an extraordinary meeting, made possible by the assiduous back-channel diplomacy of National Security Advisor Henry Kissinger, his Chinese interlocutors in general, and Premier Zhou Enlai above all. Of course, there was also Ping-Pong. China extended an invitation to the U.S. table tennis team as a gesture of goodwill in 1971, setting the stage for the political rapprochement a year later. It was perhaps the most important moment for the game, ever, save the occasional family bonding experience that still takes place in garages, dens, and fluorescent-lit basements throughout the world.

But neither Ping-Pong nor elaborate banquets in Beijing radically altered the cold peace between China and the world. The opening between China and the United States was largely confined to politics. While there was a lessening of tension and an increase in diplomacy, that was the extent of it. Until Mao's death in 1976 and the resulting turmoil in the two years after, China remained as cut off from its neighbors and the world at large as it had been at any point in its long and complicated history. Relations with the Soviet Union, nominally a cousin and an ally in the global Communism-versus-capitalism battle, were at best frosty. Within the ruling elite of the Chinese Communist Party, there was substantial resistance to closer ties with the West or even the East. The first decades of Communist rule, coming on the heels of more than a century of pressure and encroachments by the West, were devoted to making China autonomous, independent, and self-sufficient. That ran contrary to integration with the world at large, even as the economic policies of the ruling party failed to improve the material conditions of hundreds of millions of Chinese people.

In 1978 Deng Xiaoping consolidated his hold on the party and the country, and he pushed through an agenda of reform and modernization. Too many of China's people were mired in poverty, and Deng wisely understood that unless that changed, the tenuous compact between the party and the people would disintegrate. Deng was an unlikely visionary. He had survived purges, internecine battles within the Communist Party, bouts of internal exile and disfavor, the animosity of the Red Guards of the Cultural Revolution, and what could best be described as an up-and-down relationship with Mao. Already seventy-two years old when Mao died, Deng was at an age when most people look back at their lives. But he had no intention of going gently into that good night, wizened and gnomelike that he was. He had the grudging respect of many of the older party cadres and the utter loyalty of a younger generation that venerated his long service to the party and marveled at his ability to escape death—political and actual—for so long.

Deng intended to remake the way that the party governed the economy. To that end, he first undertook agricultural reform and began to abolish the collective farming system. Then he allowed for the creation of a few select special economic zones along the southern coast. These zones were allowed to design their tax regimes to be more hospitable to private industry and foreign business ventures, and to give individuals more latitude to do business separate from the mandate of the state. In spite of the Communist Party's hostility to the West, the main criteria for the zones were that they were proximate to centers of Western commerce and trade—namely, Hong Kong, Macau, and in related fashion, Taiwan.

This limited opening was meant to be a laboratory, but the hunger of people for more autonomy and for raising their standard of living led to a rush of activity. Trade spiked dramatically, as did industry in formerly sleepy regions such as the Pearl River Delta north of Hong Kong. That did not please many in the party, who would not speak out directly against Deng but who could fall back on deep-seated and widely shared ambivalence about trade and too much entanglement with the West. Many old-time party members held fast to the belief that fewer exports were better than more, and that no imports were better than some. There was also resistance to welcoming foreign capital into the closed loop that was China's economy in the 1970s and early 1980s. Many feared—rightly, as it turned out—that once foreign capital began to flow into China, the days of Maoism and even Chinese Communism would be numbered.[1]

But there was no going back. Throughout the 1980s, while the pace of reform sometimes accelerated and sometimes sputtered, it never ceased. The results were impressive. Economic growth averaged nearly 10 percent during the 1980s, while inflation was moderate. Some years growth was 7 percent, some years it neared 15 percent, but the overall trend was up. That said, the starting point was so low that even such rapid growth still left China a poor country compared to the rest of the world. It would need many more years of growth before it would even enter the ranks of a "middle-class" nation. And the big-picture statistics masked huge regional variations. While the new economic zones thrived and expanded rapidly, many parts of the country, in the interior and in the western provinces, grew not at all.

During these years, Deng championed an approach of "crossing the river by touching stones," which meant being flexible, nimble, and heterodox. There was also a concept of "one country, two systems," which meant a socialist system governed by the absolute authority of the state and the party for the bulk of China, while for the special economic zones and eventually for Hong Kong (once it was unified with the mainland) market forces would be predominant. There would be one state and one government, but there would be two distinct approaches. These ad hoc, somewhat confusing policies had wider implications for China's development. While Deng may have been clear in his own mind about the differentiation, he was at heart a pragmatist who shifted plans, labels, and slogans to fit the needs of the moment. It was left to others to debate and flesh out the implications of his ideas.

The result was a system in flux. Some resisted the move toward more openness with the world and fought the very idea that market rules should have a place in China. Others wanted the opening to go faster and extend more broadly throughout Chinese society. Most of the discussions occurred behind a veneer of party unity, but soon the debate began to seep out in public. Intellectuals and poets joined the discussions, while millions in the special economic zones set up small business enterprises and cast off the bland ideological straightjacket that had stifled change and growth for the past decades. Of course, the fact that the government relaxed its restrictions and was less prone to the indiscriminate use of force as a tool of control allowed for that loosening.

Part of the debate was purely about the best path to modernization and economic growth. But with that came the more radical debate about democracy and political openness. Inside the party, there had long been discussions about democracy within the framework of Communist Party rule, but now there were rumblings about democracy as a separate reform that could jeopardize party rule. By the end of the 1980s, some of the defenders of democracy were making their claims in public. While they were assailed as "bourgeois liberals" bent on undermining the revolution, the fact that they were even able to publish and discuss their views in public without being arrested and jailed was more notable than the acrimony they generated. Of course, they did face harassment, and when certain invisible lines were crossed, they could be stripped of their posts, confined, and in other ways silenced. The rising volume of these debates was the direct precursor to the democracy movement that culminated in the Tiananmen Square protest during the spring of 1989.

These developments were largely invisible to the outside world. There was an increase in the number of foreign tourists in China (though given the complete absence of tourists previously, any number would have represented a significant increase), and there was a sharp rise in the number of Chinese students studying abroad. But the internal dynamics of Chinese society were watched only by academics and to some extent intelligence agencies. The former did a relatively good job tracking the changes and the debates but tended to see China's evolution through a prism of "Communism and the party, bad; democracy and the market, good." Intelligence agencies were mostly focused on counting men in uniform and numbers of missiles, and on predicting whether China would take action against Taiwan.

Though the party was always on guard against internal challenges, the central leadership, including Deng, was surprised by what happened at Tiananmen. While the square had been the scene of protests in the past, including just after Mao's death, what made the spring of 1989 different was that students from other parts of the country journeyed to Beijing to join the movement. That in turn spawned other protests throughout the country, which united a hodgepodge of dissidents, factory workers, peasants, and students, each of whom had their own grievances and shared only a common anger at the party and the central government.

The swift and brutal end to the movement did lead to a period of repression and fear. Many thousands were arrested and jailed, and more were detained and beaten as the government used its considerable powers to end any possibility of a revival. But like the general in his labyrinth, Deng retreated and recouped. He knew that something had not gone according to plan, and he was determined to set a future course that would not see a repeat of the protests on the one hand, or the chaos that he saw as endemic in China's past on the other. China over the previous 150 years had been buffeted by a never-ending series of civil wars, invasions, and self-imposed crises, and Deng was determined not to perpetuate a destructive cycle that had left the country on the sidelines of history.

First he had to protect his own flank. There was a risk after June 1989 that he would be ousted by younger hard-line factions who would hold him accountable and use the protests as an excuse to clamp down on reform and shut China off from the world once again. Deng believed that would be tantamount to digging the collective grave of the party and the future of China. As a result, he renewed his commitment to reform and decided that the pace needed to be accelerated, the scope expanded, and the results magnified. Unless more people saw material improvement in their lives, and quickly, there would be nothing but trouble ahead. Always armed with an aphorism, Deng remarked, "We certainly must not stop eating for fear of choking."[2] Continuing on the path of the 1980s remained an imperative, Tiananmen notwithstanding.

Deng's willingness to embrace a market economy and adopt an open door approach to the world at large was anything but ideological. Years earlier, observing party members anguishing over some proposed policy, Deng had remarked, "Black cat, white cat, what does it matter as long it catches mice?" The ends above all mattered for Deng, and both before and after

Tiananmen, the goal was the continuation of the Chinese state led by the party for the betterment of all of China. The material prosperity of the masses was an integral component to that end, and he had the foresight to understand that the rising affluence of neighboring Asian countries such as Japan, Singapore, South Korea, and Thailand was making it impossible for the party to maintain legitimacy unless it delivered on the promise of prosperity.

Looking back, we now know that China embarked on a path of economic modernization that managed to transform the country more quickly and more effectively than anyone could have imagined. At each stage along the way, of course, other paths were available, many of which might have led to very different outcomes—including the collapse of the government, much as the ossified government of the Soviet Union fell apart in the early 1990s. Historians and scholars tend not to narrate the past in light of future outcomes. That can lead to selective memory and to emphasizing details and decisions that were understood to be more important only because of what happened subsequently, even if other things were more important at the time. In China of the 1980s and early 1990s, it was far from apparent that the outcome would be a dynamic market economy that would end the Communist experiment and leave in its wake something new and unprecedented. Most people at the time believed that Deng's policies would result in a modern, more open, and more prosperous Communist China, not the fusion of China and America. But in charting the evolution of Chimerica, the paths that were taken matter more than those that weren't.

In 1992 the pace of reform accelerated again, due once more to Deng's initiative. China had suffered a recession in 1990–91, and the reform agenda had come under attack. To shore up support, Deng took what would become a symbolic trip to the south. Touring the special economic zones, Deng proclaimed his enthusiasm for more change, and everywhere he went, he celebrated the notion that getting rich was consistent with the goals of the party and the state. In Shenzhen, which would soon become a metropolis of millions of people and would be one of the anchors of the industrial boom of the Pearl River region, he announced that there was no inherent conflict between a market economy and a state-planned economy. Deng's ability to hold simultaneously to contradictory ideas was either the mark of a genius or a madman, but he had a better read of the pulse of his society than anyone else. He was willing to embrace contained turmoil and his tour was taken—rightly so—as a green light to plunge into the untested waters of the markets without fear and without inhibition.

The 1980s had seen the first tentative steps of foreign companies coming to China to set up production. That had already been happening in Taiwan and greater Hong Kong for decades, so it was not completely alien for foreign companies to look to the Pacific Rim for business and manufacturing opportunities. But the reforms of the 1980s, even with the dispensations granted to the special economic zones, still left it difficult for foreigners to conduct business. Private property laws were ill-defined, and all initiatives had to be structured as joint ventures with domestic Chinese counterparts. While foreign companies could invest in China, they faced a variety of hurdles if they wanted to get their money out of the country.

What happened in the 1990s removed many of the restrictions on both foreign and domestic companies. Before, domestic Chinese who wanted to set up anything larger than a cottage industry had to go through elaborate and at times bizarre steps to function legally. Banks could not lend to private, nonstate-owned entities, and private organizations could legally employ only a handful of people. While tens of thousands of small businesses existed, the limited scale created barriers to growth.

Some party members were able to circumvent the restrictions by setting up entities underneath the umbrella of the Communist Party; these wryly became known as "red hat capitalists." By affiliating with party entities, red-hat entrepreneurs were able to set up companies without being shut down for being "capitalist." That was still a dirty word. Until the early 1990s and in spite of the energetic support of reform emanating from Beijing, it was still forbidden to be a capitalist, however loosely and arbitrarily that was defined. You could be involved in profit and industry; you could strive to get rich; but you had to do so in a manner that seemed consistent with the rule of the party and the people. The lines were vague, but crossing them was dangerous.

In 1992 the United States was about to plunge into the Internet revolution, and the European Union was celebrating its giddy first days. But in China, the economy—for all the ferment of the past decade—was still barely in the twentieth century. The north, in the heartland of what had been Manchuria, was a decrepit industrial Rust Belt. Steel, cement, guns, aluminum cans, bicycles, and other daily commodities of Chinese life were made by vast state-owned companies that employed tens of millions of workers without reference to quality, demand, or need. The production quotas were set in arcane and arbitrary fashion, in theory referencing the five-year plans that were drawn up by the central governors of the party. In practice, quotas and goals often fell short or overshot—usually the former where quality was concerned. Cars were a rarity; there were fewer than nine million in the early 1990s in a country with a population of more than 1 billion. Not surprisingly, there was a dearth of paved road for a country China's size, and rail lines were inadequate. That made getting anything from point A to point B in China arduous, time consuming, and expensive. Energy, then as now, was supplied primarily by coal. The oil fields of

Daqing in the northeast, which had provided enough oil both for China's domestic consumption and for exports, were rapidly being drained.

When Deng reignited economic development in 1992, no one could have possibly envisioned that within 15 years, society would be radically altered. It was as if Deng had sprinkled high-growth pixie dust everywhere he went, and the results were skyscrapers, roads, factories, ships, airports, and the entire phantasmagoric spectrum of the modern world—along with dystopian pollution, steroidal urbanization, and social ferment.

Recounting what has happened in China since the early 1990s always carries the risk of sounding hyperbolic. Books and articles list in mind-blowing and mind-numbing detail the statistics that demonstrate China's growth, from its prodigious consumption of metals and raw materials such as copper, iron ore, cement, steel, and aluminum, to its gigawatts of new power plants, its new roads, new airplanes, new cities, new world of 400 million cell phone users, and 100 million Internet users, and on and on. The problem is that no language can adequately capture the magnitude of the changes *and* the speed at which they happened. It may sound hyperbolic, but in fact, language offers a pale guide to what took place. Time-lapsed photography might offer a better gauge, though even that would sanitize the lived experience.

Take the case of Pudong, across the river from central Shanghai. In the late 1980s, before it was declared a special economic zone, Pudong—as so many fondly recount—was composed of scrappy fields, rudimentary factories, and apartment blocks. Today Pudong is an icon and a cliché, epitomized by the looming Oriental Pearl transmission tower, thrusting a third of a mile into the sky, with its bulbous middle perched on massive tripod legs, lit at night against a backdrop of 100-story buildings and miles of high-tech factories that stretch beyond, hovering over the river with the colonial buildings of the Bund illuminated by neon, the aging historic Peace Hotel lost in the fray, and barges flashing liquid crystal billboards in some real-world replication of a *Blade Runner* fantasy.

For China to make a decisive and definitive great leap forward, there were two imperatives. The population had to become urban, and the grip of the state-owned enterprises (SOEs) had to be broken. Until the 1990s, these SOEs dominated the Chinese economy and accounted for more than three-quarters of all industrial production. They were the classic expression of the command economy, and of state ownership of all vital aspects of production. These enterprises were often so vast that they were ministates unto themselves, responsible for the housing, feeding, educating, and health and elder care of their hundreds of thousands of workers.

One of the pillars of the reforms initiated by Deng was that the SOEs had to be overhauled. You could promote and spur private enterprises all you wanted, but unless the behemoths changed, critical mass would be impossible. The state enterprises were used to operating in a tight web of party, local cadres, provincial officials, and the central government in Beijing, which collectively arrived at targets, quotas, and, of course, prices. Quality was often abysmal—and in the case of certain types of goods such as food or mechanical goods, fatal when defective. Death sometimes drew official attention and forced changes at a particular plant. But on the whole, the state enterprises were inseparable from the system that had evolved since 1949. There were entrenched interests, bureaucratic inertia, and hundreds of millions of people whose lives, literally, depended on their employment by these organizations.

That said, it is easy to make a bit too much of the "old system." It had emerged in the 1950s, but in between the stops and starts of Mao, the dislocations of the Great Leap Forward in the 1950s, and then the wrenching disruptions of the Cultural Revolution of the late 1960s, it had been buffeted by shifting and contradictory laws, varying mores, and rotating leadership. It is vital to recognize that while the changes of the past decades in China have been dramatic, Chinese society has been in constant flux since the late nineteenth century, with rarely a period of calm, peace, or security. First there were the encroachments by the powers of the West starting in the 1840s; then wars and internal revolts that left millions dead, and led to the fall of the Manchu dynasty in the early part of the twentieth century; then violent rebellions that lasted years and took the lives of millions more. While Shanghai between the wars was a miniversion of Europe, the rest of the country in the 1920s and 1930s was dominated by warlords who broke alliances as impulsively as they made them and put down arms less often than they took them up. There was also the civil war between Communists led by Mao and the Nationalist government of Chiang Kai-shek and his American supporters, and a Japanese invasion and occupation that began in 1933 and lasted until the end of World War II in 1945, with a death toll that will never be precisely known but must have been in the tens of millions.

The war with Japan would have been enough to unhinge any society, but the civil war between the Communists and the Nationalists continued after the defeat of the Japanese and flummoxed the American expeditionary forces in central China, even with their tough, ornery, and thoroughly upright general, "Vinegar Joe" Stilwell. That conflict ended, of course, with the Communist takeover in 1949, followed by a complete refashioning of the agricultural system, years of famine, state-led industrialization, and then a self-inflicted ideological frenzy during the Cultural Revolution that sent millions of urban, educated people to the countryside and led to the indiscriminate purging, persecution, and often death of those seen by student cadres as disloyal to the vision of Mao.

So when the post-Mao period saw yet another turn of the wheel, this time away from reliance on state industry and the command economy, it was hardly the most unsettling development that hundreds of millions of Chinese had faced in the past decades. In fact, it was a more benign upheaval, and one that at least promised a better outcome. In that sense, the blood of Tiananmen, real and ugly though it was, hardly compared to the violence of China's twentieth century, and that may be why it left fewer scars in China itself than in the public imagination throughout the world. Yes, internal censorship in China has all but erased what happened at Tiananmen, and that also explains the lack of greater internal shock waves. But decades of turmoil, death, and violence may have inured Chinese society to being shocked that an authoritarian government might actually use lethal force and kill people in order to maintain control and defend itself against those who questioned its legitimacy.

Intending to revitalize the state enterprise system was one thing. Doing it was another. The reforms included setting new targets, holding senior managers and local party officials accountable for meeting them, and allowing individuals in positions of authority greater latitude in determining how best to meet those targets. While these measures all looked good on paper, in practice they had little effect. Many state-owned companies were industrial giants, makers of steel or generators of power, but they also included the major financial institutions, especially the four primary national banks and their thousands upon thousands of branches. That meant that even when targets weren't met, or when desired profit margins weren't achieved, if there was insufficient income to meet payrolls or procure new materials, these enterprises invariably turned to the state-owned banks, controlled by local officials who were as beholden to the regional party cadres as the officials running the factories or the power plants. The result was that loans were given, more money flowed, and, barring some special case, nothing consequential happened when managers failed and plans fell short.[3]

After 1992, the central government took more aggressive steps to curtail bad loans to nonperforming companies and to further encourage both urban entrepreneurs and innovative village and town enterprises. The result was that select rural areas became manufacturing centers. One of the more lauded of these was the town of Wenzhou and its satellite settlement Qiaotou, which in short order came to dominate the global button manufacturing industry, producing more than 60 percent of the world's buttons by the end of the 1990s. Wenzhou also cornered the market for cigarette lighters, with a consortium of several thousand small manufacturers eventually producing nearly three-quarters of all the lighters sold globally. Another mass-market product that became a regional specialty drew more prurient interest: sex toys. While some criticized local entrepreneurs for producing them, to the residents of the city, it didn't much matter whether the product was lighters or dildos, as long as there were global buyers.[4]

Farther south, many of the factories of the Pearl River Delta also began as "town and village enterprises," which weren't saddled with the moribund legacy of the state enterprises, nor with the massive payrolls of underemployed workers. As the number of those so-called TVEs mushroomed, the role of the state-owned companies started to diminish as a percentage of overall activity.

At the time of his southern tour in 1992, Deng was already 88 years old. His one-time protégé Zhao Ziyang was under house arrest, having taken the brunt of the blame for Tiananmen, and the factions opposed to further economic opening had come close to seizing the momentum before Deng undercut them. Somehow, Deng managed to find coteries loyal to him and, more important, loyal to his vision and his urgency. He could lead the orchestra, but he was getting too old to play all the instruments. While Deng himself was extraordinary—and whether one likes what he did, that much is hard to deny—it would have been little surprise if his immediate successors had stumbled. Instead, led by the dual characters of Jiang Zemin and the more junior Zhu Rongji, they not only continued what he had started but magnified it, sharpened it, and perfected it.[5]

Jiang's political career was made in Shanghai, which had been the center of commerce and modern China before the revolution, as well as a melting pot of Western and Chinese business interests. Because of that, Shanghai had earned the distrust of Mao and the party, and that never fully eased during the chairman's lifetime. Only in the 1980s did the central government begin to allow Shanghai to breathe. As party secretary of the city, Jiang had been integral to the revitalization of the region and the birth of Pudong as a new industrial city. At the same time, he also supported the suppression of the protests in June 1989, and his combined profile as both economic modernizer and party loyalist was a key element in his elevation to the presidency just underneath Deng in the early 1990s.

While Jiang was credited with the rebirth of Shanghai, his lieutenant and slightly younger comrade Zhu was also instrumental in reversing Shanghai's decline. Zhu's career had in many ways been as speckled as Deng's, with periods when he was purged from the ranks and in danger of worse, and times when he found favor with his superiors and demonstrated an unusual combination of grit, creativity, and foresight. Foreign diplomats confessed amazement at Zhu's acumen and his steel-trap memory. He also had little tolerance for corruption and incompetence, which mitigated the cronyism and favoritism that is a chronic weakness of bureaucratic states and authoritarian regimes. Transferred to Beijing as Jiang's star rose, Zhu soon had a prominent role in moving along reform at the People's Bank of China and from there rose to the premiership under Jiang.

Steered by the two men, the Beijing government became not just an advocate of reform but a driver. Jiang and Zhu were strong proponents of more regional experimentation. The privileges that had been confined to a small number of special regions were extended much more widely and aggressively throughout the country in the 1990s, though not so quickly that the old order would collapse before a new one could be established. As the number of private enterprises ballooned, the state-owned enterprise system, already challenged by Deng, began to change rapidly and permanently.

Perhaps most significant was that by the late 1990s, state-owned enterprises were allowed to lay off workers; select banks were allowed to pursue state companies for payment on loans and to take punitive actions for nonrepayment; and many restrictions on the size and scope of private companies were lifted. As many as 50 million workers lost their jobs. That was a profound shock to millions who had long been accustomed to the "iron rice bowl" that had provided cradle-to-grave care—not very good care, but better than nothing. Other state enterprises simply folded, which would have been unthinkable well into the 1980s. For most of the previous decades, it was no more likely for a state company to go bankrupt than it was for a government agency to close.

State-owned companies had become a weight holding back future growth. They consumed capital without reference to productive output; they held on to workers both capable and inept; and for the most part, they produced subpar products and delivered mediocre service. There were, of course, exceptions, but the reforms promised to allow productive state enterprises to survive and thrive while letting the others expire. The surge in unemployment was a shock, but also an opportunity, as some of those workers were then able—and willing—to find new employment in vibrant private enterprises. That often entailed moving, which tens of millions each year were now able to do as the government lifted the once-stringent restrictions on internal travel and migration.

The disintegration of the state enterprise matrix was the proverbial case of pulling one thread and seeing the entire tapestry unravel. The vacuum created by closing thousands of old factories and businesses had to be filled, and was. Millions of workers had to find new employment, and while many lacked the skills to enter the new workforce, millions more did. The movement of workers from old industrial regions and rural areas that were shifting away from the state collective system meant an urban influx that was in itself an essential ingredient to the new economy. The urban population went from 25 percent in 1990 to nearly 40 percent at the end of the decade, which meant that as many as 200 million people relocated. Urbanization in turn sparked a different approach to owning property. Many of those who relocated at first worked for factories and were housed in dormitories or units owned by the employer. But the influx into places such as Shanghai, Guangdong, Shenzhen, and Beijing led to a dramatic shift in attitudes and laws. People clamored for their own apartments, and in a move that would have astonished and dismayed the party traditionalists of an earlier era, the government allowed people to have title to their own homes. As the state enterprises shed workers, they also were permitted to sell off assets, including housing units, and these were eagerly bought. Later in the decade, the urban housing market became a prime area of financial speculation, which was one of the unintended consequences of China's embrace of the free market.

It is hard to overemphasize the importance of urbanization to what has taken place in China over the past 20 years. In the

United Kingdom in the nineteenth century and the United States in the early twentieth century, urbanization was a key ingredient to industrialization and rapid growth. The same was true of China in the 1990s. Cities with burgeoning populations had to spend increasingly large sums of money on new infrastructure, which included roads, water and sewage systems, buildings, public transportation, bridges and tunnels, power plants and power grids, and then the whole gamut of consumer infrastructure such as shopping centers, schools, and homes. Initially that activity was most notable in the Shanghai region and southern coastal regions, but by the end of the decade, more and more was happening in other coastal areas and also farther inland, in areas such as Chengdu, Chongqing, and Wuxi.

For all the reform, it wasn't as if the state enterprises disappeared. The banking system—dominated by four large banks; steel, coal, oil, gas, and power companies; telecommunications, both for fixed lines and for wireless; and much of the health care system remained state owned. The difference was that managers of these companies were increasingly held to performance standards, were given more latitude to improve operations, and were rewarded for optimal performance and penalized for subpar results. Much has been made of the endemic corruption that was a logical outcome of a system that married public and private with little visibility into the inner workings of party and government elites. But the focus on corruption is misplaced. What changed in China in the 1990s is more significant than what remained the same. Yes, local party officials could instruct a bank to grant a loan to a construction project run by another official, whether or not the project was economically viable or whether the loan would ever see any payments. Yet some of those projects needed to be built regardless of short-term viability. Take, for instance, a road connecting a new city to a port before there was enough traffic to merit it. One road may have been a waste; thousands meant that China built a modern infrastructure that gave it the capacity to grow even faster.

Another development, which would have ramifications later on, was the beginning of a domestic stock market, one in Shanghai and another in the southern Pearl River city of Shenzhen, in the early 1990s. All of the initial listings were state enterprises, and purchase of the shares largely benefited the companies, not the shareholders. The markets were one way to inject money into moribund companies, and once the initial offerings were complete, the exchanges had difficulty attracting investor interest. The markets were also closed to foreign capital, including Hong Kong, which made them that much more illiquid. Some of the larger, more established state companies were allowed to list shares in Hong Kong, and that gave foreign investors their first opportunity to "own" a piece of mainland China's growth. Most of the trading, however, was dominated by speculators and not until more than a decade later would these equity markets become a more significant aspect of China's transformation and Chimerica's rise.

The final piece of an immensely complicated puzzle was a quiet yet radical decision made by Jiang Zemin and Zhu Rongji. After Deng died in 1997, the two new leaders not only pushed ahead, they pushed beyond. Deng had focused on opening China to the world and overhauling its internal means of production. That had led to increased contacts with the world at large, but those relationships were still a fraction of overall economic activity in the early 1990s. Jiang and Zhu understood, or at least their actions suggested that they understood, that the next step was to weave China into the global economy. Rather than simply opening the sluice gates in select regions and allowing foreign capital and foreign business to participate, they planned to make China a full participant in the global economy.

And the one way to do that was to join the primary driver of the global economic system, the World Trade Organization.

Deng had set the precedent, going so far as to sign the General Agreement on Tariffs and Trade that was the precursor to the WTO. But Zhu went further. It was not enough to reform the bureaucracy, alter the culture of the state enterprises, and push ahead with urbanization. Rather, Zhu declared that "China's economy had reached the point where it could not further develop without being restructured." Instead of directly managing the economy, the party and the central government would move China evermore toward a market economy, whose success would be determined not just by internal yardsticks but by China's ability to attract global capital and produce goods that were competitive in global markets.[6]

That said, Jiang and Zhu were also highly attuned to the risks of changing too much too fast. They had watched, as the world had watched, the evolution of the economic reforms in the former Soviet Union. They had observed with dismay and alarm the Soviet collapse, and they were even more troubled by what took place in Russia soon after. With the Russian economy in shambles and production sinking rapidly, the leaders of Russia in the early 1990s took dictation from the United States and financial institutions such as the World Bank and the International Monetary Fund. That led to the sudden opening of the Russian economy to the world, and especially to foreign capital. But the Russian system could not withstand the influx, nor could it change quickly enough to be competitive in a global marketplace. China's leaders learned several lessons watching Russia unravel: reform, but do so in a controlled way; change, but set your own pace; globalize, but in stages; attract foreign investment, but on your own terms.

From one perspective, the evolution of China's reforms took place without much reference to the world at large. Party leaders vied for power; factions jockeyed for position around Deng and then Jiang; and academics and intellectuals debated with party officials about the pace, nature, and scope of reform and what amount was consistent with Communism, what was not, and how much in fact needed to be. Most accounts of these years—in China itself, in contemporary Western media, and in books written largely by Western academics and journalists—treat China as a closed nation involved in a major internal transition. And it was. But although that internal reconfiguration was necessary for the economic fusion of China and America, it was not sufficient.

By the time China entered the WTO in December 2001, it had already been fundamentally altered not just by the reforms discussed so far but by the expanding presence of foreign companies doing business throughout China. We will get to the story of how China joined the world market and how the market changed China, but for now, there is still a missing element. Tentatively in the late 1980s and more boldly and aggressively in the 1990s, Western companies started to probe the China market. With stops, starts, and considerable growing pains, they established a foothold and began to see results from their efforts and their investments. These companies, many of them American, were integral to the transformation of China, but that would be only half the equation. China also transformed them. In the United States, and in the Europe of the first days of the European Union as well, the 1990s were a heady period of optimism and giddy belief that anything was possible. Underneath that veneer, however, all was not quite so rosy. The free-market model was running into headwinds, and growth was beginning to peak. Groping for answers and for solutions, corporate leaders tried almost everything. Few of them believed that China was the answer. As it turned out, it was.

CHAPTER 2

The New Economy and the Not-So-New Economy

I N T H E U N I T E D S T A T E S, the 1990s have been hailed as a period of unrivaled prosperity. The decade did begin with a sharp and painful recession, which turned the brief euphoria after Iraq was evicted from Kuwait into a deep malaise about the present and future state of the economy. In areas such as Southern California, dependent on the defense industry for jobs and economic activity, the recession was especially painful.

Nationally, the housing market turned down sharply, and no place was spared—including the usually resilient New York City. While the overall picture began to improve in late 1991, well into 1992 most Americans still felt anxious. The unemployment rate spiked to more than 7 percent, and 1.5 million people lost their jobs. Burdened by too much debt and an inflated housing market, the national economy contracted, and the brunt of the pain was felt in manufacturing and in the financial service sector. While statistically the recession was not particularly deep, public sentiment plunged, and it took the election of William Clinton over incumbent president George H. W. Bush in 1992 to shake the public mood out of its deep despondency.

The economic rebound after 1992 was dramatic. In typically manic-depressive fashion, American culture turned optimistic almost as quickly as it had sunk into deep gloom. Clinton, having run on the pithy campaign mantra of "It's the economy, stupid," entered the White House just as the economy was improving. No doubt, the subsequent policies of his administration more than facilitated that recovery and eventual expansion, but there is also no doubt that some of it would have happened anyway.

The economy of the 1990s, however, did more than just recover. The numbers don't necessarily reflect what went on. For the next eight years, the gross national product grew above trend, averaging between 3 percent and 4 percent a year until 2000. The actual figure wasn't spectacular, but it came with extremely low inflation and, in time, very low unemployment. There was also a rise in efficiency and a steady decrease in the price of oil, as well as a relatively steady decline in interest rates. The job market seemed particularly strong, and between 1992 and the end of the millennium, the number of employed jumped by almost 20 million people.

The numbers, however, tell only one part of the story of the United States in the 1990s, and, in fact, not really the most important story. Those numbers have been used by detractors and defenders of the Clinton era to bolster or undermine the case for the period being one of great shared prosperity, but macroeconomic statistics are a poor barometer of culture or of what many people actually experience. And as Alan Greenspan, the longtime and controversial chairman of the Federal Reserve, astutely observed, many of the tools for assembling data were even then inadequate to the task of gauging the economy. What happened in the 1990s, in short, presented a challenge to our desire to measure everything to the nth degree. The data said that things were good; the zeitgeist said that things were extraordinary.

In one respect, the 1990s were a harbinger of today. The problem that Greenspan and others identified, of data and the tools to collect it not being up to the task of gauging what was actually happening, hasn't gone away. It has gotten worse. That presents serious obstacles to how we grasp and interpret the implications of Chimerica. If the national agencies delegated to compiling data on the state of the American economy were unable to measure what was taking place in real time in the 1990s, they are even more behind the curve today, when national economies are becoming units in a global system of hundreds of economies and subeconomies colliding against one another and interacting with one another like so many atoms in a reactor.

The economic turnaround was bolstered by the passage of a balanced budget act in 1993 that dedicated the Clinton administration to a path of fiscal discipline. That was atypical for Democrats in the White House, and it has often been cited as a reason for the quick reversal from recession to expansion and for the rather heady and steady growth that followed. But in truth, the sudden explosion of activity could not be primarily credited to government policies, however astute, and the unexpected surge in optimism that coursed through American society had roots quite different from who did what inside the Washington Beltway.

By 1993, many Americans already had personal computers, but most of what they did on their PCs was limited by software they purchased at stores. There was some level of communication via group message boards, and there was some rudimentary e-mail offered by closed-end services such as America Online, Prodigy, and CompuServe, which combined had fewer than two million subscribers. But in the next two years, that changed dramatically. There was one reason: in 1993 and 1994, the Internet acquired a new element called the World Wide Web.

Created at a research lab in Switzerland, the Web was a software program that allowed users to go to fixed pages housed on external servers without needing to establish joint communication with those servers first. To put it another way, before the Web, Internet users had to establish two-way contact, much like a phone conversation between two ends of a fixed line. The Web made it possible for Internet users to access sites in one direction, much like we watch television or go to a movie theater. That in turn made it possible for a vast expansion of the amount of information transmitted and shared via the Internet. With the help of a browser called Mosaic, created by a group of graduate students at the University of Illinois at Urbana-Champaign, the Web soon became the hottest thing in the United States.

The glee that met the commercialization of the Web and the new technologies for accessing it could be compared only to earlier revolutionary inventions such as the lightbulb and the airplane. True, some in the close-knit world of computer geeks and software engineers resented and despaired at the commercialization, but most simply jumped aboard the quickly accelerating bandwagon. Almost as soon as the Web made its debut, Silicon Valley venture capitalists and Wall Street bankers took up the cause. The result was a wave of financing, investment, and initial public offerings that took these early iterations and magnified the scope of the activity many times over.

The explosion of activity around these new technologies in turn spurred substantial investment in communications infrastructure, especially fiber optics, wireless telephone devices, and cable. The goal was to speed up the rate of information transmission over traditional phone lines and then cable lines to allow for more data to be accessed via the Web more quickly, with greater graphic variety. By the late 1990s, incredible strides had been made in semiconductor technology and its ability to house more and more data and in hardware devices. Most important for the lives of millions, home computers became much faster and more capable of storing larger amounts of information.

In short order, the activity generated by these technologies—along with the virtuous circle of new investment giving rise to industries dedicated to the development and commercialization of the new technologies which then began to alter the lives of millions of ordinary people both in the United States and throughout the Western world, which in turn spurred more investment—became known simply as "the New Economy." Within a few years, the New Economy had assumed a central place in the culture, to the point where other issues and concerns were pushed to the periphery of public life.

It may seem odd to be reading a condensed history of the New Economy in a book about the fusion of China and the United States. What, after all, does the story of the World Wide Web, America Online, and cell phones have to do with Chimerica? The answer: just about everything.

The fact that these stories are rarely combined says a lot about how we tend to understand the world. For the sake of clarity and simplicity, different areas of life are treated as distinct. Foreign affairs are separate from the economy; interpersonal relations are distinct from politics; where to eat has little to do with how to manage your 401(k); and so on. Look at any newspaper or Web site. The science section is set off from the business section, which is separate from sports. Those sections then have subsections, so that someone intensely interested in baseball may never read anything about car racing. These types of distinctions make it easier for us to analyze and understand a complex world. Sometimes the lines make sense. Finding the best restaurant in Houston, London, or Tokyo does not require curiosity about the Olympics. But at other times, simplicity has a price: it distorts how the world works.

The New Economy, both as an economic phenomenon and

a technological one, was an imperative precondition for the evolution of Chimerica. Without the communications and information revolution of the 1990s, the United States and China could have developed close ties. The international economic order could have become more global and less national, as it had been doing for centuries. After all, both the European Union and the World Trade Organization emerged without the benefit of the Internet, just as the United Nations had before them. But the New Economy made possible the fusion of systems without the planning of any government and without anyone fully noticing the fusion as it was happening.

The New Economy gave rise to multiple innovations, but for Chimerica, the most important was the information technology that made it possible to break down the supply chain into multiple parts separated by thousands of miles. For most of the twentieth century, the factory model dominated industrial production. Even when companies went global, they tended to copy the model that had worked in one place and then reproduce it in another. If a Japanese automaker wanted to set up a factory in the United States, it replicated the production system that was the norm in Japan and then produced cars in America in a similar fashion. The same was true of a retail company. As it set up stores in other parts of the world, it used the template that had worked in the home country. The reason was sometimes a lack of creativity, but usually there was also a pragmatic impulse. Each business unit in each separate country had to be self-sustaining, and the only methods managers understood were the ones that they knew. That meant replicating the same model no matter where the business was located.

There have always been exceptions to the rule, of course, and generalizations such as these are just that. But for the most part, until the 1990s, supply chains were either centralized by a company or set up locally in a manner that mirrored the home country. Sometimes that worked well, sometimes less so, but it was the only feasible method. In almost all cases, it was easier for companies to produce goods proximate to the market where they were sold, and usually too expensive to do otherwise. Even if a company wanted to standardize operations across multiple companies and markets, there were significant obstacles, ranging from different laws and regulations, to the complete lack of global standardization of the many different tools and technologies needed to produce whatever it was the company was in the business of producing. The result was cookie-cutter models on the one hand and huge regional and local variations on the other. Even the largest multinational corporation didn't have global supply chains per se; they simply had operations around the world, many of which functioned as their own silos that filtered profits back to the central organization.

The technologies of the 1990s created a radical shift in how businesses operated globally and how things were made.[1] The matrix of new information technologies allowed for much greater levels of real-time communication and access to data from distant sources. The simplest example of what changed is the factory floor. Before the 1990s, a manager had to be on premises or near the factory, often in an office overlooking the floor. He could assess written reports, but he also needed to go down on the floor and observe what was happening in order to troubleshoot and problem-solve and to make sure that the line was functioning at capacity. As a result of the information technologies of the past 20 years, however, a manager in central Illinois can know more about what is happening in a factory in Shenzhen than he could have known about the factory floor spread out in front of his office window 20 years ago. Inventory-tracking software makes it possible for one centralized data base, accessible by multiple users anywhere in the world, to determine what is where and in what quantity. That makes it possible to manage global supply chains and production networks to a degree that was simply impossible in the past.

But for these technologies to become ubiquitous, they needed to be adopted widely, and for that, they needed to be priced attractively. That meant scale, and that in turn was one reason for the massive influx of capital and investment in New Economy companies of the 1990s. Earlier on, many people grasped the inherent potential of the Internet and wireless communications, both for business and for individual consumers. What was needed was investment, and beginning in the 1990s, some of that started to come from an unusual source: the stock market.

The symbolic eruption of the New Economy euphoria occurred when a company called Netscape, which had perfected the Mosaic Web browser, went public on August 9, 1995, and went from a preliminary price of $14 a share to $75 a share by four o'clock that afternoon. While it wasn't the first of the spectacular Internet initial public offerings, it was one of the more dramatic, and it helped propel the New Economy to the epicenter of popular culture. The stock market had already risen steeply since 1990, but the late 1990s saw it go on a bull-run of epic proportions. The technology-heavy Nasdaq index went from below 1,000 in 1995 to just over 5,000 at its peak in March 2000. But it wasn't simply the fivefold increase in the index that marked the era; it was the degree to which the fusion of the Web and the stock market dominated popular culture. The birth of the Web led to a substantial increase in the volume of trades on the exchanges, as individual investors for the first time were able to buy and sell shares online. The Web was also fertile ground for content, which sent journalists, editors, and writers flocking to the new medium.

By the late 1990s, the New Economy was a cultural obsession. According to one article written in early 2000, "It's been dubbed the 'new economy' for the simple reason that no one has ever seen anything like it: an era in which growth and innovation have created jobs that never existed, boosted productivity to new heights, and drive the economy forward . . . It's an era when everything seems to be on the cusp of getting better, faster, cheaper, more accessible, and more profitable." It was a heady vision—and an unrealistic one—but for a time, it was enchanting.[2]

In many ways, it was a very American-centric obsession. While European countries witnessed their own investing mania in Internet and telecommunications companies, the tone was largely set by Wall Street and Silicon Valley. And also by Main Street. By the late 1990s, it seemed as if everyone was investing in the market, talking about the market, watching the market. The hottest deals for the new Internet company collectively became known as the dot-com boom, and you could hear taxi drivers, bus drivers, waitresses, secretaries, and schoolteachers debate the virtues of the latest golly-gee-willickers company with as much passion and sophistication as an investment banker. Never had more people been trading in the market directly, and the euphoria led to ever-higher bids for shares in the hot companies, which in turn led to more euphoria. By the year 2000, as many as 100 million Americans owned stocks.

As for the world at large, few Americans seemed to care. The United States had gone from being deeply immersed in the Cold War, when foreign affairs were central to public discussion and popular concerns, to being focused on the market and new technologies, with little regard for anything else. The attention paid to the ins and outs of Apple or Microsoft crowded out attention that might otherwise have been paid to public policy or the world at large. Again, this is painting with a broad brush; there were people who cared deeply about other things, and for many millions of Americans, the ups and downs of the market or of the New Economy had little impact on daily life. But the culture was obsessed, to the point where one member of Congress complained during the Monica Lewinsky sex scandal that Americans were more concerned about their stock portfolios than they were about what was happening in government. Of course, it didn't help that much of the government in 1998 and 1999 was itself obsessed with the minutiae of who did what to whom in the confines of the Oval Office, which was hardly a recipe for enlightened public service. Rarely had Washington seemed more sordid and less relevant. Perhaps it was for the best that Americans were not all that concerned about government, though they did follow the impeachment trial of President Clinton with the same zeal as a celebrity trial. Given the high drama and low characters, how could they not?

All of this meant that few people in the United States noticed the radical changes taking place in China. Yes, there were China experts at the State Department, in the White House, at think tanks, and in universities. Occasionally, some issue would flare, and China would be in the news—as when U.S. planes mistakenly bombed the Chinese embassy in Belgrade, Serbia, during the NATO action against the regime of Slobodan Milošević in May 1999. The bombing led to angry reactions in China, where many did not believe that the U.S. military, with its advanced technology and experience, could have made such a mistake. Instead many Chinese assumed that the destruction of the embassy had been an intentional message to China that for all its progress, it was still weak militarily. The sense of humiliation was compounded by the timing. It was a delicate moment for the two countries, and the bombing occurred just after Zhu Rongji had made an official visit to Washington to gain support for China's entry into the World Trade Organization. The visit had not gone as planned; Congress raised objections, and Clinton was too weak politically to force the issue. Zhu returned to China without the deal he felt he had been promised, and then the embassy was bombed. That in turn gave Zhu's opponents in China an excuse to rally public opinion against the United States, and protestors turned out in force in front of the U.S. embassy in Beijing.

As we will see, this crisis threatened to derail the progress toward what would become Chimerica, but in the United States at the time, it barely registered. Images of angry Chinese mobs shouting slogans against America in Beijing made the news for a few days and did nothing to smooth relations, but China didn't hold public imagination for long. That was reserved for the market and the Internet.

The New Economy mania generated an illusion of both American affluence and power. Like all good illusions, these contained a good deal of truth. With the sharp rise in the stock market as well as low inflation and decent job creation, many Americans did experience a positive change in their material circumstances. A much smaller number saw substantial gains, and these received the lion's share of attention. It felt as though every day there was a new story of a dot-com millionaire, often a twentysomething with a hope and a dream who managed to raise money for an idea that had no discernible way of making money but seduced sufficient numbers of people with the promise of great things to come. As for the power of the United States in the world, Americans correctly perceived that with the end of the Cold War and the collapse of the Soviet Union, there were no credible conventional military threats to America's global position. While the European Union collectively was as populous and on a per capita basis as affluent as the United States, its cohesion was more of a desire than a reality.

In spite of the tenor of popular culture, however, tens of millions of people in the United States did not share the benefits of the New Economy. In fact, as many as 50 million people were at or near the poverty line of $17,000 a year for a family of four, and even an income of several thousand dollars more than that didn't translate into economic security or well-being. The United States had started to shed traditional manufacturing jobs in the 1970s, and that trend continued in the 1990s—even though some of the pain of that was masked by job creation in other areas, especially technology and health care services. Some of those jobs were in high-tech manufacturing, but most were not. The problem was that the places where jobs were lost were not typically the regions where jobs were created, and years as a factory worker did not tend to qualify someone to pick up and move to parts of the country that were adding jobs for knowledge workers.[3]

One reason for the change in employment was caused by the very information technologies that were being heralded for generating new opportunities. Computers, software, and the Web meant that traditional production could be done with fewer people. In the 1980s, the rise of Japan raised concerns about how the increased mechanization of production lines was making many jobs obsolete. In the mid- to late 1990s, however, the trend accelerated. It wasn't only the factory floor that was affected. The financial services industry, for instance, staffed by millions of people managing accounts, relationships, and paper flow, was disrupted. The most obvious example were the automated teller machines that sprouted, seemingly overnight, in the most unlikely places—including not just bank branches but also convenience stores, movie theaters, airports, and shopping malls. These were greeted gleefully by many consumers, but one consequence was to reduce the number of people needed to work as tellers.

So while part of the culture was extolling the virtuous circle of the market, the Internet, and the technology boom, another part was quietly seething. High school students in parts of the country formed investing clubs, but high schools in other areas had a significant proportion of students whose parents had lost jobs and hadn't found new ones at the same income level or with the same security. The degree to which many felt left out of the prosperity of the 1990s wasn't widely recognized, either in Washington or in the media. And for that reason, when officials from around the globe gathered in Seattle in November 1999 to formalize the next round of regulations for the World Trade Organization, no one thought it would be a particularly big deal. Turns out, it was.

Not that there weren't warning signs. An earlier meeting of trade negotiators in Melbourne, Australia, in 1997 had triggered massive protests, but that was a world away for the American psyche and not considered a reference point. There had been a strong push against the creation of the North American Free Trade Agreement (NAFTA) in the early 1990s, forever immortalized by the maverick—to put it mildly—campaign of billionaire Ross Perot for the presidency in 1992. In railing against the formation of NAFTA, Perot famously predicted a severe loss of jobs to Mexico, as high-paying factory work would inevitably give way to low-paying factory work just on the other side of the border. You would be able to hear "a giant sucking sound" of all the jobs whooshing south, he warned, and for his pains and his millions spent on the election, he garnered an astonishing 19 percent of the vote.

But when Perot ran again in 1996, that percentage declined to just over 8 percent. It was generally assumed that the prosperity of the Clinton years had trumped earlier fears about the effects of trade liberalization and the laissez-faire trade regime symbolized by NAFTA and by the World Trade Organization. The Clinton administration believed firmly that closer economic ties with the world and greater levels of trade and economic activity were part and parcel of a stable international system, and Clinton officials worked assiduously to build that system. They were also aware that these issues had little popular appeal and that with each year further from the Cold War, Americans grew less interested in and less willing to dedicate time, energy, or resources to the world at large.

That had created a sense of urgency within the administration. Given the paucity of interest in international affairs during the 1996 campaign, the second Clinton administration believed Americans needed to be reminded that it was in the national interest to stay engaged globally. That included members of the government itself. In Congress, said one administration policy document, "Many questioned the need for robust American leadership and engagement in the post–Cold War era." That had to be countered. Said one memo written for the incoming secretary of state, Madeleine Albright, in December 1996, "at no time since the colonial period has American prosperity depended more profoundly on effective participation in, and leadership of, the global economy." The memo then specifically cited the need to integrate China into that system as one reason among several for continued U.S. focus on shaping the global economy.[4]

The talks in Seattle were supposed to further that agenda. Instead they unraveled in the face of thousands of angry, masked protestors who blocked the streets, set fires, and spread chaos. Some of them were anarchists whose primary goal was to disrupt and wreak havoc. But others were animated by more specific grievances, against the mantra of free trade, against the "Washington consensus" that viewed increased global commerce and economic activity as the greatest good for the future of the world, and against the inequalities and failed promises of the New Economy and its will-o'-the-wisp dreams.

"People before profits!" That was one of the slogans shouted by the men and women who flooded the streets of Seattle. One of the cornerstones of Clinton's economic policies was the liberalization of trade throughout the world and a lowering of barriers and tariffs. The underlying belief stemmed from one of the classical tenets of economics: namely, the law of comparative advantage. In theory, if goods and services were not constrained by artificial costs such as import and export restrictions, they would be provided by companies and countries that could offer them at the lowest cost and the highest quality. While tearing down trade barriers would create short-term disruptions as some companies failed when exposed to global competition, in the long run, it would be a recipe for greater prosperity, not just for corporations and the people who ran them but for all consumers everywhere. The most productive companies would come to dominate; that would make them profitable, but it would also make them able to sell their products for less as costs declined. Access to cheaper goods and services would in turn benefit the end customer.

But what the protestors in Seattle saw wasn't a benefit to them as consumers; it was profit to corporations as producers. Around this time, the term *globalization* entered everyday use, and then as now, it managed to be vague and unsettling at the same time. For those in favor of the Washington consensus, globalization was a self-reinforcing system that extended the benefits of capitalism to increasingly large numbers of people. For those who had watched in helpless frustration as the warnings of Perot went unheeded—as NAFTA sailed through, and the New Economy boom made billionaires out of a random assemblage of computer nerds and venture capitalists—globalization was the cause of all that had gone wrong. Joseph Stiglitz, an acerbic critic of globalization who was once chief economist at the World Bank, noted the views of the protestors in Seattle and the views of cabinet secretaries in Washington were so diametrically opposed that it made one wonder if they were even talking about the same phenomenon. Where one saw increased wealth for all, the other saw declining living standards and rising insecurity. Where one group applauded greater connectedness globally, the other saw threats to domestic culture and an unravelling of the ties holding society together.

For many millions, the New Economy was like the proverbial candy shop, and they were the ones standing outside, noses pressed to the glass, able to look and thirst without the means to sate. Television shows presented images of "middle-class" lives that were in fact available only to the affluent; magazines heralded the dawn of a new era, replete with gadgets and toys that only a minority of the population could afford; and all the talk of the endless economic expansion, the end of the business cycle, and the coming days of Dow 36,000 seemed like a hollow promise that only a select few would enjoy. Seattle was a harsh reminder of the reality of the 1990s in the United States: it was an era of the New Economy, and of the not-so-New Economy. There were winners, and they dominated the discussion. There were losers, and they were left out, overlooked, and ignored. Both were right—and neither.

In their utopian vision for a world made new by technology, the Web, and the market, the boosters of the New Economy overstated and underdelivered. No one has more astutely described the nature of capitalism than the Austrian economist turned Harvard University professor Joseph Schumpeter did in the 1930s and 1940s. Calling the system an endless process of "creative destruction," Schumpeter identified the disruptive reality that underlies capitalism. The proponents of the New Economy, however, emphasized the creative and gave short shrift to the real-world harm caused by the destructive. The argument seemed to be won by the New Economy partisans. Seattle disrupted the meeting but not the WTO itself, which continued to expand and gain members. The economic figures reflected the growth in the economy and the increase in productivity. The challenges of those on the other side of the glass were less visible.

When the stock market began its precipitous reversal in 2000, the New Economy started to deflate. Within a year, its obituary was being pronounced and the entire period was quickly recast as a bubble, a fraud, and a mirage. Economic growth contracted at the end of 2000 and into 2001, as the Clinton era came to an end. Within short order, it was New Economy RIP.

That story line of the 1990s should sound relatively familiar, but that doesn't make it entirely correct. Even as the partisans were touting and the antiglobalization groups were assailing, there were other story lines underneath the radar. While many perceived that the benefits of the New Economy were accruing disproportionately to corporations and monied elites, the view from those corporations was somewhat different. In fact, unless you were a new technology company in the 1990s, chances are that you felt disoriented and overwhelmed. If you were the CEO of a traditional retail or industrial company, you were bewildered by the words and ideas coming out of the mouths of Silicon Valley entrepreneurs. In all likelihood, you were also skeptical. But it was difficult to proclaim that skepticism when those new companies' stocks were skyrocketing and yours remained earthbound.

Companies such as America Online, Amazon.com, and Yahoo!, which hadn't even existed before the 1990s, suddenly had a market capitalization greater than established giants such as Caterpillar and 3M. For many traditional corporate leaders, the world was topsy-turvy. They had done business the way they were supposed to do business, and now they were stuck driving their '57 Chevy in the slow lane. The rise of the New Economy shocked the corporations of the old economy. They were routinely portrayed as dinosaurs, lumbering idiots locked in a brick-and-mortar world and about to die a slow and humiliating death. Many predicted that they would soon be replaced by the nimble online upstarts who were constructing a virtual world of industry and commerce. Unwilling simply to roll over and die, and at a loss about how to turn back the seemingly inevitable tide of change, the mavens of the old economy hunkered down and did some serious soul-searching.

The result was a strategy to go to where the growth might be, not just where it was. That meant looking not just at new technologies but for new markets. They searched the world and asked: What isn't yet integrated? Where are there consumers who aren't being served? There were many answers, and China was one.

Very few companies had coherent, clean strategies. Hodge-podge was more typical than rigorous blueprints. And it wasn't as though these executives had all been complacent before the 1990s. Even before the technology revolution, corporations had been aggressively pursuing new markets. American and European companies had followed the growth of Western power in the nineteenth and twentieth centuries and set up enterprises in Latin America and India. In the twentieth century, the United States was particularly aggressive in doing business south of its border, in Mexico, the Caribbean, Chile, Peru, and Argentina. European companies prospered in the United States, and the commercial ties across the Atlantic long predated the technology boom of the 1990s. Those ties had in turn been strengthened by earlier technology booms, by the invention of the telegraph and then the jet engine, and by innovations in shipping.

It would, of course, suit a simple thesis to say that the challenges of the New Economy sparked a move by old companies to find new markets and thus discover China. That was part of what happened, no question. But some of the move to China happened before the New Economy boom, and then accelerated because of it. Some happened because of the various and particular personal relationships that pop up all the time: for instance, an American businessman who knew a banking friend who did business in Hong Kong and heard that it might be possible to make money on the mainland because of the reforms begun by Deng; or a division head of a Taiwanese company that manufactured low-cost goods who was turned on to the idea of sourcing in China because his Taiwanese floor manager had a cousin setting up joint ventures in the special economic zones.

In addition, some companies went to China simply out of desperation or last hope, both before the challenge of the New Economy and because of it. The relentless pressure of the market forces corporations to grow; those that don't, die. In the late 1980s and into the 1990s, companies that found themselves losing market share to competitors looked to China as a Hail Mary pass. The irony is that some of the companies that flourished in China and created the foundation of Chimerica were domestic losers, the middling brands that hadn't kept pace in their country of origin. Those who went to China in the late 1990s, were often the ones on the losing side of the New Economy. Their desperation made them take risks far afield. In China, in spite of themselves, they had first-mover advantage, and some of the costs.

There is no one story of how U.S. companies made their way to China in the 1990s. But the common theme is that the ones who went first did so because they had reached the limits of their business model in the other markets that they were in. A select few went to China simply because they were global and went everywhere, but many more went because they saw few other options. These same companies had struggled to integrate the technologies of the New Economy that everyone seemed to believe were a necessary component to doing business in the modern world. Old economy imperatives thus met New Economy pressures, and the path—to the surprise of almost everyone and the intent of almost no one—led straight to one of the last places on earth that still officially embraced the antithesis of capitalism: a Communist country with a closed economy, a few cracks to let the outside world in, and 1.3 billion people hungry for the market.

CHAPTER 3

So Good, You Suck Your Fingers

M UCH WAS MADE DURING the Tiananmen protests of the small-scale replica of the Statue of Liberty, standing as an inspirational symbol of hope in the middle of the square. Like everything else that was celebrated in those giddy weeks, it was swept away when the protests were dispersed. Yet, another symbol, less vaunted but immune to the currents that buffeted China in the spring of 1989, survived. During those days of May, thousands of students took nourishment from both the highs and lows of American culture. If the statue represented the highs, then Kentucky Fried Chicken, the fast-food restaurant just off the square and looking out at Mao's tomb, surely represented the lows.

On October 6, 1987, *Kend-de-ji jia-xiang-ji* opened its doors for a trial run before its formal opening six weeks later. It was no ordinary outlet of the American chicken chain. Occupying three stories and 12,000 square feet, it had cost more than $1 million and had a seating capacity of more than 500, along with 150 staff. A two-piece meal of "Kentucky hometown chicken" and a soda cost as much as the average Chinese worker earned in a week. One Beijing resident scoffed, "I don't see this as competing with Peking duck." The American slogan so familiar to millions in the United States—"finger lickin' good!"—received a Chinese makeover and became "So Good, You Suck Your Fingers," but only after an initial translation snafu that yielded the less-than-appetizing Mandarin line: "So Good, You Eat Your Fingers Off." Two statues of Colonel Sanders stood sentinel on either side of the main entrance. Given what happened nearby just over a year and a half later, there was a certain irony to the décor inside the restaurant: photographs of a Manhattan skyline, a poster that read "America—Catch the Spirit," and a large picture of the Statue of Liberty.

Initial reaction to the outlet in Beijing was a combination of bemused and excited. The food was far too expensive to appeal to everyday workers, and while many flocked there for the experience, repeat business was an economic challenge. The restaurant initially did a booming business among foreign tourists, who were relatively few in number but could at least be counted on to make an appearance at the square to tour the Forbidden City, gaze on the Great Hall of the People, and view Mao's embalmed body. "This is the best location in the world, so we built the largest Kentucky Fried Chicken restaurant in the world," said Tony Wang, the regional vice president who had overseen the store's opening and its creation. His optimism was not universally shared.

At least one prominent U.S. newspaper predicted a mediocre end to what was widely regarded as a mediocre business. "Kentucky Fried Chicken will have trouble finding customers because Beijing is the capital of a nation that invented fast food . . . The theme will lose its effectiveness when other fast-food restaurants break into the Chinese market . . . McDonald's, we are told, is thinking of opening a franchise there." Less than five years later, business was so strong at the Beijing flagship that another 200 seats and several thousand square feet were added. Twenty years later, Kentucky Fried Chicken, now known in China simply as KFC and part of the conglomerate called Yum! Brands, was the most popular foreign brand in China, with nearly 2,000 locations, double the number of McDonald's stores, making incredible profits and growing at more than 30 percent a year, every year.[1] And even more striking? While KFC in China represents less than 7 percent of Yum's branches globally, in 2008 those 2,000 locations accounted for nearly a quarter of the entire company's profits worldwide.

Kentucky Fried Chicken does not usually elicit much enthusiasm. Compared to sexy, zeitgeist companies like Amazon in the 1990s or Google and Apple today, Kentucky Fried Chicken and parent company Yum! Brands are decidedly middlebrow. The franchise generated more than its share of derisive sneers from a business media that preferred the snarky charm of Wendy's advertising in the 1980s and 1990s or the marketing savvy of McDonald's. That makes KFC's China story all the more dramatic.

It's hard to imagine a more American company. Founded by Harland D. Sanders in Corbin, Kentucky, it was a mildly successful venture for the next 25 years. Sanders was the classic rags-to-riches story, born in 1890 in Indiana. He never made it beyond sixth grade, and in 1930, after years of wandering from job to job and state to state, he opened a gas station with a restaurant attached called the Sanders Court & Café. He began to fry chicken and was good at it—so good that he invented a recipe with, yes, 11 secret herbs and spices. He also perfected a different way to fry the chicken, using a pressure cooker to speed up the process. The restaurant was so popular that Sanders applied for and was granted the honorary title of colonel by Kentucky's governor in 1936.

But it was the recipe and not that first restaurant that transformed the colonel's chicken into a national treasure. Sanders and his café couldn't keep up with demand, so he began to share the recipe with franchisers. By the mid-1960s, there were 700 Kentucky Fried Chicken branches, and quality across the various restaurants was notably high—in stark contrast to the problems that beset the company in the 1970s and 1980s. The decline occurred after Sanders sold the business in 1964 for a small sum and a lifetime salary. The chain grew quickly in the following decade, but at a cost. As the number of franchises grew into the thousands, the ability of corporate headquarters to maintain uniform standards waned, largely because management had a more decentralized approach to the business than fast-food rivals such as McDonald's. Whereas the hamburger giant dictated almost every detail to its franchisees, Kentucky Fried Chicken gave more autonomy to local and regional managers. That worked as long as management was intent on hiring only highly capable managers who shared a similar vision, but when the company was then sold to a larger conglomerate in the early 1970s, the chain saw an exodus of older, more experienced executives and a concomitant slide in both profit and quality.[2]

The 1980s were kinder to Kentucky Fried Chicken. Growth returned and quality improved, but corporate stability was another matter. The company was sold yet again, this time to R. J. Reynolds Industries, the tobacco giant that was diversifying its portfolio of companies to include snacks, fast food, and soft drinks. The primary advantage of having Reynolds as a parent was its commitment to spending money on expansion. While the U.S. market wasn't totally saturated, the real opportunities for growth lay elsewhere, especially in the barely tapped markets of East Asia. With the possible exception of the German economy, the Pacific Rim was then the most dynamic area of the world, anchored by the rising might of Japan and its hungry consumers. Thailand, Korea, and Taiwan were also seeing a rising middle class looking for ways to spend their growing disposable income. Kentucky Fried Chicken had one advantage: while the preparation may have been exotic relative to the native cuisines of these various countries, chicken was familiar everywhere.

The merry-go-round continued for Kentucky Fried Chicken when it was sold by Reynolds to PepsiCo in 1986. Reynolds had been an early and aggressive player in the China market, largely because it saw an opportunity to sell cigarettes, and during its brief ownership of KFC, plans were made to open a flagship store on the Chinese mainland. Already the branches had been popular in Hong Kong, and the company had high hopes for expanding into the virgin Chinese market.

The decisions were made at corporate headquarters, but the implementation was left to regional managers with their own ambitions and their own passions. That was true under normal circumstances, but it was even truer in the uncharted waters of an untapped market. At the center of KFC's China story is Ta-Tung (Tony) Wang, who was born in Sichuan in 1944 and fled to Taiwan with his family just before the Communist victory on the mainland in 1949. Like many urgent young Taiwanese in the 1970s, he went to the United States for an education. He earned a master's degree in management from the Stevens Institute of Technology in New Jersey and then another from New York University during the height of the nitty-gritty 1970s.

Taiwan then as now had close ties with the United States, both diplomatically and economically. The American government was explicitly committed to defending Taiwan's security, and for the first decades of the Cold War, the island was a flashpoint. Cut off from access to mainland China, Taiwan looked elsewhere for markets for its exports, and it became a global center of cheap manufactured goods, especially electronics. Ties with the United States notwithstanding, the two countries were far apart culturally, and the anything-goes attitude of America in the 1970s widened that gulf.

Tony Wang was comfortable in both cultures and fluent in both languages. But unlike many of his peers in the United States, he wasn't focused on sex, drugs, and rock 'n' roll. He wanted to get ahead in corporate America and took a job with Kentucky Fried Chicken in 1975. It was a difficult period for the company, and management was part of the problem. Given his ambitions, Tony chafed at the hidebound traditionalism of the senior executives and many of the franchisees. He urged his bosses to think bigger about opportunities in the international arena and Asia in particular. He believed that the Asia branches were not reaching full potential because they were run by Americans with a rigid and provincial attitude about how things should be done. The reaction to his proposals was lukewarm. Dissatisfied, Wang left KFC to head up a new fast-food franchise venture in northern California. That led in the mid-1980s to an opportune meeting with the mayor of the northern Chinese city of Tianjin, who had come to San Francisco to urge Chinese-American business to set up shop in China.

Tianjin falls into the category of a major Chinese city that most people outside of China have never heard of. In the 1980s, it was the third largest metropolis in China, with a population of seven million, slightly less than New York. Like other coastal cities, it was just starting to cast off the cobwebs of the past sclerotic decades. Barely 90 miles from Beijing and the primary port for the capital, Tianjin enjoyed a gateway location, enough proximity to Beijing to be part of its economic orbit, and enough distance to experiment without the central government hovering ominously. It also had a charismatic mayor who took to heart Deng's green light to get rich, open doors, and embrace the global market.

One thing led to another, and soon Wang formed a partnership with the Tianjin city government that led to the opening of a joint venture fast-food restaurant called Orchid Food. Its success forced Wang's former bosses at Kentucky Fried Chicken to take notice, and they persuaded him to return to the company to lead strategy for the mainland. R. J. Reynolds may have given the green light, but it took Wang's ambition to move KFC executives to think seriously about expanding into mainland China. While he still had concerns about the corporate culture of the company, the opportunity he was being offered outweighed those. He took the job, energized by "the personal challenge to develop KFC in China."

The company did have enough experience in the region to feel comfortable with making a commitment to the mainland. The success of the Hong Kong franchises was a positive sign, but no one before Wang had been given the mandate for leading the effort on the mainland. And as Wang and anyone who actually knew the region understood, while Hong Kong was an island off the coast of China, for all intents and purposes, it could have been on the other side of the world. Having been a crown colony of the British Empire since the middle of the nineteenth century, Hong Kong was a hybrid culture, more like Singapore than Beijing, and a thriving commercial and banking hub. It had never gone through the turmoil that buffeted China throughout the twentieth century, and its Cantonese residents had a long and on the whole positive experience as part of the global market.

So while Hong Kong was an example of the potential that China offered, it was not a relevant model for doing business on the mainland. That said, there were no viable models for doing business on the mainland, which meant that anyone trying to enter the market was faced with a tabula rasa. There were no rules to break or precedents to honor, and no mistakes to learn from. That made it all the more surprising that the KFC experiment worked so well.

The most crucial issue for Tony Wang in 1986 was deciding

where the first restaurant would be. Tianjin was one possibility; Shanghai was another. But in the end, Wang decided on Beijing. The capital city had a population approaching 10 million people; it drew both foreign tourists and domestic visitors; and it had a large student population—a key demographic for the experience that Wang wanted to create. Wang also found key allies in the capital, including Beijing's powerful mayor, the city's tourist bureau, and the Bank of China. After two years of negotiations with the Chinese authorities—who may have welcomed the idea in theory but were still largely unused to and ignorant of the ways of American and multinational businesses—work began on the giant outlet.

The grand opening of the Beijing KFC was an unequivocal success, but it took years for the company to expand its presence to other parts of China. Much of the country was off-limits well into the 1990s, and Wang and his bosses were wary of going too fast. They wisely believed that it was better to plan and test each store meticulously and weigh the pros and cons of each city rather than roll out restaurant after restaurant and see business sag or the concept fail. Five years later there were only 10 locations on the mainland, concentrated in northern cities. While the Tiananmen location soon became the busiest and most profitable branch in the world, it was still a novelty, a Western artifact in a society that was closer to Mao than to the market.

Given the prevalence of KFC in China today—not to mention the ubiquity of every major Western brand in every major Chinese city—it's easy to forget just how odd that three-story franchise was for Beijing before and after the Tiananmen protests. The vast majority of people in China had more familiarity with ration cards than with currency, had spent more of their lives working either on farms during the Cultural Revolution or in immense state-owned enterprises, had no television or telephones, little electricity, could travel only with a permit, did not own and could not own any property, wore traditional Mao suits, and made their way either by foot or by bicycle. Even in the more sophisticated metropolis of Beijing, most Chinese had never encountered a Westerner in their lifetime and had never eaten Western food. They didn't know one brand from the next, and aside from a few students who had studied abroad, they were as unfamiliar with Kentucky Fried Chicken as a resident of Kentucky was with fried crickets, goose testicles, roasted silkworms, or a Guizhou Province delicacy called the "three squeals," made from rat embryos.[3]

So the sudden appearance of a three-story, brightly lit, gleaming, and clean Kentucky Fried Chicken outlet was an alien experience, welcomed as a novelty and as a symbol of everything that Deng Xiaoping had been advocating. People went not because they liked the food; they went because they wanted to take in, literally, an experience of the modern world that China was rapidly, eagerly, and adamantly trying to enter. In fact, many of the patrons confessed that while they recognized the food as chicken, they didn't really like the way it was prepared, and they certainly didn't appreciate the various exotic side dishes such as coleslaw. They went because being there was a statement about where they wanted to be. Little did Tony Wang, the mayor of Beijing, or the thousands of initial patrons know that a few chicken wings would be the harbinger of a new global system.

But first there was the unexpected caesura after June 1989, and then the hurry-up, go-slow corporate response. Kentucky Fried Chicken was acutely aware of the looming threat of McDonald's entering the mainland market. McDonald's was one of the leading global brands, along with icons such as Coca-Cola, and in China the company was pursuing a strategy of expanding via the southern cities of the special economic zones. It was assumed that McDonald's would eventually surpass KFC in China, as it had in most parts of the world. But Tony Wang was able to turn what should have been a liability and a losing cause into an advantage.

Kentucky Fried Chicken was unable to draw on managers from other parts of the world, in part because of the decentralized franchise structure and in part because KFC didn't have the same rigorous approach to training people. As a result, the chain was forced to turn to local talent. But there was a problem there as well: there was no local talent. Anyone who was in their 30s or early 40s in China had spent their formative years on rice farms or in education camps—not in business. They may have been willing, but they had no experience. Needing Mandarin speakers, Wang along with the regional management team decided to look to Taiwan.

That made perfect sense; it was also insane. Taiwan's very existence as an independent nation was a continual reminder to the Chinese government that the Communist victory in 1949 was incomplete. Ruled by Chiang Kai-shek, his descendents, and the Kuomintang Party he had founded, Taiwan was protected by the United States and had for many years presented itself as the only legitimate Chinese government, albeit in exile. There were no formal diplomatic relations between the two countries (why would there be, when China didn't even recognize Taiwan as an independent nation?), trade was officially banned, and no flights or ships went between the two countries.

Yet relations were more complicated than they appeared, and many Taiwanese had made their way to the mainland, especially in the 1980s, as new opportunities beckoned. Kentucky Fried Chicken hired more than two dozen Taiwanese to manage the mainland expansion and serve as managers for the new stores. They were given considerable room to adapt the brand to its local milieu and to work with municipal governments and enterprises to decide on locations and marketing. The result was the first step toward re-creating KFC in China. As it expanded, it acquired local characteristics, and as it began to succeed in China in the 1990s, China began to reshape the nature of the entire company, its global identity, and its overall performance. Kentucky Fried Chicken thought it was going to China to find new outlets. It did, but then those outlets—vibrant and profitable—began to set an example for the rest of the company in other parts of the world.

First there were the dramatic, high-profile locations. The company pursued that strategy in other parts of the world outside of the United States, but in China, it reached a whole new level. In the words of Allan Huston, then president of KFC International, the goal was "to obtain the most visible piece of real estate available." KFC wanted to be on the Fifth Avenues of the developing world. Location became part of the branding. In a country such as China, where there were few major media outlets and advertising was in its infancy, a flagship store doubled as a marquee and a billboard.[4] Because the company's strategy demanded prime real estate and dramatic openings, it often took several years to go from deciding on a city to opening the first branch there, which was why there were still fewer than a dozen outlets six years after the flagship's Beijing debut. The model in successive cities was similar; in places like Nanjing, it included strategic partnerships with local politicians and grandees. In each new city, a grand opening was a major event in local social and business life.

The next hurdle came with the opening of Kentucky Fried Chicken's 9,000th store, in Shanghai in 1994. Located in one of the grand hotels on the Bund, it was another showy location on the waterfront in one of the most spectacular neocolonial buildings that had epitomized Shanghai in its glory before World War II. The opening of the branch on the Bund attracted nearly as much fanfare as the opening of that first outlet in Beijing.

Shanghai then was establishing itself as the economic power-house of northern China and reasserting its primacy as a commercial hub. It helped that both Jiang Zemin and Zhu Rongji had emerged from the Shanghai branch of the Communist Party, and they energetically supported the teeming city's ambitions. The Bund represented the past and present of Shanghai, but it was Pudong across the river that represented the future. Culture, restaurants, and shops adorned the grand waterfront, while the factories and gleaming new skyscrapers were across the river. When it opened in 1994, the KFC on the Bund was the hippest spot in town. It allowed young and increasingly affluent Chinese consumers to dress up and be seen as modern.

Being hip made it possible for KFC in Shanghai to charge high prices, as it had in all of its China venues. In absolute dollars, the cost of a meal was less than it was in the United States, but relative to the costs of supplies and labor, it was three to four times more profitable. Chinese customers came to KFC on the Bund not to eat a quick meal but to linger, hang out with friends, impress a date. Being there and being seen was a goal unto itself; the food was almost an afterthought. KFC had grown globally because it sold a commoditized unsexy product—there is nothing as ubiquitous as chicken. It had developed a system of franchises that left local store managers to oversee their business, and the result was fast food of modest quality and minimal cost. That entire equation was turned upside down in China.

At the Shanghai outlet, the model was refined even further. Local managers tweaked the menu and added a few items designed to appeal specifically to Chinese taste. On the menu were coconut and mango juices, and Tsingtao beer, served on trays by teams of waiters standing at the ready. There was a children's area with special hostesses giving out gifts and toys. In addition to the ever-present Colonel, there was a new addition called "Chicky." After several years of operating in China, KFC's managers had done enough customer surveys to realize that the Colonel was not quite the welcoming, avuncular figure to the Chinese that he was to the Americans. Instead he was seen as a rather stern grandparent. That was not the image the company was trying to cultivate, and Chicky was born.

How does one describe Chicky? Imagine a fluffy chicken suit with white feathers, an orange beak, and a blue beanie. Chicky quickly became a kid favorite and appealed to Chinese families far more effectively than the Colonel had. Soon Chicky was as integral to KFC in China as the Colonel had been to KFC in the United States. It was only a matter of time before Sanders himself received a posthumous makeover in China, which happened after the millennium, when all statues of the Colonel were clothed in traditional Chinese Tang suits. Remarking on what KFC had learned from China, Allan Huston said, "You can't think like an American company starting an American business in a foreign country. You have to think like a local." That is easier said than done, especially for companies with a rigid model that has worked adequately. Usually, only desperate or innovative companies adapt to different conditions and alter their model, and the former are usually desperate because they lack the competence to make those changes even if they recognize the need to make them.

The grand opening of KFC in Shanghai coincided with another step along the path to Chimerica. In the spring of 1994, President Clinton made a much-debated and controversial decision to delink China's most-favored-nation trading status from its human rights record. After Tiananmen, U.S. policy makers had been torn between the desire to open China to Western and American business interests on the one hand and to take a strong stand against the autocratic Chinese government on the other. The first two years of the Clinton administration had seen a powerful push toward human rights as a defining feature of American foreign policy in the post–Cold War era. On that score, China was squarely in the sights of the human rights lobby.

The economic opening notwithstanding, Chinese officials could still imprison people on political charges, habeas corpus was an unfamiliar concept, and freedom of speech was allowed only as long as the government wasn't criticized. The tension over human rights has been one of the primary areas of discord between the United States and China over the past 20 years, but the issue was not quite as straightforward as it seems. Early in the Clinton administration, powerful voices advocated a stringent policy against China, including the refusal to grant it the most-favored-nation status that was essential to closer economic ties. Clinton had campaigned in 1992 on a plank criticizing the Bush administration of "coddling" Chinese dictators. That made the decision in May 1994 to separate economic considerations and human rights issues all the more striking.

Under U.S. law, revoking China's most-favored-nation status would have triggered the imposition of high tariffs on Chinese imports, as well as restrictions on what goods could be exported to China. Because China was classified by the U.S. as a "non-market economy," the president was required to renew China's status every year. That turned China policy into an annual debate in Washington, and many in Congress wanted to revoke China's status as a way of punishing the regime and forcing it to comply with Washington's timetable on political reform. Of course, Deng and his successors in China were not prepared to alter their approach to reform under coercion from the United States, and they made it clear to U.S. officials that they had no intention of being dictated to.

While trade between China and the United States had expanded, in 1994 it was still less than $40 billion. But it was one of the fastest-growing markets for U.S. goods at the time, and the prospects for more in the future were impossible to ignore. In the end, Clinton decided that his administration would not make trade with China contingent upon China's human rights record. While he promised that the United States would continue to press China toward reform, he announced in May that trade would not be the primary source of that pressure. He explicitly criticized the Chinese leadership for failing to make progress on human rights, and in announcing the renewal repeatedly chastised Beijing for its violations, but he concluded that using trade was not likely to force change and that the United States government had "reached the end of the usefulness of that policy."

In typical Clinton fashion, he managed to alienate almost every side. The Chinese were offended by what they saw as American arrogance and condescension, while human rights advocates in Congress and in the press excoriated Clinton for placing commerce above morality. *New York Times* columnist A. M. Rosenthal bitterly condemned Clinton: "Politically, the Chinese Communists have taken a new prisoner—the president."

Over the past 20 years, U.S. policy toward China has been clouded by a messy mix of realism, idealism, and capitalism. China in turn has had its own internal debates about how much ideals should dictate policy and how much pragmatic self-interest should. Deng and his successors abandoned the ideological excesses of Mao, but the United States never resolved the contradictory strains in its China policy and still has not. For most of the 60 years after 1949, however, the United States could approach China from a position of power. No one questioned that the U.S. had greater economic, military, and global clout than China, and U.S. policy toward China evolved in that context. In 1994, for all the changes that China had undergone care of Deng's reforms, that dynamic remained. But the presence of Kentucky Fried Chicken and other companies indicated that the balance was shifting, even though Americans and Chinese remained largely unaware of it.

There was one group that was unequivocally thankful for Clinton's May 1994 announcement: businesses such as KFC that saw China as their next great market. The president of Kentucky Fried Chicken, John Cranor, flew to Shanghai to open the branch on the Bund just after Clinton's fateful decision. "The door to China is open wider. Now U.S. firms can go full speed in China," he said. "By permanently de-linking human rights and U.S. economic investment, President Clinton has removed uncertainty from our China business," Cranor concluded. "We do not have to worry about the potential for deteriorating relations between China and the U.S." After cutting the ceremonial ribbon, Cranor and other senior executives took a walk down the crowded Bund accompanied by 100 Chinese children dressed like Colonel Sanders. They then took a boat ride across the river to Pudong, where there were more speeches and a dance performance from the chicken-clad kids accompanied by the Shanghai Symphony Orchestra.

Relieved that the U.S. government would not place further obstacles in the way, Cranor capped off the day with an announcement that he had intended to shelve if the decision in Washington been different: KFC would spend $200 million to expand to 45 Chinese cities by 1998. KFC had identified China as its most promising future market. Other companies shared that sentiment, including General Motors, Chrysler, Boeing, and Caterpillar.[5]

The belief that 1994 would mark an end to the tension in U.S. policy was, to say the least, overly optimistic. But the Clinton decision was still a watershed. It gave a green light to businesses to go to China, and allowed companies that had already made their first forays, like KFC, to accelerate their plans. The U.S. government still retained some restrictions and sanctions that had been in place since Tiananmen, which included defense contracts, technologies deemed sensitive, and some punitive tariffs. But the critics of Clinton's decision were correct in their assessment of its import. By uncoupling morality from business, Clinton accelerated the rush of U.S. businesses into China and set back the agenda of those who wanted to use economic ties as a carrot to induce the Chinese government to change the nature of the political and legal system in China.

After 1994, those issues went into remission. What did not change was the American belief that the United States had the power and the right to dictate to the Chinese. The hardball option may have been put on hold in 1994, but few Americans considered the possibility that their leverage might fade. For their part, the Chinese government continued to view the U.S. government with suspicion and occasional paranoia, even as more U.S. and global companies began to set up shop in China as part of joint ventures with local Chinese enterprises. These years, not so long ago in time but Jurassic compared to today, were a jumble of improvisation for companies. There was little precedent for what they were trying to do and only the barest of legal frameworks in China for doing it. Global trade agreements also did not cover the vagaries of the relationships that were being forged. The result was an exciting, discombobulating, often frustrating, and sometimes highly lucrative set of arrangements developed on the fly by businesspeople trying to do business with one another.

KFC went to China and became the most recognized brand name in the country, with thousands of outlets and hundreds more opening each year, but 20 years ago that was a dream. It was also a dream that Western companies and adventurers had dreamt for centuries, and those dreams had almost all ended as nightmares. The lure of the Chinese market, the hope that if every person in China bought one of whatever it was that someone wanted to sell that would mean hundreds of millions sold, had animated merchants ever since a thirteenth-century Venetian explorer named Marco Polo journeyed to the court of the great Kublai Khan and wrote back glowing reports of the wonders and riches he discovered in the Orient. Throughout the nineteenth century and early twentieth century, Western companies and governments tried—and mostly failed—to profit from China. The British had some success with Hong Kong, and for a time between the two world wars, Shanghai was an international entrepôt for Western business interests. But 1949 wiped the mainland off the face of the commercial map and left only memories.[6]

The sheer difficulty of doing business in China in the late 1980s and early 1990s deterred many companies. Lack of clarity about property ownership, deeds, intellectual property, banking structures, and how to get capital out once it had gone in were one set of problems. Poor infrastructure, few roads, inadequate rail lines, and erratic electricity were others, as was the fast-changing, chaotic nature of the Chinese legal system as it pertained both to foreign businesses and domestic rights to participate in a private profit venture. If you were in charge of a company doing well in the United States or Europe, China posed hypothetical opportunities and real-world risks. You might make a lot of money one day, but first you had to invest a lot of money without any clear timeline for generating returns.

Companies such as KFC, which were struggling to remain competitive globally while being passed from one corporate parent to another, had an incentive to take chances. For them, the risks were skewed toward doing business as usual. Certainly some companies, like General Electric and Nike, which had strong franchises in the United States and elsewhere and innovative management teams, also looked to China simply because of the potential and took steps to enter the market in the 1990s. But few had the kind of success that KFC and others like it did.

As Chinese began to eat more at KFC and treat it as part of their lives, their sense of what the modern world meant evolved as well. Food is food, certainly, and it's not as if KFC represented some groundbreaking experiment in cuisine. But it was different from a noodle cart or a food stand in a marketplace, and not at all like a traditional Chinese banquet hall dripping with formality and pomp. It looked and felt "other," and to its Chinese patrons, it became a symbol of the new and the modern rather than an aspect of traditional or native culture. While the same could be said for any Western chain in any non-Western country, the difference was that in most parts of the world the Western company called the shots and had the power. What happened in China was different. There the sheer size and potential of the market combined with the degree to which the government still controlled access changed the equation. As companies went to China, they couldn't dictate terms; they had to negotiate. They couldn't impose an agenda; they had to improvise. The result was the gradual formation of a new system, one which began with humble, greasy, eat-your-fingers-off chicken, and then extended, in equally modest fashion, to how one looked while eating it.

CHAPTER 4

Avon Comes Calling

A VON PRODUCTS, THE NEW YORK–based cosmetics firm plagued by poor earnings and takeover threats the past two years, is venturing where few American companies have gone recently: China." So began a story in the *Los Angeles Times* on June 18, 1990, reporting on the beginning of Avon's new gamble overseas. While China was hardly the first international market that the company had attempted to tap, it was by far the largest and held the greatest promise of lifting Avon out of its decade of doldrums.

In many respects, Avon was more alien to traditional Chinese culture than KFC. Founded in 1886 as the California Perfume Company by a New York door-to-door salesman named David McConnell, Avon a hundred years later had retained the model of selling door-to-door long after most companies had moved to stores. Under the slogan of "Avon Calling," the company became a cultural icon in the United States by the middle of the twentieth century. What began with perfume expanded into a broad range of cosmetics. And what began with a male salesperson soon morphed into one of the largest employers of women, as the Avon Lady established herself as a fixture of rural and then suburban America, bringing her bag of goodies to housewives across the country.

By the middle of the twentieth century, Avon was also expanding into other countries, starting with Canada, but soon encompassing dozens of others. China, of course, was not an option, given its closed economy, antipathy to the material obsessions of the Western world, and rigid enforcement of a universal dress code of drab Mao jackets. But with the opening of the Deng era, Chinese women were eager to break free of that unisex past, and lipstick and facial cream were two easy pathways toward personal autonomy and self-expression.

The expansion of Avon into China started inauspiciously with arduous and ultimately unsuccessful negotiations between the company's representatives and the Beijing government. Avon's management wanted to begin its China experiment in the north, in the heart of the country. Beijing, however, was ambivalent. The direct-selling model alarmed and confused them, and the unwillingness of Avon to open stores struck both the Beijing government and potential joint partners as odd and inexplicable. As a result, Avon turned its focus south to the special economic zones of the Pearl River Delta, and it was there that the Avon ladies began to peddle their wares.

The initial discussions were given the green light by Avon's then chief executive officer, Hicks Waldron. Waldron came from Heublein, which had owned Kentucky Fried Chicken before its sale to R. J. Reynolds, and he had been part of KFC's turnaround before being hired by Avon to energize what was then a sagging cosmetics business. But the strategy Waldron pursued at Avon failed. He went for big and brash acquisitions and tried to extend Avon into other areas, most notably—and disastrously—into health care. Under his watch, cosmetics sales did begin to turn around, but the strength of the beauty franchise wasn't enough to compensate for the sharp losses and write-downs from the failed health care acquisitions. The company had negative cash flow for 7 of 10 years, which in plain English meant that it was losing money rather than making it.

The brand shed more of its already-waning luster, and during that troubled period, the China strategy was born.

Before the Communist Revolution, China had its peddlers who sold their wares, as well as small merchants who set up stalls on streets. Some of those had survived even during the most radical periods of the Communist era—too small to suppress and offering needed services in the alleys of Beijing or the winding lanes of Sichuan towns. But peddlers were not large-scale businesses. They were lone individuals or perhaps families, serving their immediate community, selling live chickens, tofu, and fresh produce as well as the occasional exotic trinket. That was a far cry from a centralized global company providing products to salespeople who were trained in a particular model, given quotas and territory, and then paid on commission. The Avon way of direct selling wasn't an overly complicated model, but it was unlike anything that had been done in China before.

Avon entered China just as the direct-selling model in the United States was in serious need of updating. Women had moved into the workforce in large numbers since the 1950s heyday of the Avon lady, and the Avon brand—which had never been aggressively marketed—had become at best quaint and at worst archaic. In China, Avon had the advantage of a clean slate. It hadn't figured out how to revamp its U.S. business, but its initial moves in China worked. As it started to recruit agents, it found that it was able to attract a more upscale demographic of both saleswomen and customers. In the United States, the company was known for modestly priced products sold to middle-class customers. In China, its first representatives were highly educated and skilled. They tended to be members of an economic and educational elite that had spent years frustrated and unable to find outlets for its energy or entrepreneurialism. Considered down-market in America, Avon was upscale in China.

When Avon came calling in the Pearl River Delta, a different market answered the door.

One of the first reps was Liang Yungjuan, a 40-year-old pediatrician from Guangzhou who had been earning all of $120 a month, which was significantly above the average wage. Like many women her age, she bristled during the conformist days of the Mao jackets, and like most, she had bristled in silence. When Deng announced that "to get rich is glorious," she embraced the message. She had not, however, found a way to live it. Avon was her ticket. She became a part-time Avon lady and quickly sold $5,000 of products, which netted her $1,500 in commissions. "Avon has given me confidence in myself," she confessed. "I'm thinking of quitting my regular job to sell full-time. My son says I love Avon more than I love him."[1]

Unlike KFC, there was no dramatic "grand opening" for Avon in China. One day there were no Avon ladies; then there were. Initially, the company planned on hiring 3,000 sales representatives, each of whom would be given a few weeks of training. The company opened a regional distribution center where the reps could obtain supplies and be briefed on new products and ongoing initiatives. The company believed that it would take years for the sales model to work in China. American managers assumed that after decades of Communist rule, the Chinese would view the profit motive as something alien and that breaking down the mores of the Communist era would occur only gradually, if at all. That proved to be a complete misreading of the culture of southern China, and it meant that the company was unprepared for how quickly its business grew.

That was understandable. According to John Novosad, Avon's regional head, the initial reaction to Avon when it began working with local officials on licenses and hiring was incredulity and confusion. Chinese officials wanted to know what direct selling was and why it was a viable business model. But the leap from those questions to embracing the model wasn't as difficult as Novosad and others had imagined. Having recruited the first class of supervisors and representatives—who totaled nearly 1,000 people—Avon managers were prepared for months of trial and error. Instead the first question Novosad received from a new hire was "How much commission do I get?"[2]

Avon also risked its reputation in the United States by moving into China. American businesses—especially publicly traded ones—were wary of the heated politics surrounding China after Tiananmen. While the sanctions imposed after the suppression did not prevent joint partnerships, there was the threat of negative publicity. But Avon needed the market more than it needed to avoid possible repercussions. In the words of then CEO James Preston, China was "a commercial endeavor—not a political endeavor. The venture will not benefit the government of China; it will benefit the women of China and Avon's shareholders."[3]

And so it did. Women like Liang Yungjuan responded eagerly and immediately, and within months in Guangzhou, a city of slightly more than a million people, there were 7,000 Avon ladies. Chinese women interviewed about why they were so eager to work for Avon described the job as one that offered an unusual degree of autonomy and self-fulfillment in addition to potential income. It also provided an avenue for self-expression and independence for women that was simultaneously radical yet did not tread into forbidden territory. Deng and his coterie had drawn a clear and bright line: get rich but don't meddle with politics. Selling Avon cosmetics had no political agenda and did not threaten the Communist Party. At the same time, direct selling was subtly subversive because it gave women an outlet that provided more than the factory floor or the state-owned enterprises ever had.

Avon provided a modicum of individual freedom in a society

where such freedom was scarce. The 1980s had seen an opening, but if you were a 20- or 30-year-old woman in 1990, you had spent most of your life living under a strict dress code, watched by local cadres, housed either in dormitories or perhaps village communes that offered little privacy, and unable to move freely from one place to another without fear of being watched and the possibility of being accused of some impropriety. Some experiences were more benign than others, and throughout the 1980s, the rigid social controls loosened. But most people—women especially—had lived lives defined by what they couldn't do and not by what they could.

And so when Avon came to China, the pent-up dreams of millions of women converged with the urgent needs of a struggling company. Avon needed supercharged growth, and China held that possibility. Fanning out from southern China, Avon set up distribution centers up and down the coast, and it finally did establish a foothold in Beijing. Initial sales of $4 million were nearly triple the forecasts. That was still a tiny fraction of Avon's global sales, but the speed of adoption in China was nonetheless surprising. Revenue doubled in 1992, and then doubled again, reaching $40 million in 1995. The company invested in new distribution centers and factories and looked forward to $250 million in revenue by the year 2000. By 1996, there were 100,000 Avon ladies on the Chinese mainland, and other cosmetics companies had followed Avon and were aggressively jockeying for position. Having had few choices of makeup and skin care in 1990, an urban Chinese woman living in a coastal city now could select from Avon, L'Oréal, Mary Kay, and Estée Lauder.

It wasn't the absolute numbers that made such a difference to Avon. Unlike the expansion of KFC in China, which added meaningfully to the global bottom line, business in China even as it grew and grew was not enough to tilt the scales for Avon overall. But there is something to the cliché of success breeding success. As Avon found new life and ardent enthusiasm throughout China, it started to reverse more than a decade of poor performance and misbegotten strategy. It was helped by other emerging markets, particularly Russia, but China was the jewel. At shareholder meetings, management began to speak of the future with optimism, and Wall Street investors took notice. Investors were reassured by Avon's refound commitment to its old model of selling door-to-door. By focusing intently on its core business and its main competency, Avon gained some grudging admiration. It wasn't anyone's idea of cool, but by the mid-1990s, with China's wind at its back, the company at least earned a nod for integrity.

There was no explicit connection between the booming China business and the hiring of Avon's new CEO in 1998, but it was a striking choice nonetheless. Andrea Jung, a Toronto-born, Princeton-educated child of a Hong Kong father and a mother originally from Shanghai, had moved quickly through the ranks at Avon in the early 1990s. Her focus was marketing, and she had been a key player in revitalizing the image of Avon and reviving its advertising and brand management. But she also honored the essential core of the business, which was the Avon lady as an independent saleswoman creating relationships with individual customers. Her efforts notwithstanding, the company went through yet another challenging period in the late 1990s. Its business in Latin America weakened in the face of economic difficulties in several countries, and U.S. sales sagged. Avon had a core constituency, but it was hardly what one would call chic and hip in an Internet age that glorified the new and different. In the era of the New Economy, Avon was the dowager aunt. Jung, who was energetic, smart, youthful, and who herself bridged cultures just as Avon was becoming increasingly global, invigorated the company, and her heritage underscored the importance of the China market.

Jung would become the new face of an old company, and in time lead it to its next phase of growth, but the years that preceded her appointment had seen another set of challenges almost as perilous as what the company had faced a decade earlier. Even China, which had shown such promise, began to falter, first organically and then because of an unexpected and potentially devastating government ruling.

First was the problem of competition combined with headwinds in the mid-1990s that were beyond the company's control. Avon was only one of several foreign firms jockeying for position in the Chinese cosmetics market. Even though the number of consumers was growing rapidly, so too were the number of products available and places to buy them. Avon's product mix was also not optimal for China. Chinese women were more willing to spend money on skin care, which was one reason why a variant of Procter & Gamble's Oil of Olay had such quick success. While Avon did shift its emphasis away from makeup and toward skin care products, that required precious time and effort. So too did altering the wholesale model as the company expanded beyond southern China. In more developed markets, Avon operated only a few large distribution centers and then shipped where needed. But China was a large country with bad infrastructure. In contrast to what the country would look like in the early 2000s, it was still a challenge to get from point A to B. There were few major roads—which made sense, given that there were also very few cars—and rail links were erratic and not extensive. For Avon, that meant investing in a larger number of small distribution centers, each of which required lengthy negotiations with regional and local authorities for licenses and partnerships.

While sales advanced steadily, the overall numbers masked other problems. The direct-selling model needed to be modified in China, because Chinese women, however ambitious, were not comfortable knocking on the doors of strangers. China was not, as anthropologists might say, a high-trust society, at least not compared to the United States. China was more like New York City, where the average person confronted with someone they don't know trying to sell them something immediately assumes a scam. Avon managers addressed that issue by urging salespeople to sell first to friends and family and then to coworkers, and build on that base.

After a hiccup in the mid-1990s, business again accelerated, and more products were made specifically for the Chinese market. Avon also created its own domestic Chinese supply chain. Raw materials were procured locally, shipped to local factories, made into cosmetics that themselves had been designed with Chinese women in mind, and then sold by Chinese women to other Chinese women. That became a point of pride to Avon's hundreds of thousands of Chinese employees and managers. In the words of one customer, "Asian skin is different, and Western products may not be ideal for us." In China, Avon learned to brand itself as a company that made Chinese products, and that made all the difference.[4]

As it adapted to the new environment, the company did what immigrants have always done: it started to go native. Management thought that it was training its Chinese salespeople how to sell. "We will select virtually anyone who wants to come in and be trained," said John Novosad, Avon's executive vice president for the region. "We'll teach them how to sell and how to network among their friends."[5] True, in those first years, they needed some training. But not quite as much as American executives in China thought. Americans carried with them the baggage of their own cultural assumptions, one of which was that China was an immature society when it came to the selling and marketing of consumer goods. It was true that China had skipped a generation or two of consumerism and also true that

American firms had become more skilled in the arts of getting people to want and motivating them to buy. But unnoticed by managers like Novosad, as Avon became more entrenched in various parts of China, it began to change as a company because of the Chinese employees who were doing most of the work and the Chinese customers who were doing all the buying.

All multinationals that expand into different markets face these issues. They each confront the unique traits, needs, and outlooks of individual countries, with their own histories, languages, and mores. Like Coca-Cola, Procter & Gamble, McDonald's, and so many others, Avon dealt with multiple countries and cultures, and its success in different markets depended in part on its ability to adjust to local conditions. But because of how China emerged as the next great player in the global economy, the story of Avon in China matters more for our world today than, for instance, the story of Avon in South Africa. And because Avon was one aspect of the superfusion of China and America, its evolution has wider ramifications.

As Avon's business spread, the government in Beijing began to look more closely at the company's selling model. It did not like what it saw. The large gatherings appeared to some officials more like revival meetings with pseudoreligious overtones than normal worker-employer conclaves. There were also concerns that the various levels of commissions at times replicated a pyramid scheme rather than a legit direct sales model. With agents taking commissions, managers taking commissions, and regional directors taking commissions, the system was open to abuse if commissions were paid to managers on goods that were distributed to agents but not actually sold. The government also suspected that prices were being unfairly inflated. Because so many people took a cut, higher prices were the only viable solution. The burden would fall to new agents, who had to buy inventory from the regional distribution centers in order to sell their wares and could be forced to pay exorbitant sums. Avon wasn't the only company using this model. Tupperware and Sara Lee set up similar operations in China, as did Amway and Mary Kay cosmetics, but Avon was the poster child.

Avon executives knew that Chinese officials were becoming increasingly uncomfortable with direct selling. But though Avon had introduced the idea, by the late 1990s most of the estimated 10 million people involved in direct sales in China were neither Avon ladies nor associated with any Western company. To allay official concerns, Avon executives made the case that their practices were fair and legal, but it didn't matter. In April 1998, the central government, with the explicit blessing of Zhu Rongji, issued a ban on all direct selling in China. In the words of the official report, "Due to immature market conditions, inadequate legislation, and immature consumer psychology, direct sales have proved unsuitable for China and thus must be resolutely banned." The government accused certain companies of using direct sales "to engage in superstition as well as reactionary and underworld gang activities."[6]

The vast majority of the abuses had nothing to do with Avon, or with its Western competitors such as Amway and Mary Kay. But the accusation that these companies were using recruitment meetings for religious indoctrination was not quite as absurd as it sounded. True, Chinese officials frequently made outlandish charges when arresting individuals or shutting down enterprises, but there were cases of representatives of these companies using the ruse of recruitment as a Christian missionary tool. Avon per se was never implicated directly, but it was perhaps guilty of spreading ideas that still sat uneasily with the official ideology of the Chinese Communist Party. The relentless focus on profit, gain, and sales quotas was not easily reconciled with the mores of an egalitarian society. Because it involved millions of individuals who were autonomous and largely unsupervised, the use of direct agents emphasized the contrast between what China still officially was and what an ever larger number of actual Chinese wanted. Undoubtedly there were cases of fraud, but the same could have been said for factories and real estate projects. In 1998 direct selling crossed the line between what China had been and what it was becoming.

For Avon, the ban should have been devastating. The company had invested nearly a decade and millions of dollars, and was just beginning to see significant contributions to its global bottom line. Under new management, Avon had returned to its core of direct selling, and now it was facing an unprecedented ban. Avon had no other selling strategy, anywhere. Yet somehow it was able to shift gears in China and survive. Having closed one door, the Chinese government inadvertently opened another, and Avon was once again transformed, this time into a high-end retailer.

When I first went to China in 2002, two things immediately struck me as odd. One was how hip Kentucky Fried Chicken seemed to be; the other was how cool Avon was. Like most Americans, I was familiar with both brands, and the words *hip* and *cool* would have been low on the list of adjectives used to describe either one. Yet there was Avon, with stores on the chic Nanjing Road in Shanghai, decorated in a trendy blue and silver palette, video screens flashing images of pouty, sexy Chinese women dressed to kill, and cosmetics under countertops and lining the walls in stores that were sleekly minimalist and decidedly upscale. Young women filled those stores, and not just any young women, but well-heeled women with attitude and income. Professionals were drawn as well, attracted by the strong aura of the modern world emanating from Avon outlets. The same experience was replicated in Beijing, in the malls near Tiananmen, and in the gleaming cities of the Pearl River Delta. In the late spring of 1998, after the ban, you could have bet with confidence that Avon was done in China. Within a few years, it was a retail powerhouse with boutiques throughout the country.

The rebirth of Avon in China was a child of necessity. The company was forced to innovate. The fact that it was able to adjust its model so radically in such a short period of time says volumes about the fluid nature of Chinese society and about the hodgepodge nature of Western companies establishing themselves in China during the 1990s. Simply put, there was no template for how to succeed and no blueprint for what to do. The same could be said for Chinese government policy, which remained a pragmatic seat-of-the-pants process governed by ends, not means, and driven by the goal of economic development. The ban on direct selling was one of many stops and starts, but China was changing so quickly that there was no such thing as absolute obstacles unless you chose to see them that way.

Because everything was so fluid, prior rules didn't apply. What should have been a death knell was instead a blip. What should have derailed a company not known for its nimbleness or creativity became an opportunity for a new way of doing business and an image unlike any version of Avon anywhere else in the world.

Avon is a prime example of Western companies transforming China and themselves being transformed. At the same time, what happened to Avon in the 1990s was part of the larger changes both in China and in relations between China and the United States, and it is fair to say that Avon executives were only dimly aware of those trends. In fact, while Avon officials (or similar executives at Mary Kay, Amway, Tupperware and the like) had contacts with regional and national officials on issues that pertained directly to their business, they were not particularly sensitive to the bigger picture.

To be fair, the inner workings of the Beijing government and the central party were opaque and purposely so. It was one thing to get to know local officials, mayors, and heads of regional councils and cadres; they could be wined and dined at banquets, and relationships could be forged. But it was rare for an Avon executive vice president to have more than a brief introduction to Zhu Rongji, most likely at a formal reception in the Great Hall of the People, where there might be a photo and a handshake but no chance to engage in substantive discussion. In China, there is an old saying, "The mountains are high and the emperor is far away." It's meant to capture the peculiar dynamic of extraordinary power in the hands of the central government in theory, and the limitations of that power in practice. For centuries, the emperor had absolute power, yet edicts in Beijing had a way of decreasing in importance the farther one got from Beijing. Unless the emperor was willing to send his army to impose the laws, it was up to local officials to implement them.

But that old saying also underscored the fact that while you could function for years without hearing from and having to deal with the central authorities, you also never knew what they were thinking and what they were planning. Mercurial and unpredictable, they could remain aloof and out of mind—until they took sudden, unexpected actions. Sometimes, those actions proved less potent in fact than in principle, especially when the government lacked the will or the means to enforce its edicts in faraway provinces. But other times, as in the case of the ban of direct sales, the fiat was potent, and swift.

In isolation, the story of Avon in China in the 1990s was very much one of a struggling U.S. company establishing a foothold in a new market and gaining traction. Viewed through the lens of Chimerica, it was also a story of a struggling multinational company finding new life in China and in the process contributing to the evolution of China away from a Communist command economy and toward a unique merger of state capitalism and mass consumerism. But there was also something else going on. Avon's zigzag was driven by the internal debates within China and within the Communist Party about how far and how fast China should embrace the market and the global economic system. The trajectory of the company was shaped by heated arguments about the virtues and vices of the market and of the West, and about the place of China and the definition of capitalism with Chinese characteristics. Avon executives, occupied with how to sell more lip cream and facial cleanser, were largely unaware of those debates, just as they were uninterested in equivalent debates within the United States about what the focus of America should be in a post–Cold War world. The outcome of those deliberations, however, mattered greatly to Avon, as the ban on direct selling demonstrated.

After the floodgates had been opened by Deng, first in the 1980s and then again with his southern tour in 1992, there was a rush of consumer activity in China. Families and individuals believed they had been given permission to acquire, and they rushed to buy consumer goods that had been forbidden or unavailable during the previous decades. Consumerism in these years went through successive waves. Initially people sought washing machines, air conditioners, and television sets. Within a few years, by the early 1990s, most middle-class families had those. Then they wanted telephones, video cassette players, stereos, cameras, and apartments. They also spent on discretionary items, like cosmetics, food at restaurants, entertainment, and fashion. By the second half of the 1990s, many of the desires for big-ticket items had been fulfilled, but the financial system simply wasn't up to the task of providing credit and liquidity for wide-scale consumer activity. As a result, China experienced yet another of a long series of hiccups, and growth ebbed almost as quickly as it had surged.[7]

The inadequacies of the banking system certainly weren't a mystery to the Chinese leadership, but identifying the problems was easier than solving them. There were four large national banks, one nominally focused on agriculture, another on smaller domestic companies, and the other two—including the mammoth Bank of China—on everything else. These banks had never operated as traditional banks in a free-market sense. Yes, they received deposits and gave loans to businesses, but until the late 1980s, those businesses were state owned and aligned with the Communist Party. So were the banks. Loans might be given, but payment terms were murky at best and rarely if ever enforced. Individual consumers were never a focus, and other than offering people a place to put their money, the banks didn't do much for individual customers.

A thriving consumer economy needs a banking system that caters to the particular needs of the individual as well as to retail businesses that exist solely to sell to people. Other aspects of the Chinese banking system were also in need of reform, especially the tendency of local banks run by party hacks to lend to local factories led by party hacks, who might also have been cousins or in-laws. Money changed hands with no regard to the intrinsic worth of the project, and no consequence if it failed to produce a dime.

During his years as premier, Zhu Rongji made reform of the banking system one of his top priorities, if not the top priority.[8] Unless China's economy was able to provide capital to meaningful projects and deny funds to wasteful ones, the country would be stuck in a loop of one step forward, one step back, with the appearance of constant activity clouding the fact that much of that activity was wasteful or bogus. At the same time, Zhu understood that you couldn't just embrace the orthodoxy of global financial institutions and shock the Chinese banking system into reform. If there had been any doubt of that fact after the collapse of Russia in the early 1990s, the Asian crisis of 1997 was a reminder. When Thailand suffered a vertiginous drop in its currency after capital flows reversed course, it set off a chain reaction that brought not only Thailand but also the high-flying "Asian Tiger" economies of Hong Kong, South Korea, Singapore, and Taiwan to a painful halt. Global financial players scrambled to rescue the plunging currencies in the region to prevent a total collapse of trade, but the lesson for China was simple: reform, but at your own pace, your own fashion, and without undue influence from abroad.

The maelstrom of the Asian crisis was also a factor that led to a pullback in consumer demand in China, which in turn affected how Avon and a host of other foreign companies were doing. Avon executives were aware of the issues affecting a broad swath of Asian economies, but they could not have known how these were interpreted by the Chinese leadership. The Beijing government had one focus: pursue policies that led to greater prosperity and stability within China, period. If that meant loosening controls and wooing foreign companies, so be it. If it meant enacting laws and passing regulations that harmed foreign companies, so be it as well.

While the country was changing dramatically, it retained the vestiges of a command economy, with five-year plans setting goals and determining the agenda for the party and the national bureaucracy. The plan that set the parameters for the last years of the 1990s stressed a more rapid and radical pace of reform for moribund state enterprises while simultaneously preserving the characteristics of a socialist state. Much like party platforms in the United States, the five-year plans were kitchen-sink affairs, and not always taken literally. But there's no question that the Chinese leadership was intent on retaining control of the unwieldy machine of the Chinese state. They wanted robust but not chaotic growth, so that tens of millions of people moving from the countryside to the cities had an opportunity to increase their affluence, and so that the authority of the Communist Party remained unquestioned and unchallenged.

No country has ever evolved without severe challenges and crises. When the United States emerged as a force in world affairs at the end of the nineteenth century, it was faced with regular economic collapses occurring every 15 to 20 years. Cycles of boom and bust were extreme, oscillating between gold rushes, land rushes, land grabs, and railroad booms on the one hand, and bank panics, mass unemployment, and labor unrest on the other. There were also violent battles between owners and workers, between whites and blacks, whites and Native Americans, whites and Chinese immigrants, and between immigrants of all stripes and citizens of all colors. The ethos may have been liberty and equality for all. The reality was a chaotic mix of high ideals and base instincts.

What China did in the 1990s took the states of Western Europe more than a century and the United States more than five decades. The Communist Party kept a tight rein on expression yet also relaxed its hold and allowed more people to enjoy more personal freedom than they had ever known. Maintaining the balance between control and greater individual autonomy was a constant balancing act. The government's ban on direct selling was a blow to Avon and its competitors, but in the greater scheme of things, it was a minor measure—born of fear and paranoia, to be sure—intended to keep the country on its unique and peculiar path.

The move toward a market economy was not without controversy in China. Chinese intellectuals and party leaders debated just how far the country could move toward capitalism without losing its socialist character. Many expressed significant opposition to the consumerism of the United States and Europe, and vowed to prevent the same materialism in China. After decades when various intellectuals were purged from the party for being either too "rightest" (which in Chinese terms meant too enthralled with the power of the market) or too "leftist" (too in love with the power of the state and the party), the contest was between those who wanted more free market and less socialism and those who wanted more egalitarianism and less materialism. The ambivalence about Avon was part of a larger questioning of capitalism and of how China would create its version of capitalism with Chinese characteristics.[9]

A world away, the United States of the 1990s was in the midst of an aggressive embrace of visionary capitalism. The fall of the Soviet Union was taken as a vindication of liberal, free-market capitalism, and the release of energy that had been pent up during the Cold War added fuel to the New Economy. Traditional companies like Avon chugged along during these years, but management felt significant pressure to keep up with the digital Joneses. By 1998, Avon believed that it was finally on the right track; that it had corrected the mistakes of the 1980s and had carved out a new niche as a dependable but not flashy company in the New Economy 1990s. Its success was due in part to connecting with a customer base that itself was not fully comfortable with the technorati who were leading the New Economy charge. Avon met the needs of the middle class in Middle America.

But in China, Avon was a neophyte. Its success had more to do with Chinese hunger for its products than with brilliant execution. But the direct-sales ban made Avon innovate; it made the company take a new tack. To the surprise of its own management, that new tack worked. Rather than a bastion of American middle-class values exported on a global stage, Avon in China turned into a hip retail outlet that offered Chinese customers a way to express their individuality and to spend their hard-earned money. The fact that Avon opened freestanding stores and counters in shopping centers, that it became a place to see and be seen, was born of necessity. And, astonishingly, it worked.

Eventually in 2006, Avon was allowed to return to its traditional model, after China joined the World Trade Organization and long after Avon had re-created itself as an icon of Chinese cool. But while Avon's return to direct selling added new luster to its already gleaming China franchise, it was the crucible of the 1990s that mattered to the evolution of Chimerica. Much as KFC re-created itself and was in turn re-created, Avon went to China and stirred up passions and desires. Unlike KFC, Avon found that some of those passions were negative and led to a backlash. While Americans saw themselves and their companies as apostles for the market and consumerism, the Chinese were not willing to become simply another market for American goods. They wanted to determine their own destiny, even while recognizing that they needed foreign capital, foreign companies, and foreign expertise in order to move forward. That was a difficult path, and sometimes invisible lines were crossed and trip wires went off.

Even when there was a step back, however, there was no permanent reversal. As the case of Avon demonstrated, when one road was cut off by a pragmatic but mercurial government, the result was more innovation. Avon was a microcosm of the changes caused when the irresistible force of American-style capitalism collided with the immovable object of China in the 1990s. What emerged was something new and different, familiar and not. And as those hundreds of millions of new consumers began to stir, as the Chinese government confronted a myriad of foreign companies all of whom wanted in, it also faced yet another challenge: not just how to manage and control the rapid growth of the market, but how to get things from where they were made to where they could be sold. China in the 1990s had big eyes and a big appetite. But moving things from one point to another, that wasn't so easy. China didn't just need a better banking system. It needed planes, trains, and automobiles. It needed transportation hubs and logistics. It needed Federal Express.

CHAPTER 5

Up, Up, and Away

H IS REMARKS WERE PREPARED in advance and delivered without much drama or even panache. Sitting before a committee of the U.S. House of Representatives in 1998, Fred Smith, the CEO of Federal Express, wanted there to be no ambiguity about his views. He had spent the prior 15 years, give or take, building up a franchise in China, which was only just starting to yield results. Each year, it seemed, some politician or lobbyist tried to reverse the course, wave the flag, and ratchet up the tension, and each year, Smith and others like him had to defend their interests and explain why it was important to maintain and deepen the economic ties with Communist China that had developed in the years since 1989.

After a brief introduction, he got right to his point: "It is clearly in the interest of American business, the American economy, and the United States government as well to normalize trade relations with China. The politicization of this extremely important economic issue for domestic constituent consumption risks eighty billion dollars in trade relationships, hundreds of thousands of jobs, and the viability of billions of dollars of U.S. investment in China. If a normal trading relationship is not established with China, the resulting retaliation and downward spiral in bilateral U.S.-China relations would deprive American companies access to the Chinese market for a long time to come . . .

"The underlying premise of the opponents of normalization that disparate treatment of China would somehow achieve its transformation into a more acceptable member of the world community is simply wrong. More outside contact with China, not less, is the only way to influence China's development in a positive fashion . . . Better economic conditions do contribute to improving the social and eventually the political climate. Federal Express and other American companies constitute a positive force for change. Federal Express began serving China in 1984 and began flying to China in 1996. Federal Express brings its best practices to the Chinese marketplace and to our Chinese partners. We daily expose countless Chinese to the efficiencies of our brand of market capitalism, whether it is in business ethics, personnel policy, management practice, or operational efficiency. We are proud of our record in China. We believe that demonstrating to the Chinese how a modern corporation conducts itself benefits not only China but the United States as well."

Smith went on to mount a strong case for China's entry into the World Trade Organization, an issue that was then becoming contentious in Washington and one that did not split along purely partisan party lines. Smith spoke not just of the potential of the Chinese market but of the manifest good that might come from more closely knitting together the two countries and the two economies. He made, in short, one of the most cogent cases for the fusion of the two systems. He spoke as the head of a leading American company who saw the potential of a transformative relationship that would be a net positive for both China and the United States, and he argued passionately that more business activity in China equaled more change for the better within China.

Fred Smith wasn't born a CEO, but he spent most of his life creating his company. He has the biography of an everyman, except for the fact that his net worth has flirted with $1 billion. He went to Yale, served in Vietnam, and has been the driving force behind one of the more important global companies of the past 40 years. In interviews, he has a sort of aw-shucks Americanism that belies his achievements, or perhaps explains them. He describes how he and his brother used to try to "beat the devil out of each other," hardly a unique childhood experience. After losing his father at the age of four, he was raised largely by his mother and later said that the experience taught him self-reliance "through a lot of hard knocks." He worshipped his high school coaches, took what he could from his Yale experience, and was deeply affected by serving in the Marines in Vietnam, where he learned how to manage people as much as how to survive battle. And when he left the military at the age of twenty-seven, he applied those lessons and started a company dedicated to the proposition that people wanted a way to get things from where they were to where they wanted—quickly, efficiently, and cheaply—and that the only way to accomplish that was to harness the power of new technologies.[1]

For all his folksy charm and everyman name, Smith proved to be a visionary who found a way to use the emerging power of first the computer and later the Internet in order to make it possible for goods to be shipped around the world in a manner that can only be described as revolutionary. It wasn't that he had the simple—in retrospect—idea of combining air and ground transportation into one seamless logistic web. It wasn't that he learned from IBM the necessity of cutting-edge information technologies. It wasn't even that he was an early disciple of management philosophies that sought ways to make each employee a partner who internalized the norms and creeds of the company and executed its processes with a high level of competence and accountability. It wasn't any of those of things in particular. It was all of them in combination.

It doesn't really matter whether or not you like Federal Express. After all, in its rigid adherence to rules and methods, it can seem a bit Stepford. But in the company's ability to get things from anywhere in the world to anywhere in the world when it "absolutely, positively" has to be there—from Christmas gifts on the afternoon of December 24 to heart transplants within hours; from components for Dell computers to flowers for a wedding banquet in Shenzhen—FedEx does what it promises and it delivers, in every sense of the word.

Fred Smith's humble name did not signify humble goals. Packages didn't stop at the water's edge, and neither could FedEx. Europe came first, but by the mid-1980s, the company began to eye China. In 1986, it set up a joint venture with Sinotrans, the largest freight shipper on the mainland. Sinotrans had been created by 1950 as the primary state-owned enterprise for international shipping and logistics. It had managed China's first modern container ports, worked with Japanese and Hong Kong companies, and established networks linking northern China to the Trans-Siberian Railway. Perhaps because the company had always had a mandate to work with foreign partners, its management was less hidebound. By the mid-1980s, Sinotrans was already contemplating its own overnight delivery services, using its network to mimic what it saw going on in the world beyond. When foreign carriers began to enter China, Sinotrans was the only viable partner.

However, like most joint ventures, there was more hope than substance in the deal between FedEx and Sinotrans, and nothing high-tech. Packages were carried on trucks, off-loaded from trains and ships. China's road network was minimal, its rail lines basic at best, and internal air travel almost nonexistent except for military transports and rudimentary service to a few select hubs. Ports such as Tianjin in the north and Guangdong in the south were connected to their immediate hinterland, but there was almost no way to transport materials throughout the country. Officials had their ways, but everyone else was left to improvise. If you wanted to get a package from inland cities such as Chongqing or Changsha to Shanghai or Fujian, you were left with old planes, creaky trains, and few trucks, none of which was dependable. Of course, in the 1980s, there wasn't a significant amount of trade between various provinces, so the need wasn't as great. There also wasn't much trade with the rest of the world. In the 1980s, China supplied barely 1.5 percent of global exports, an astonishingly low figure given how high it would later climb.[2]

But given the rumblings of economic reform and the willingness of the Communist Party to do deals with foreign businesses, the needs of China were about to change. As long as its economy was inward looking, detached from the outside world, with each province its own mini-economy, there was no pressure to create a national infrastructure. As Deng's reforms took off, however, that became unacceptable. The difficulty of getting goods and people throughout the country had been an advantage for Mao: the only organizations that could function nationally were the party and the central government. Individual provinces were cut off from the outside world and from one another, and while local officials enjoyed a good deal of control, they could not extend their reach or meaningfully challenge Beijing. The needs of a centralized Communist state, however, were not the needs of a market state. If China was to make its economic great leap forward, it would need more than will and desire. It would need to be able to get things from point A to point B.

FedEx, however, did not go to China intending to serve masses of Chinese. The company harbored no illusions that millions of individual Chinese were clamoring for overnight deliveries. Its goal for China was to answer the needs of Western companies doing business in China, and to compete and win against its two main rivals, United Parcel Service and DHL, which was a subsidiary of Deutsche Post. DHL entered earlier and was poised to win the business of European firms; UPS came soon after and extended the heated rivalry with FedEx to yet another corner of the globe. The competition between UPS and FedEx has been unusually intense, because they perform essentially the same services and have no other major rivals save for the U.S. Post Office in the United States and carriers like DHL in other parts of the world.

Because the two companies have dominated their industry—especially in the United States—their rivalry is a favorite case study for business schools and management gurus. On one side, there is the employee-owned United Parcel Service, of the ubiquitous brown trucks and a willingness to work with multiple partners. On the other is FedEx, of the catchy marketing slogans, focus on technology, and a desire to control and micromanage every aspect of its business. In China, FedEx tried to create a network on its own, relying on local partners only when strictly required, and moving as quickly as possible to owning its own planes, its own fleet of trucks, and its own logistics. UPS, on the other hand, spent years building relationships with local Chinese companies—first Sinotrans and then others—shipping packages on other people's trucks, leasing other companies' planes, and partnering with different agents in multiple cities.

By the late 1990s, FedEx had captured 13 percent of the market, while UPS lagged behind with 5 percent. Both were still behind local Hong Kong competitors as well as DHL. In that respect, neither strategy proved dramatically successful, but FedEx's approach was unquestionably more costly. In 1988, the company paid nearly $900 million for a local air carrier called Flying Tiger Line, which controlled a Japan-to-China route that FedEx coveted. It spent another $70 million in 1995 for a cargo carrier called Evergreen. That was on top of the hundreds of millions more for beefed-up logistics centers in both the Philippines (meant to be a hub for South Asia, including southern China) and Taiwan.[3] The company also hired thousands of employees in China, and in 1996, after more than a decade of investment and preparation, it began to fly its own aircraft in and out of China from the United States and locations in Asia.

The massive investment of time and money was one reason that Fred Smith was so adamant when he appeared before Congress that day in 1998. His company had made substantial commitments and investments on a hope and a dream and had yet to see a return on its capital. While the China air-freight market was the fastest growing in the world in the 1990s, it remained midsize compared to other markets. Relative to FedEx's $12 billion in annual revenue in 1997, for instance, China barely registered, although Asia as a whole did. But it was the potential of China, combined with clear evidence that it was indeed on the verge of taking off (pun intended), that enticed FedEx and its competitors.

The lure of the China market proved irresistible. But it was not simply a function of size. Size alone may have fed the centuries-old "China dream," yet unless those dreams could somehow be turned into reality, some companies would get burned and the rest would learn the lesson and stay away. It took the concerted efforts of the Chinese government to attract foreign businesses, and to set up a system that allowed foreign companies to make considerable investments with at least a decent chance of getting their money back and their money out.

As Western companies contemplated China as a market, they recognized the risks. Similar risks, after all, existed in other countries. American and European companies in Brazil, for instance, had their assets seized or sold by the military government in the 1970s. Western oil companies had faced a wave of nationalizations in the Middle East in the 1950s and 1960s in places like Iran, while companies in countries like Indonesia, not exactly warm to its former colonial masters, were forced to sell property, sign over deeds, or depart entirely. Even in more stable parts of the world, there were often crippling constraints. India, led first by Jawaharlal Nehru and then his daughter Indira Gandhi, embraced democracy but not free-market capitalism. They wanted to modernize India by relying on domestic industry, and viewed foreign businesses—especially Western ones—as not much better than the British who had ruled the country until 1947. In their minds, Western companies sought only their own interests and would strip India of its assets and take any profits out of the country. Given how multinationals functioned, those fears were not unreasonable.

For most companies, going global in the second half of the twentieth century was simultaneously fraught with danger and bursting with opportunity. In order to offset the risks, U.S. companies often turned to the U.S. government for help. Sometimes that help came from the U.S. Department of Commerce, which acted as an unofficial global lobby group for American businesses abroad. Companies also used industry groups like the U.S. Chamber of Commerce and various trade associations to pressure Congress and the White House to pass legislation or enact regulations that would create favorable conditions for global commerce. The World Bank and the International Monetary Fund also exerted leverage on countries outside of Europe and the United States and demanded as a condition of granting loans or financial assistance that countries craft a regulatory regime that was friendly to foreign investment.

What companies wanted most were assurances that their investments would be protected and that if they put capital into a country, they could get it out. A company might be willing to accept restrictions on selling property in another country, but not on its capital. For a global corporation such as FedEx or

Avon, doing well in one market helped the overall bottom line only if profits could be pooled with other profits. If there was a chance that income from a country could be trapped there, that was less appealing. While companies might accept restrictions initially in order to establish a foothold, they usually agitated for fewer constraints rather than more. In short, companies want to be able to do business globally without barriers on the flow of capital or goods. Countries and governments, however, often want to retain or tax capital to use it for their own benefit. While the desires of companies and countries are sometimes in sync, very often they are not.

The attraction of China was that it offered a market of unparalleled potential. But there was a cost. Chinese laws, combined with the lack of a legal framework designed to accommodate engagement with the outside world, made it difficult for foreign companies to dispose of property or to extract their profits. In other parts of the world, those types of restrictions usually repelled foreign companies. Why bother investing time and money in a country that would take and take and offer little in return?

For many countries outside of Europe, the need for foreign investment, expertise, and capital led governments to change their laws and accept—often in sullen resentment—the "Washington consensus" that demanded a variety of preconditions for investment. The phrase, coined by a Washington think tank in 1989, initially referred to the suite of conditions for Western investment in troubled Latin American economies. These included having clearly established property rights; a free-floating currency whose value would go and up down depending on global currency markets; privatization of state-owned enterprises; a cap on the amount of sovereign debt; a commitment to lowering the costs of doing business in the country, ranging from tax breaks internally to lowering duties on goods produced by foreign companies; and less government spending relative to overall economic output. By the 1990s, what had begun with Latin America was extended as orthodoxy to the rest of the non-Western world.

China, however, offered few of these benefits. It had a currency that could be exchanged only at the official government rate and by the government-controlled central bank. It had high tariffs on imported goods, limitations on how much a foreign company could own of any business in China, and a legal system that made the enforcement of contracts between a foreign entity and a Chinese one difficult if not impossible. It also had a central government that spoke in welcoming tones about foreign business yet maintained these barriers and was further limited in how much it could force individual provinces to open their doors to foreign companies. In short, China should have been undesirable. Foreign companies should have taken one look at the obstacles and risks and taken a pass. Instead they tripped over one another to get in, and they spent billions in the process.

As early as the late 1970s, the Chinese government saw the appeal of attracting foreign business and capital. After all, if you can get someone else to pay, why not? In 1979 the government passed a law making it mandatory for any joint venture with a foreign company to have at least 25 percent of its capital come from outside the country. Deng and his coterie always believed that China's transformation would occur much more quickly if knowledge and capital from abroad were actively involved. Other countries had the will and desire but were unable to attract the attention. Beginning in the 1980s and accelerating in the 1990s, China began to draw more foreign investment than anywhere in the world.

Some of that, to be fair, came from ethnic Chinese who had been living and thriving in countries like Malaysia, and some came from Taiwan and Hong Kong, which were both foreign and not. Hong Kong businesses had long coveted the opportunities of the mainland, if only the Chinese government in Beijing allowed it. The rapid expansion of the Pearl River Delta region in the 1980s and 1990s was supported by Beijing but also funded in part by Hong Kong. Businessmen such as Li Ka-Shing, who had been born in China but grew up in British-controlled Hong Kong, poured billions into ventures in southern China during these years, fully—and it turns out correctly—expecting that after Hong Kong reverted to China's control in 1997, those investments would be worth many times more.[4]

But foreign investment wasn't just local, ethnic, and regional. It also flowed from global multinationals. In the 1990s alone, FedEx's purchase of a local air carrier, its construction of new airport facilities, and its spending on logistics capabilities throughout Asia in order to serve the China market, amounted to billions of dollars. That was hardly justified by current business. As of 1995, trade between China and the rest of the world was less than $300 billion, a fraction of the $2 trillion it would become a decade later; its trade with the United States was barely $50 billion. Yet foreign direct investment in the country amounted to between $30 billion and $40 billion a year during the 1990s.

FedEx wasn't investing for business as it existed in those years. It was investing for what it hoped would happen later. As we now know, its wildest dreams came true. But it wasn't just foresight. By investing what they did when they did, FedEx and other companies helped make their dreams real. They thought they were putting money to work in order to capture part of this ephemeral potential. What actually happened is that their investments were part of why that potential was realized.

It's a vital distinction. The traditional view is that these companies set up shop before the full potential of China was realized, spent years losing money while the Chinese government and society underwent radical changes, and then in the late 1990s and the first years of the twenty-first century began to reap the rewards. The transformation of China is seen as an internal development that U.S. and other multinational companies were able to exploit, and which the Communist Party leadership under Deng and then Jiang Zemin encouraged. That misses the deeper story. The activities of those U.S. companies and multinationals in China itself were an integral part of China's transformation, and the capital they invested was essential to the changes that took place.

Without that capital, China would have been like a super-sized version of any number of emerging-market economies that hungered for modernization but lacked the means. In order to attract foreign investment, other countries had made significant compromises. From Brazil to Thailand, governments allowed global institutions such as the World Bank along with the U.S. government to set terms and dictate reforms. Though many business and political leaders of those countries voluntarily bowed to the Washington consensus, the power dynamic was clear: the West and above all the United States had the power and the money and could therefore set conditions.

But in China, the familiar pattern was turned on its head. China had neither the capital nor the expertise to modernize, and it lacked the legal and political infrastructure that the Washington consensus demanded. Yet foreign companies and governments made every effort to get in, and while they urged the Chinese to adopt the reforms being pushed on the rest of the world, the unwillingness of the Chinese government to move at all or move quickly did not act as a deterrent. Instead, foreign companies were told to do business on terms acceptable to China, and they did.

As FedEx poured money into a losing venture, the optimism of its CEO was in inverse proportion to actual returns. Yes, he and others could point to the staggering growth of China's economy during these years, at rates of 9 percent, 10 percent, or even more if the stagnant regions of the country were excluded. The areas that mattered to companies such as FedEx, Avon, and KFC—the coastal cities of the special zones in particular—were growing as much as 15 percent or even 20 percent a year. Yet unlike emerging economies where that pace of growth was almost always accompanied by runaway inflation, China was able to keep a lid on inflation because the government kept a tight hand on the currency, interest rates, and the pace of reform outside of the special provinces. And because foreign companies wanted access at all costs, China didn't have to worry about the destabilizing effects of the Washington consensus.

China was thus able to have the best of all worlds: the cream of global companies clamoring to get in without the loss of sovereignty, economic dislocation, and even chaos that usually accompanied their entry. Rather than making radical concessions to foreign capital, foreign capital made the concessions. Companies accepted limitations that they never would have tolerated in other markets. China was thereby able to draw in foreign enterprises, attract investment, and still control the timetable and its degree of openness to the world.

The fact that China owed nothing to foreign creditors was also an advantage. Burned into the collective Chinese psyche was a memory of indebtedness to the powers of the West and how those debts became an excuse for ever-greater Western control over China's domestic affairs. The Washington consensus was in many ways a function of debt and leverage. Most countries that were hungry for development needed loans, and Western governments and international financial institutions were the source. In return, they could dictate the terms under which such loans would be given. But China refused to go cap in hand to foreign lenders, and had the luxury of not needing to.

The direct investments of companies like FedEx did more than further the ambitions of Fred Smith. They formed the foundation of a new capital base for the future growth of the country. China was thus able to modernize not at the expense of its own economic sovereignty but instead at the expense of foreign companies. These not only invested billions of dollars—which, given the size of China's economy in the 1990s was a considerable portion of the overall output—they also sent managers, hired local employees, and with their joint-venture partners transmitted knowledge and experience. That combination of money and knowledge, which China obtained almost free of cost, was essential to the evolution of not only China itself but to hundreds of multinational companies and to Chimerica. It was part of the glue that bound the two economies together.

The uniqueness of China's relationship with the financial and economic centers of the world cannot be overstated. It is the only country in the past six decades that has been able to modernize, industrialize, and "Westernize" according to its own timetable and according to its own rules. Deng may have decided that China needed to wrench itself into the modern world, but he probably could not have imagined that the modern world would accommodate China's growth and adapt to it. Yes, Western companies pressured the Chinese government for speedier reform of its legal system to protect contracts and intellectual property, and the U.S. government among others advocated everything from reform on human rights to allowing the currency to appreciate. But these urgings were not ultimatums, and the consequence of China not doing what Western powers wanted when they wanted it was not the withdrawal of business or capital but even greater levels of engagement and commitment.

Throughout the 1990s, China was one of the fastest-growing economies in the world, and the express delivery business grew even faster, at a rate of 30 percent per year.[5] FedEx alone served nearly 100 Chinese cities by the late 1990s and had begun to operate direct flights in and out of the country. Though service was rarely overnight, it often managed to get packages to where the customers wanted them in less than two days, which for a country that had barely had enough cars and trains to facilitate the movement of troops and basic necessities a few years before was quite a feat.

Much of the traffic and the business helped other U.S. and, multinational companies to increase their level of activity in China. A regional headquarters in Hong Kong or Guangdong or Shanghai used FedEx to get packages to factories in Fujian or Wuhan or documents to law offices and ministries in Beijing. The ability to do so was one factor that allowed so many foreign companies to take root on the mainland quickly and, in the greater scheme of things, easily. Though few companies and managers involved in the arduous task of building a China business in the 1990s would have described the process as easy, it was certainly less complicated and time consuming than mining in central Africa or exploring for oil in remote regions of the world. The presence of FedEx and its competitors UPS and DHL was one of many factors that propelled the turbocharged evolution of China.

The proliferation of foreign companies on the mainland had profound effects: they offered a model of modern industrial capitalism that Chinese businesses wanted to emulate, and they helped spur the Chinese government to focus on infrastructure. Yes, part of the reforms ushered in by Deng included significant spending on roads, ports, power plants, and urban development. But until the early 1990s, those projects were regional and radiated from the special economic zones. Vibrant regional pockets were necessary to move China forward, and they acted as gateways for global business and commerce. Yet they weren't on their own sufficient. For the next wave of growth, China's cities and regions needed to be linked internally to one another, and only the central government could get that done.

That is precisely what happened in the 1990s and into the first decade of the twenty-first century. At the time of Tiananmen, China was a bicycle society. A decade later, it was becoming a car culture. Cars required highways, and so the road network was aggressively expanded—to accommodate passenger vehicles, yes, but first to make trucking easier. Development of inland cities required rail networks to transport containers from ships that unloaded their cargo at coastal ports, and that in turn necessitated more trucks and more roads to distribute the products housed in those containers. Rapid economic growth put pressure on the power grid. Upgrading it wasn't an early priority but became one later on when major urban centers and manufacturing centers were faced with brownouts and blackouts.

To put these trends in perspective, at the time of Tiananmen, there wasn't a single expressway in China. Just over 10 years later, there were 15,000 miles of expressways, and that would double in the next decade. Nearly 25,000 miles of new single-lane and double-lane roads were also added each year. That was matched by thousands of miles of rail lines, significant expansion of ports from Tianjin and Dalian in the north to Hong Kong and Shenzhen in the south, and dozens of new and expanded airports.[6] With that infrastructure came new factories, and office buildings and apartment blocs for the millions who staffed those factories and offices. That in turn led to more consumer activity and more demand for goods that had to be shipped by land, sea, and rail.

FedEx didn't cause any of this to happen, at least not by itself. But it was one element. It provided a highly visible model, especially for the state-owned companies that were its partners. Sinotrans, which was the initial partner of both FedEx and UPS, learned more from the experience of working with these international shippers than it ever could have if it had only been able to watch from afar or hire a few managers who had begun their careers under the corporate tutelage of Fred Smith. Employees and managers of Sinotrans took one look at how FedEx managed its business, planned for the future, and designed a strategy for the China market and realized how much change was necessary before China could compete. They might have understood that intellectually or in the abstract, but seeing FedEx in action from the inside was to know that reality at a core level.

Still, for most of the 1990s, the promise of China remained just that: a promise. Companies throughout the world, from the United States as well as from Europe, Hong Kong, Taiwan, and other parts of Asia, invested billions of dollars without seeing significant returns. Those dollars were vital to China's growth, but at the time, the spending could be justified only because of faith in the future rather than profit in the present. That was why Fred Smith and other business leaders trekked to Capitol Hill each year and made passionate pleas for maintaining China's most-favored-nation status and for deepening and expanding ties with China. If the U.S. government slammed those doors shut because of objections to China's human rights record or tensions over Taiwan, those investments would be lost, and China might once again prove to be the dream that became a nightmare.

The trends that began in the 1990s—with U.S. companies investing heavily in China in order to access the new market and gain advantages from low-cost manufacturing—unfolded in the context of heady economic times in America. Even though some sounded the alarm about China as a competitor for U.S. jobs and as a potential rival of the United States on the global economic stage, China was still too small an economy and U.S. confidence was still so strong that these concerns paled in comparison with the sense of opportunity. Business leaders like Fred Smith were the heroic figures of the era, along with titans like Jack Welch of General Electric, Jeff Bezos of Amazon, Steve Case of America Online, and a host of other celebrated names. Concerns about China had less traction than hopes and dreams about China emerging from decades of Communism to become a partner in the ever-expanding pie of global capitalism.

As it turned out, both the hopes and the fears came true. But in the late 1990s, FedEx started to see its years of work pay off, as did hundreds of other companies that began to profit from a real China market. China, in turn, continued to navigate its own course of state capitalism. The government avidly pursued economic modernization, spent heavily on infrastructure and rural reform, and led the charge while simultaneously determining priorities and setting the pace. Once it was clear that the special economic zones had achieved critical mass, banking and financial reform rose to the top of the agenda.

There was one other priority, which was fully in sync with the needs and desires of the foreign businesses and investors such as FedEx. If the changes were to be permanent, China needed to be tethered to the global system. The only way to do that was to become even more open to the world, and that would require more than willingness on the part of the Chinese government. It meant joining an organization that didn't even exist when Deng initiated his reforms, an organization that existed solely because its members wanted it to, that had no way to enforce its decrees yet was reshaping the commerce of the world. It meant joining the World Trade Organization, something that almost didn't happen and would have led to a rather different world had it not. We will get to whether that was good or bad for the world at large, but how it happened, and the debates around whether it should have, set a tone for the relationship between China and the United States that has lasted until today.

CHAPTER 6

Free Trade and Its Discontents

T HE NEGOTIATIONS COULDN'T HAVE come at a worse time. Since his election in 1992, Bill Clinton had been a champion of global free trade. He had campaigned strongly supporting the North American Free Trade Agreement (NAFTA), which had aroused substantial opposition and anxiety in the United States. The concern was that as trade barriers fell and protections for U.S. manufacturing and agriculture decreased, factories would be shuttered and farms would be foreclosed. Ross Perot, who ran as an independent attacking government profligacy and warning of the doom of the U.S. economy if NAFTA were passed, managed to garner his aforementioned 19 percent of the vote in 1992 and 8 percent in 1996 based largely on his stand against free trade. Free trade may have been part of the Washington consensus, but it wasn't part of the Main Street consensus.

For more than a decade, beginning in the 1980s, the Chinese leadership had worked with counterparts in the United States and Europe to integrate China into the global economic system. During that time, the system evolved, and the most notable change was the replacement of the post–World War II General Agreement on Tariffs and Trade (GATT) with the World

Trade Organization (WTO). Given how rooted the WTO has become in popular consciousness—and often not in a positive way—it's worth remembering that it came into being only in 1995, and rather quietly and uneventfully. Acronyms and trade associations are not the stuff of legends. They generate yawns in popular consciousness, except for rare moments when they trigger utter panic about loss of control.

Both China and the United States panicked in the late 1990s. The Chinese economy had a brief swoon during the Asian crisis, but at the time, it didn't seem like a hiccup. It seemed as if the model of opening and liberalizing might not be such a good idea, given what had happened to countries such as Thailand and South Korea, which were caught in a currency tsunami that nearly reversed decades of progress. In the United States, with a thriving New Economy and expectations of a world without economic cycles, the fear was different. What if by advancing the needle of free trade with China, the delicate equilibrium created only so recently in the post–Cold War world was disrupted? And what if allowing China to join the WTO ended any possibility of pressuring China to open up politically?

Of everything that happened on the road to Chimerica, the entry of China into the World Trade Organization may have been the most important. Agreed to in 1999, the formal entry occurred in December 2001, in the wake of the events of 9/11. American attention, as well as the focus of Europe and much of the world, was fixed firmly on al-Qaeda, the Taliban, Afghanistan, and the global challenge of terrorism. History, however, is littered with events that seemed of utmost importance at the time only to fade in significance over the years and crowded with moments that were overlooked at the time and were only later identified as turning points. Because the act of joining a voluntary trade organization is neither heroic nor fraught with peril, because it involves no visible bloodshed or loss of life, it rarely receives the focus given to battles and crises where the future seems in doubt and at stake. China joining the WTO may be one of the more pivotal events of the modern world, but it will never make for grand narrative.

Trade negotiations are long, arduous, and dull. They involve hundreds of industries, thousands of products, and an incalculable number of emotions. There is hardly a country on the face of the earth that doesn't try to shelter its farmers from the disruptive effects of world trade. For much of history, the number one challenge facing societies and their governors was securing a consistent and sufficient food supply. Allowing global trade to determine the health of domestic agriculture strikes most countries as no saner than ceding national defense to other nations. Yet food is a commodity like any other, which can be abundant in one place, scarce in another. It is a central part of trade negotiations, and one of the reasons for the tortuous negotiating process.

Another hot-button issue is domestic industry and manufacturing. Developing countries fear—for good reason—that their industries won't be able to withstand open competition from more sophisticated, wealthier rivals. Developed countries want—understandably—to be able to sell their goods and services to as wide a range of customers as possible, without hurdles and with some guarantee that contracts will be respected. International trade organizations, first GATT and then the WTO, seethed with these tensions. Each time a new member applied to join, especially one as large and potentially dominant as China, these and other issues were front and center.

For much of the 1990s, the trajectory for China joining the WTO seemed straightforward, and relations between China and the United States became warmer than they had been at any point since the Communist takeover in 1949. The Clinton administration was led not just by the president but by globally oriented economic advisors such as Lloyd Bentsen, the first Treasury secretary, and then by Robert Rubin and his deputy, Lawrence Summers, as well as by the chairman of the Federal Reserve, Alan Greenspan. All believed that more global trade would ultimately benefit not just the United States but the entire world. America was feeling confident, affluent, and powerful, with visions of a new world order cemented by Internet-enhanced capitalism and a Pax Americana that would result in a future of peace and stability around the globe. The fact that China, the last remaining pillar of what had once seemed to be a formidable Communist challenge, was rushing to cast off its Maoist clothes and don the garb of the West was taken as further proof of the ascendancy of American capitalism.

The Chinese government under Jiang Zemin was intent on joining the WTO, both as a symbol that China was prepared to take its place among the leading nations of the world and as a sign that the reforms of the past decade were legitimate, permanent, and leading to more prosperity for the people. The appointment of Zhu Rongji to supervise negotiations for China's accession to the WTO was in itself an indication of how serious the government was. Zhu was the second most powerful official in the Chinese government, not a trade delegate who might toil in relative obscurity. Assigning the task to him was a powerful message by Jiang Zemin that the changes set in motion by Deng would be permanent.

Even in autocratic societies, however, governments cannot race too far ahead of popular sentiment. In those parts of China that had seen rapid growth and new affluence, there was also a surge in nationalism. Chinese nationalism, both before the victory of the Communists and after, was laced with distrust of the "imperialist" West that had come so close to occupying the country at the end of the nineteenth century and in the early decades of the twentieth. While feelings of animosity toward

Japan may have burned more intensely after the brutal years of war between 1933 and 1945, lingering anger toward the West tinged with feelings of humiliation coursed through Chinese society as surely as the American dream of homes, cars, and independence ran deep in American culture.

These deep currents of distrust were never far from the surface. Each time some American senator or congressional representative raised questions about human rights, the lack of democracy, or the rule of law, China heard the echo of imperialists past who had treated the Middle Kingdom as a land of corrupt naifs who were neither equal in intelligence nor in ability. When U.S. negotiators objected to China's demand that it be treated as a developing nation rather than a developed nation, Chinese interlocutors heard in those demands an insidious plan to undermine China's sovereignty and place it once again under the thumb of the West.

In the United States, meanwhile, the old legacy of friendship with China that defined the Nationalist period before 1949 was offset by a deep-seated suspicion of any country governed by the Communist Party. That was further colored by the recriminations that followed 1949, when a witch hunt of "who lost China" went hand in hand with a determination never to allow Communist China to join the international community. The opening that occurred in 1972, when Nixon made his stunning and surprising visit to Beijing to sit and talk with Chairman Mao, created the foundation for a new relationship based on mutual interests rather than incompatible ideology and bitter history, but the legacy of distrust burdened the U.S. side as well.

Still, after weathering the aftershocks of the Asian crisis, the Chinese leadership was resolved to push ahead. Having the luxury of not being in debt to any of the Western nations, China's bargaining position was stronger than most "developing" countries, who often were in the position of petitioning the United States—and by extension the European Union—for membership in a club that was created by and dominated by the wealthier nations. While Zhu recognized that concessions would have to made, and probably steeper than many in China would support, the nature of China's system of state-run capitalism insulated the country from some of the risks associated with joining the WTO. China still maintained tight control of capital flows in and out of the country, and that acted as a dam against the flood of global capital that too often deluged developing nations. In addition, Zhu planned to hold the line on timetables. Even if he agreed to steeper reductions of taxes and more openness to foreign companies doing direct business in China itself, he would not compromise much on speed. His tactic was simple: agree with the general goal of having China be part of the global trade system but insist that the lowering of barriers occur gradually over the course of a decade. Russia in the early 1990s had been crushed by too much too soon; China would not make that mistake.

China's tough stance caused friction in the United States, where many members of Congress as well as business leaders judged China's economy to be of a different order than the typical developing economy: more layered, more sophisticated, and with much greater potential to become a competitor. Those concerns were justified, but China in the late 1990s was still a far cry from what it would be just a few years later. It remained a predominantly agrarian, poor country with pockets of reform along the coast and large swaths of the old industrial north that were kept from collapse by continued injections of money by the state.

Countless preliminary meetings and thousands of hours of discussion by ministers and trade officials hashed out the innumerable issues. A very partial list of these included: When and on what terms could U.S. and foreign insurance companies do business in China? When and how much would quotas for wheat and citrus be reduced? What percentage of a Chinese telecom company could a foreign entity own? What types of retail banking could a foreign bank do and at what date? How much protection could be maintained for China's domestic industries, such as steel and textiles? Where could foreign law offices operate? Once these issues were addressed, the final stages were left to the premier of China, Zhu Rongji, and the president of the United States, William Jefferson Clinton.

Though the WTO was a global organization consisting of hundreds of members, the United States, by virtue of its size and power, could de facto veto almost any measure. Other members could also band together and effectively block action, but if China wanted to join, the U.S. Congress had to agree. As a result, when the negotiations entered their final phase in the spring of 1999, all the old qualms about China came to the fore in Washington. Those then dovetailed with vehement reactions in China against the move away from Communism and toward a global trade and economic system then dominated by the icon of free-market capitalism, the United States.

Ready to resolve all outstanding issues, Zhu traveled to Washington in April 1999. The city was then consumed, as was much of the nation, with the unfolding soap opera of the Monica Lewinsky scandal. Little else received much media attention, not the intervention of the United States to secure the independence of Kosovo, not the continued tensions over the no-fly zone in Iraq, and not the visit of the number two official of China to discuss what would be the most significant development for China and the Western world in decades.

Zhu went on a charm offensive, offering interviews and making public appearances to a degree that was normally unthinkable for a Communist Party official, let alone one of his standing. Speaking with the *Wall Street Journal*, he asserted that

China had made innumerable concessions to U.S. demands, especially in its willingness to relax restrictions on foreign ownership of Chinese companies. "You may ask me why China is making such concessions," he said. "The reason is . . . because we want to protect the overall picture of friendly cooperation between China and the U.S. . . . in order to build toward a constructive strategic partnership . . . We have felt all along that China is not a rival of the United States, let alone an enemy of the U.S., but rather is a reliable friend."[1]

While a CEO with millions on the line—a CEO like Fred Smith and hundreds of others—would have agreed, others were not so sure. Any deal that would signal acceptance of Communist China, of its autocratic government and its questionable (in the eyes of the West) record on human rights, as well as its lax enforcement of contracts and intellectual property rights, was seen by many as immoral, misguided, and not in American interests. The left interpreted the strong support of the business community for normalized relations and increased trade as a naked and cynical play for more profit at the expense of the American worker and even at the expense of American economic security. Some on the right clung to the rigid ideology of the Cold War which had declared any Communist regime anathema and demanded a rejection of China until democracy trumped Communist dictatorship. Many opponents, left and right, feared that the deal was simply a ploy that would give China access to American capital and know-how so that the Chinese Communists could use that knowledge to enhance their military, strengthen the state, and then seize Taiwan and confront the West at some point in the early twenty-first century.

While the American public may have been glued to the Lewinsky affair, the White House and the trade negotiators tried to act as if it were business as normal. By the end of April, Zhu and Clinton had ironed out the remaining issues. Though China was allowed to retain its status as a developing nation, Zhu made a host of concessions to U.S. demands, particularly on telecommunications. Because this was still in the midst of the height of New Economy ambitions, telecommunications assumed almost as much importance as agriculture. Zhu agreed to much more openness to foreign telecom companies, as well as to more protections for U.S. textile companies. Yet in spite of Zhu's Herculean efforts, in mid-April Clinton informed him that he would not yet endorse the deal or bring it to Congress. Too weakened by the endless tide of negative press and the ongoing impeachment hearings, Clinton did not feel that he had the political capital to navigate a deal through a Congress that was at best ambivalent about it.

It was a devastating moment for Zhu and for backers of the accord. The Chinese premier had staked his prestige on the deal by making the negotiations so public. To leave Washington without the high-profile press conference replete with cameras flashing as he shook the president's hand and the encomiums of how the new accord would cement years of friendship and prosperity for the two countries was to leave with his proverbial tail between his legs. Opponents in China were waiting to take their shots. Unless Zhu received the explicit support of Jiang Zemin, his own position would be in jeopardy after such a visible defeat.

The weeks that followed seemed to seal not only Zhu's political fate but any hope of future convergence of the economies of the United States and China. In addition to the Lewinsky scandal and sordid details about taped conversations and stained dresses, the headlines were full of talk of Chinese nuclear espionage at the Los Alamos National Laboratory in New Mexico. A Taiwanese-American scientist named Wen Ho Lee had been arrested on suspicion of feeding secret technology to China, and the assumption almost everywhere (which turned out to be unwarranted) was that he had indeed spied for the Chinese government. His case had negatively impacted Zhu's visit, but things deteriorated even further when a congressional committee released its report.

Chaired by Representative Christopher Cox, a Republican from California who would later become chairman of the Securities and Exchange Commission (SEC), the committee had conducted months of secret investigations that went far beyond the accusations against Wen Ho Lee. The so-called Cox Report unequivocally declared that the People's Republic of China had been stealing U.S. nuclear technology throughout the 1990s and that those secrets would allow the Chinese to develop a sophisticated nuclear arsenal more rapidly than had been anticipated. The report also asserted that "U.S. policies relying on corporate self-policing to prevent technology loss have not worked . . . Corporate self-policing does not sufficiently account for the risks posed by inherent conflicts of interest, and the lack of priority placed on security in comparison to other corporate objectives." While the report was actually written in January 1999, its contents were not made public until May, just as Zhu was returning to China with the status of the trade deal in jeopardy.

The Cox Report was inflammatory enough. The gods must have been displeased, however, because its release came on the heels of the inadvertent bombing of the Chinese embassy in Belgrade by NATO jets that were then pummeling Serbia in order to coerce its regime to withdraw from Kosovo. The American government promptly apologized to China and claimed that the bombing was a mistake based on inaccurate maps, but in China, that claim was greeted with skepticism bordering on derision. How could the world's most sophisticated military possibly make such a colossal mistake as to destroy the Chinese embassy in the middle of a Serbian city? The bombing triggered a wave of protests in China, which included thousands of angry students marching in front of the U.S. embassy in Beijing and throwing stones at the compound. Though the protests couldn't have continued without the acquiescence of the government, some in the United States were convinced that they were actually orchestrated by the government.

It's impossible to know how the protests began, but the notion that nothing in China could happen spontaneously, or that any nationalist sentiment in China was a creation of the government, is to misconstrue the nature of Chinese society. Yes, it was (and still is) an autocratic, secretive government that zealously attempted to stifle dissent and control political expression. But it was also a government by a Communist Party that had millions of members and ruled more than a billion people. Provinces had a good deal of autonomy, and from time immemorial, always had. The desire of Beijing for control exceeded the ability of Beijing to control. Nationalism in China bound society together but had its more troubling elements. It tended toward xenophobia and suspicion of the outside world, especially the West, and toward an aggressive stance about Taiwan and its continued independence. The embassy bombing ignited populist Chinese nationalism as surely as it literally ignited the building in Belgrade.

But in the United States, the protests were taken as a sign of official Chinese displeasure and a transparent effort to further sow dissension and drive the two countries apart. Cox was dismissive. "The organization of anti-American demonstrations has laid bare the manipulative nature of the Communist government." Cox believed that Beijing "used the protests to gain leverage in negotiations" with the United States over the terms of accession to the WTO.[2] Anti-American sentiment in Beijing was met in equal measure by anti-Chinese sentiment in Washington. Even before the bombing, officials in Washington had released the draft agreement that Zhu had wanted to finalize, and the only purpose of the release was to torpedo any chance that the deal would be passed. Longtime opponents of closer ties, such as Republican senator Jesse Helms of North Carolina and Democratic senator Ernest Hollings of South Carolina, pointed to the protests in Beijing as an "I told you so" to justify their earlier opposition. By the end of May, the chances of China and the United States coming to a resolution appeared slim indeed.[3]

Yet even the protests were not quite as they seemed. Anti-American sentiment may have run high, but the crowds that stoned the American embassy in Beijing were wearing Nike baseball caps and Disney T-shirts.[4] That alone, of course, says much about the globalization of trade and goods but nothing about the hearts and minds of the Chinese students who wore them. A similar observation has been made about the Iranian students who stormed the U.S. embassy in Tehran in 1979 and took Americans hostage. To don the mantles of modernity is not to endorse its mores. But by 1999, China was already enmeshed in the West and in Western capitalism, and by its own choosing. It wanted to become integrated into the global system and to become integral to it. But pride and a strong sense of historical pique also led to wariness of the United States and sensitivity to anything that smacked of capitulation. For several days after the Belgrade bombing, that took the form of extreme belligerence. "The campus is seething," said Xiao Nan, a junior at Beijing University, during the protests. "People are gathering all night talking about strengthening the Chinese military, and attacking Clinton. America and Clinton have become a . . . target for Chinese anger."[5] Students, of course, are not known for moderation, and strong words were only that. But with tempers high and relations deteriorating fast, it seemed as if the momentum that had propelled China and the United States to move ever closer since 1989 had halted and was about to move in reverse.

To almost everyone's surprise, it did not. Quietly but quickly, both governments moved to restart the negotiations. Instead of doing that in the public eye, the discussions occurred in private and in secret over the summer. Zhu assumed a lower profile in Beijing, leading some observers to question whether he had been demoted by Jiang. While he had certainly been dinged, he continued to steer the course. Having committed his career to continuing on the path begun by Deng, he made a tactical shift away from greater public openness and back to the older modus operandi of working behind closed doors. Clinton also decided to pursue a lower-profile path and work privately with allies in Congress, of whom there were many but who had to tread carefully lest they be seen as apologists for China or complicit in the scandals engulfing the White House.

While public opinion in both China and the United States tilted against closer ties—at least in the form suggested by the WTO—government and business leaders wanted to move forward. As had been true with the debates over NAFTA, more free trade was what business and government elites craved, not what many people wanted. Nowhere in the world was free trade an easy sell, an irony that was lost on most. At a time when the word *globalization* was entering common parlance, anxiety over what that entailed was rising. The shiny bauble of the New Economy masked a great degree of anxiety about what this new world meant. While Silicon Valley entrepreneurs were getting super-cool rich, millions of Americans were feeling the shudders of the destructive part of "creative destruction." The promise of a world enhanced by computer productivity had the downside of a world that required fewer workers to produce the same products. Added to the perils of technology, there was the threat that China posed to the American worker. China, much like Mexico a decade earlier, was seen in the United States as a real and present competitor for jobs, a competition that China would win because the average wage was so much less than it was in the United States. The result was that anti-Communism blended with fear of job loss and anxiety about wage stagnation to form a powerful bloc that questioned closer ties with China and more intimate ties with the world at large.

Having been caught in a compromising personal position, Clinton was in a compromised political position. Distracted and politically hobbled, he could no longer argue as persuasively that globalization offered bountiful opportunities for Americans. In the absence of strong and consistent messages from Washington, opponents were ceded the public field. In China, meanwhile, opposition came from entrenched interests like the old state enterprises and hard-line voices in the Communist Party. Zhu had been tireless in his efforts to force state companies to become more competitive, and his efforts to overhaul the banking system were met with strong measures from those who had never embraced Deng's policies in the first place. Zhu wanted to open China to greater global competition through the WTO because he believed that it would hasten the demise of ineffective and moribund state companies in China. That was precisely why the managers of those companies and their many allies in the party opposed him and his plans. They could also manipulate popular opinion, by fanning the anti-Americanism that smouldered beneath the surface or by raising the question of worker rights and who would protect them.

After months of radio silence, the two governments announced in mid-November that an agreement had been reached. The U.S. trade representative, Charlene Barshefsky, concluded the deal with a photo-op handshake with her counterpart, the Chinese trade minister, Shi Guangsheng. While neither had, of course, acted without the explicit green light of their bosses, the fact that it was them and not Zhu and Clinton was an astute tactic: make the deal seem like any other trade agreement rather than a symbol of a brave and scary new world. Optics notwithstanding, it was anything but a garden-variety trade agreement.

The announcement was, unsurprisingly, hailed by business leaders. "This certainly makes it more favorable for us to invest," said an executive at the high-tech Texas Instruments. Even though the amount of ownership foreign firms could have of companies in China was more restricted than the United States had initially wanted, the agreement provided for a timetable for the percentage to increase. Foreign banks were initially not allowed to do retail banking, but over the course of several years, they would be able to expand their operations to include an ever-wider variety of services to Chinese consumers and businesses. The same was true of other industries, including automobiles and insurance. General Motors, for instance, welcomed the provisions that would allow it both to own a larger percentage of its joint ventures and eventually to set up a finance arm in China along the lines of GMAC, which provided loans and leasing to the majority of GM customers in the United States at the time. As a result, even as GM's business in the United States hurtled downward, it became extremely profitable in China. The agreement also set a timetable for a decrease in import tariffs for agricultural goods, and a decrease in subsidies for Chinese exports of food, steel, and a host of industrial goods that China had been protecting and underwriting. Most of the subsidies would be phased out over time, as would the barriers, but in general, the transition would be complete by 2005.[6]

It still remained for Congress to ratify and for the leadership in China to overcome the resistance of the state enterprises that were facing demands for efficiency and privatization coming from Zhu along with the looming threat of greater foreign competition. While China had agreed that the U.S. could maintain some restrictions on textile imports—a major issue, given that

China could make everything from bras to T-shirts to sportswear more quickly and less expensively than any American factory—the concessions cast a harsh light on the long-term implications. The same could be said of China's willingness to crack down on the more egregious pirating of intellectual property.

No matter what each government promised, however, the nature of the agreement and of the WTO itself was to channel the tide of global commerce toward comparative advantage and away from national interests. Comparative advantage, one of the basic tenets of modern capitalism—enunciated by the early nineteenth-century economist David Ricardo and others since—holds that in theory, a free market will allocate capital where it is most efficient, and goods will be made where costs are low. While a country may suffer the loss of an industry, its consumers will in turn benefit from the lower costs of goods and services they want being made somewhere else more cheaply. So went the theory. In practice, reality was messier. Lost jobs were lost jobs; changing patterns of trade and production may have benefited the many, but whenever those changes happened, they also hurt those who depended on the status quo. Add in the disruptive effects of technology, which was even more responsible for obsolescing older modes of production in the United States, Europe, and throughout the world, and you had an agreement that fit economic theory but remained politically explosive.

In short, barriers and protections phased out over time were still barriers and protections phased out. Making the date 2005 gave some breathing room, but opponents of the deal saw through the timetable and to the heart of the issue: once barriers came down, once production went to where it was most efficient and least expensive, and once companies and capital began to focus on markets where there was the greatest potential for future growth, the ability for any one country to control its economic fate would diminish. And once those forces were unleashed, there would be no going back.

The sense of foreboding explains the violence in Seattle at the end of 1999, when the ministers of the WTO met to discuss the next round of global trade agreements. China and the U.S. had come to their agreement, and China was about to conclude a similar negotiation with the European Union. But even without the China factor, popular sentiment in the United States and others parts of the world had been turning against unmitigated free trade. The contest pitted those who believed in an ever-greater embrace of globalization and its benefits for global capital against those who believed just as ardently that the net effect was to benefit a few wealthy corporations at the expense of the many.

The meeting in Seattle brought together representatives from 135 countries and was greeted by a ferocious outpouring of anger in the streets not seen since the Vietnam War. The result was tear gas, riot police, broken bones, arrests, shattered glass, burning cars, balaclava-clad men and women glaring at armored police, and bystanders caught in the fray. The protestors—who numbered in the tens of thousands—were a mix of peaceful activists uncomfortable with the lack of specificity about environmental protections and labor rights along with a small number of anarchists who saw the WTO as the next, dangerous stage in the establishment of a global government in thrall to business interests. The largest union organizations in the United States, including the powerful AFL-CIO (American Federation of Labor and Congress of Industrial Organizations), opposed further extending the scope of free trade and of the terms of China's admission to the organization. "Our view is that once China comes into the WTO, we have no leverage to raise the worker-rights problems anymore," said a spokesman for the AFL-CIO.

These concerns weren't ignored by the Clinton administration. Both Clinton and his vice president, Albert Gore, genuflected to the need for more worker protections embedded in global trade agreements. But for the unions, those reassuring words paled in comparison with the thousands of clauses detailing duties on every possible good and service, with scant reference to labor rights, workplace conditions, or environmental issues. And the fact that leaders of both parties in the United States—including two men poised to become their party's nominee for president: Gore and Texas governor George Bush—endorsed the overall expansion of the WTO and the entry of China did not give comfort or assurance that the issues raised by the Seattle protestors would ever be addressed.[7]

The debacle in Seattle was dramatic but did nothing to halt the trajectory. The ministers left, shaken by the virulence but determined to plow ahead and secure in their belief that more openness globally was in everyone's interest. After the flurry of attention to China and global trade, the U.S. press moved on to the cresting of the Nasdaq market in March 2000 and then the steep collapse of both the stock market and then the Internet and telecom bubbles. In Europe, attention turned to internal affairs and to the debates over enlargement of the union and further measures to cement the federation. In China, Zhu returned to the difficult work of internal reform, especially in the banking and financial sectors. And then the events of 9/11 interrupted the world and shifted focus yet again, toward the challenge of terrorism, the intractability of Afghanistan, and the place of the United States in the world. Relations with China had been strained prior to 9/11: in April 2001, a U.S. spy plane collided with a Chinese naval fighter over the South China Sea and had to make an emergency landing at a Chinese military airfield. The plane was returned to the United States only after the Chinese had taken it apart, studied it, and presumably copied it. However, tension over the incident was offset by the awarding of the 2008 Olympics to Beijing with the support of the United States.

In short, with these few exceptions, after 1999, the China-U.S. relationship assumed a low profile in both China and the United States. Even when China officially joined the WTO in December 2001, it was at most a two-day story, quickly relegated to the business pages and pushed aside for more pressing concerns such as the rumblings about Afghanistan and the whereabouts of Osama bin Laden. In China, the focus was on the continued integration of Hong Kong, the emergence of Shanghai as a financial center, and the impending leadership transition as Jiang Zemin began his gradual retirement in 2002.

The frame of the debates in the late 1990s and into the first years of the twenty-first century gave little indication of the deeper forces at work. On the face of it, the discussions and controversies were garden variety. Nations and states had been dancing these diplomatic two-steps for centuries. While the scale and scope of global organizations such as the WTO or the United Nations were particular products of the twentieth century, when it came down to it, there was nothing all that "new" in the disagreements between China and the United States, or between the EU and China, or between any of the several hundred national governments that made up the map of the globe. Ministers still huddled in closed chambers and were still appointed by governments that were in turn influenced by various interest groups, of which businesses and their leaders were one of the more powerful.

Nations still defined their self-interest in ways that ended at their national boundaries, though the history of the twentieth century had led to a widespread acceptance that there was such a thing as a global commons and a common good and that at times, giving up some sovereignty to a body like the UN or giving resources to something like the World Health

Organization might serve self-interest more than going it alone. International relations, starting with security concerns and extending to economics, were understood in terms of state-to-state, *bilateral* relations, or in terms of many states working together in a *multilateral* fashion. Yes, the world was abuzz with thousands of nongovernmental organizations, from Greenpeace to Doctors Without Borders and so on and so forth. But the dominant framework remained the nation-state, defined by its borders, its bureaucracies, its armies, central banks, and individual currencies.

Here and there, you could hear notes of something different. The technologists and Silicon Valley visionaries were forever spinning dreams of a borderless world, linked through the ether of the Internet and the Web, of communities finding one another and connecting with one another without the intervention or participation of the state. But those were abstract concepts in a concrete world. Even the apostles of trade without barriers spoke in terms of an expanding pie that would feed the needs and ambitions both of individuals and of states. One day, perhaps, state governments would wither, or a new supergovernment along the lines of the European Union would become the norm for the globe, but weak or strong the sovereign state would still be the core unit.

So the interaction between China and the United States and between China and the world at large in the 1990s was still defined by states and ministers, and by companies that identified themselves first by their country of origin, by where they were headquartered, which capital market gave them primary funding, and what language was their internal lingua franca. Businesses may have understood that global markets transcended any one state or international governing institution, but the individuals who ran them were as rooted in their own nation-state as anyone else. Thus, as China prepared to enter the WTO, it was perceived as simply another step in the ongoing game of nations and the ever-shifting balance of power between business and government, between capital and the state, between managers and workers.

It was not, therefore, seen as what it was: the step that changed the system from something familiar into something not. It was not yet another document agreed to by two parties; it was the birth of a new paradigm. Even today, many would dispute that notion. Many will dismiss the idea of Chimerica altogether, especially in light of the earthquakes that shook the global financial system in 2008 and 2009. There is also the very problem of proving the existence of an entity that in traditional terms does not exist. From the vantage point of Washington and Beijing and from the perspective of more than a billion people in China and 300 million in the United States, the world is still defined by national borders and national identity. The fusion of China and America may exist, but in the minds of most, it doesn't.

The nation-state mindset is one obstacle. But so is the absence of data. There is almost no data proving that China and America have become one economy. And to understand why that is, and before we turn to the rapid evolution of this new system in the years after 9/11, we need to take a step back and look at how we understand economies and how they have, until now, been measured.

CHAPTER 7

Data Duped

T HE FOUNDATION FOR THE fusion of the American and Chinese economies was laid in the 1990s, but only after 2001 did Chimerica fully emerge and begin to reshape the world. Most of the anomalies of the first decade of the twenty-first century, including the movement of interest rates, the cost of goods, the stagnation of wages in the developed world, and— especially in light of the meltdown of 2008—the proliferation of credit in the United States and Europe along with the related buildup of savings and dollars in China were due to the emergence of China on the one hand and the symbiotic relationship between China and the United States on the other.

So, too, is the stability of the global economy relative to the past 200 years. Many people, no doubt, do not experience the economic landscape today as stable, especially given recession and the 2008–09 collapse of the credit and stock markets. But those crises did not produce the chaos and social breakdown that was characteristic of early periods, however wrenching they felt. That comparative stability is also a product of the U.S.-China fusion. If all this is the case, however, why have so few noticed?

The simple answer is that almost no one has been looking. More precisely, no one is paid to look. There are two reasons: the profession and practice of economics and the way that data about the world is collected. It's not that either is inherently flawed but rather that neither has caught up to the world as it now is.

Think about it: most of what we think we know about the world is derived from a suite of statistics. Those statistics are compiled by various people from a variety of sources, ranging from government agencies to international organizations to businesses. We all rely on data assembled by others in order to form a snapshot of what is going on, because none of us is in a position to observe most of what takes place on the globe. How much oil is consumed daily? The commonly accepted number is 87 million to 88 million barrels. We know that because someone in the Organization of the Petroleum Exporting Countries (OPEC) or at the International Energy Agency (IEA) compiles that information, as do the major oil companies themselves. We take that statistic on faith insofar as none of us actually counts every barrel. We take on faith that some reputable group has spent the time and energy to reduce a complex system to a simple number, and we then use their data to make conclusions about prices, supply, demand, and future trends. The same could be said of almost every piece of information we use.

Some data are more basic than others. Oil consumption and iron ore production are arithmetic. The amount produced is counted and added up. Even here, adjustments are made by the statisticians. It's not as if all 88 million barrels were lined up and counted physically. Instead, refineries, national oil companies, private companies, and government agencies release their own figures, which other groups then assemble. Not all appear at the same time, and some are fuzzier than others. So even a basic calculation such as global oil consumption can present challenges and become complicated in practice.

Other data are more abstract, which makes the process of compilation more complex. Take the rate of inflation. First the concept has to be defined. Then ways need to be invented to measure it. Today in the United States, the most common measure of inflation is a statistic calculated by the Bureau of Labor Statistics called the consumer price index. Every month, the statisticians at the BLS survey the prices of a wide range of goods and then calculate how much those have changed since the month before. The basket of goods in the surveys is not "weighted"—that is, their relative importance in the index doesn't change whether more or less is consumed. Periodically, the weights are adjusted, but from month to month, they aren't. That means that if gas prices are very high one month and as a result people don't drive as much the next, the decreased consumption doesn't get factored into the relative importance of gasoline to the overall inflation picture.

In addition to the basket of goods, the BLS tries to factor in the cost of homes. Unless a home is actually sold, the increase or decrease in its nominal value isn't included directly in inflation statistics. In order to capture some of the price movements of a home, the statisticians created something called "owners' equivalent rent," which attempts to determine the value of the home by assessing what the current rental value would be if the occupants had to pay rent rather than a mortgage. That component alone makes up nearly 30 percent of the entire monthly price index.

The creation of the consumer price index is an elaborate process that attempts to provide one simple, synthetic figure for anything but a synthetic, simple reality. The same is true for any number of statistics, ranging from the unemployment rate to the gross domestic product to the national savings rate. All of these use some combination of surveys, quantitative metrics and adjustments, and all of them are subject to revisions to the initial figure as more data become available in subsequent months and years. Methodologies also change. But each time the methods are changed, after someone identifies an issue or a limitation and tries to remedy that, it becomes more difficult to compare the data over time. The way inflation is calculated today is not the way it was assessed 20 years ago, which means that comparing the stated inflation rate in the consumer price index in 2009 to what it was in 1989 is like comparing a 2009 Ford to a 1989 Ford; they are made by the same company, but they are radically different cars.

These data points, however, are the only guideposts we have to assess "the economy." Yet even that basic concept assumes that there is such a thing as "the economy." No question, each country, trading bloc, and geographic region is intimately affected by economic ebbs and flows. But the phrase "the economy" suggests something else. It suggests that there is this unitary, closed system that can be quantified and described and that the figures used to do so provide a useful picture of activity within that system. Most of us then take those characterizations of "the economy" and apply them generally to most people living in the system. The assumption is that if "the economy" is weak or in recession, then most people are negatively impacted, as are most industries and businesses and regions.

Not necessarily. There are huge regional variations in most countries, and especially in larger countries such as the United States, China, and the individual members of the European Union. The economic conditions of Omaha, Nebraska, may tell us nothing about the condition of Las Vegas, and the problems of Leeds, England, may have no relationship to the strengths of Manchester. The same could be said of Beijing rather than Changsha, Paris as opposed to Marseille, and Rome compared to Palermo. Sometimes, both pain and profit are spread evenly, but many times, one area is thriving while another suffers. That can be true of industries as well, which sometimes parallel geography and sometimes not. Pittsburgh faced challenging times in the 1990s even as Silicon Valley began to thrive, partly because it was saddled with the old industries that had collapsed even as Silicon Valley thrived from the influx of investment capital and new technology and telecommunications companies.

But there is an even larger issue. Most statistics were invented by governments in order to measure what is going on in the nation-state that they are governing. The U.S. consumer price index was created in 1919. Many of today's statistical benchmarks were established during the late nineteenth century and the first decades of the twentieth century, as were the agencies responsible for producing them. The most common measure of national economies is the gross domestic product, the GDP, which most people believe is the best indicator of a nation's economic health. Yet GDP as a statistic has existed only since the 1930s, when it was used to help the Roosevelt administration figure out whether its innovative but untested New Deal programs were succeeding in ameliorating the systemic issues that had led the stock market to lose nearly 90 percent of its value, 25 percent of the U.S. workforce to lose its jobs, thousands of banks to shutter their doors, and the sale and production of goods to plummet.

The indicators that we use to assess the health of "the economy" have become enshrined in national politics and bureaucracies, in almost every country in the world. As more states formed throughout the twentieth century, they copied Western nations and that included establishing government agencies to calculate things like GDP, inflation, and the unemployment rate. Businesses, investors, politicians, and individuals use that data to formulate plans, assess what they believe the future holds, and make decisions about everything from the national budget to corporate hiring to whether or not to take the family on a vacation to Disney World or its equivalents. Some of those countries have a thriving middle class who take cues from the data; others have little more than subsistence farming, where statistics matter only to a small governing class, the nongovernmental organizations advising them, and foreign investors circling the scene.

The statistics were created at a time when most economies were either industrial or agrarian, composed of workers who made things rather than the service-oriented economies prevalent in the developed world in the latter half of the twentieth century and into the twenty-first. During the 1990s, in fact, the traditional measures failed to register any changes in things such as worker productivity even as computers and the Internet so clearly began to alter the way most people work. Though anyone working at any company could say without question that the advent of computers and the Web allowed for greater efficiencies, that wasn't showing up in the official statistics. The reason was simple: none of the statistics had been developed when there were computers, and there was no method to capture the amorphous nature of work when it took place on a computer screen rather than a factory floor. All of those automated bank teller machines, for instance, allowed financial institutions to process more transactions with fewer employees, which in turn enhanced their profitability, albeit at the expense of labor. But that fact was all but invisible in national and official productivity statistics in the United States, which barely registered any improvement in the productivity of financial services companies throughout the 1990s.

There is an even deeper issue, however. It isn't just that technology outpaced the ability of government statisticians. The very foundation of the data is now outdated—and not just the data, but the economic theories on which they are based.

Almost every piece of information we have about economics—or, more precisely, macroeconomics—is based on the notion that the nation-state is the primary unit of an economic system. Economics as a profession emerged in the mid to late nineteenth century, along with other social sciences such as sociology, history, and political science. There had been philosophers of economics before then, towering intellects such as Adam Smith and David Ricardo, who framed much of Western thinking, but it wasn't until the second half of the nineteenth century that economics emerged as a self-defined profession.

Over the next century, the profession developed rules, gathered information, and formulated hypotheses about both human behavior and economic systems. The goal was to solidify economics as a science, which meant testing hypotheses to prove or disprove their validity. That was the core of the scientific method: repeatable experiments that could gauge the validity of theories. That made sense in a laboratory. You could endlessly set up the same experiment with the same variables. How does a chemical react with another chemical? Start with chemical A and add different amounts of chemical B and record what happens.

The problem with economics as applied to societies is that these experiments are possible only as a mental exercise. No one gets to freeze society in one place and test different variables to study cause and effect. Did the Great Depression happen because the U.S. government didn't respond the right way? It's a fascinating question, but it would be easier to answer if you could endlessly start in 1931 and modify what actually happened with what might have happened to study the consequences. Economists have been able to test certain theories as applied to individual behavior. Do people rationally pursue their self-interest? That is one of the fundamental hypotheses of traditional economics, and to test it, economists have devised numerous experiments with control groups of several dozen people. Then variables can be changed, behavior studied, and conclusions drawn. But what can be done at an individual or small-group level is impossible for society.

The belief that economics is a science with laws has deeply

affected how the world is understood by economists. It has led economists in academia, Wall Street, and the government to pay attention to some things more than others, and to attempt to explain anomalies in terms of laws they believe exist. As we shall see, that has led to a chronic inability to appreciate the nature of the U.S.-China relationship. But there is another legacy that has been equally crippling: the assumption that the nation-state is the primary economic unit, and that it should be analyzed as a closed system.

The idea that the state is an economic unit made perfect sense for most of the twentieth century. Indeed, at the time that economics emerged as a discipline, the state was the single most important system in the world. National governments defined and defended borders; issued the sole valid currency for inhabitants inside those borders; chartered and ran central banks that were responsible for the accounts of the government and for the basic oversight of the financial system within state borders; taxed goods, entities, and individuals; established the rules and conditions for the importation of foreign goods and the exportation of domestic goods; and determined how and to what extent foreign individuals or businesses could own property or do business within state borders.

As the twentieth century progressed, the state took ever more active roles in economic life within its borders. Governments looked for ways to lessen the cycles of boom and bust, expansion and contraction, that had been ubiquitous for as long as anyone could remember and had been sources of instability, chaos, and war as well as the breakdown of social order and revolution. The turmoil of the Great Depression helped cause World War II; the economic ambitions of various European countries led to adventures in colonialism that often created more burdens than rewards; dislocations in industry and labor led to strikes and internal violence in both Western Europe and the United States; and inflation, hyperinflation, and insufficient access to affordable food were the sources of unrest and uprisings, from Mexico in the early part of the twentieth century to China between the two world wars.

Because so much economic activity was determined by the state and ended at the state's borders, it made sense for economists to define the macroeconomic system in terms of the state. Traditional economics didn't just view the state as a system; it held that the system had to be in equilibrium, which meant that all inputs should be balanced by an equivalent numbers of outputs, that supply and demand should be equal, and that prices should find their natural level based on activity within the state. As economics and macroeconomic theory became more sophisticated, the equilibrium notion still remained at the core.

One example of that notion is trade. For the system to maintain equilibrium, it is thought, a nation's imports should not exceed its exports and its exports should not exceed its imports. If one is greater than the other, then the nation's trade is considered to be imbalanced. The same is the case for a state's current account, as well as balance of payments, relative to other states. Currency and foreign exchange rates also shape the balances. If more money is owed abroad, then that country is said to have a current account deficit; if more money has been lent to foreign entities, then there is a current account surplus. In either case— surplus or deficit—the system is not in a state of equilibrium, and because equilibrium is what the system strives for, those imbalances have to be addressed and rectified so that the system returns to a state of equilibrium. If a country is importing more than it is exporting, then eventually its currency has to decrease in value, making its own goods less expensive abroad and foreign goods more expensive at home, which in turn should mean more exports and fewer imports. Or if the current account deficit yawns too wide, money has to be paid back, inflation has to increase (thereby making it easier to repay), and borrowing has to slow until the gap closes.

These principles may have originated and been fleshed out by academic economists, but they have become enshrined in both politics and business. Traditional economics, which includes everything from the idea that the market is composed of rational actors to the principle that a nation's accounts must be in balance, have become, in the worlds of business and government, "laws" of economics that are as immutable and unchangeable as "laws of nature." Though these ideas evolved gradually over the course of the twentieth century, they remain ensconced in businesses and governments, even as some academic economists have either moved on to other questions or have themselves challenged, questioned, and modified some of the basic hypotheses of traditional economics. Research economists have questioned the idea of rational actors and the very idea of a state as an equilibrium system, yet most of the economists who help shape government policy and Wall Street behavior remain wedded to the basic notion of the state as an economic unit and to the belief that there are laws of economics that demand that it rest in a state of equilibrium.[1]

In truth, business and government economists are not paid to do abstract research. They are not paid to sit back and contemplate new models. They are supposed to analyze and parse the available data and make predictions about likely future trends. And they are paid because there is some perceived specific need that their function addresses. Deep thoughts may be a societal necessity, but outside academia, they are rarely seen as necessary enough to divert otherwise precious resources. There are, of course, exceptions. In flush times, companies sometimes set up think tanks that allow creative minds to cogitate about big ideas. But such units are usually the first to go when times are tight.

In general, an economist employed by a financial institution is supposed to make sense of the bewildering array of data that spews forth from government agencies and corporations, as well as from industry associations and other groups that produce regular statistics about consumer sentiment or housing activity or retail sales. These economists are also used as a vital source of information by various clients. During the time that I served as chief economist for a Wall Street firm, I spent considerable time speaking with brokers and financial advisors who wanted a read on current conditions, a sense of where the indicators were pointing (up or down), and what the implications might be for the price of stocks and bonds. They needed that guidance in order to decide how to allocate their clients' money and where to invest. While individuals in that position may have contrarian or creative ideas about which data are reliable and which aren't, which theories accurately point to likely outcomes and which don't, their primary role is to explain the data and provide analysis for clients rather than test and reformulate basic tenets such as equilibrium and rational actors.

Government economists can be found in most departments, and appear in force at the Federal Reserve, the Treasury Department, the Office of Management and Budget, and the various statistical agencies such as the Census Bureau and the Bureau of Economic Analysis. The Federal Reserve has hundreds of economists working at its 12 branches, many of whom do substantial and sophisticated research on questions such as why and how does labor productivity improve, and how can one calculate the "wealth effect" from higher home and equity prices (or conversely, the "poverty effect" from sharply lower prices). Staff economists help Congress figure out what the budget shortfalls will be in the years ahead based on likely tax receipts and industrial output. Others work with their agencies to predict exports versus imports, domestic sales, interest rates, currency movements, and other factors that impact the national budget and the overall economy. And of course, the most important use of these economists and those statistics is to set the parameters for entitlement spending. Their analysis determines Social Security benefits (which are keyed to the rate of inflation) and sets the budgetary requirements of Medicare and Medicaid.

In short, the bulk of the information we have on economies is gathered either by government agencies or by businesses and business associations. Governments collect data in order to make decisions about spending and to assess the efficacy of programs and the stability of the system. Inflation figures aren't assembled in order to tell the average man or woman something meaningful about his or her personal fortune or lack thereof; inflation statistics and unemployment and trade figures are compiled to provide the government with signposts, to set spending targets, and to predict future revenues. State governments do the same thing. Other data—on retail sales, on layoff announcements, inventories, and housing starts—are provided by business associations to help companies in those industries assess trends and plan budgets accordingly. For instance, a very weak retail or chain-store sales figure might make a large retailer think twice about leasing more space at a mall or planning too aggressively for new stores.

In order for data to be collected, someone has to need it and someone has to pay for it. All those economists and statisticians and surveys cost money, and even in flush times, money allocated for those uses has to be budgeted and justified. Government agencies have certain questions they want answered, either to formulate policy or execute it. Companies, whose primary goal is to maximize returns for shareholders, need specific information that pertains to their particular business. Even academics have questions that interest them or are relevant to their field and those that don't or aren't; to obtain new information, they must look for grants and funding to support that research.

The result is that even in a world awash in information, there are significant holes in the data that we depend on to understand the world. To put it another way, the mass of information disguises all the things that we don't know and don't even bother to examine. It's been said that no one knows what they don't know. In the case of the data and formulas used to describe the world of economics and business, the illusion of certainty is based on a false sense that we have adequate data to draw definitive conclusions.

One consequence is that no national government perceives an interest in spending significant time and money to assemble global data. Some multinational companies do, but only in narrowly defined areas. Oil companies work intensively to assess global oil supplies and energy needs; a company like General Electric attempts to gauge global demand for power turbines. But these still leave significant gaps in what we know about the global system. Some of those gaps are filled by international organizations. At the end of World War II, a number of global institutions were created, including the United Nations, the International Monetary Fund, the World Bank, and NATO. Each of those also employ people to collect data. Unlike national governments that focus on national issues or companies that focus on industry issues, these organizations are transnational. They therefore attempt to collect global data, but their mandates limit what they examine. The World Health Organization focuses, not surprisingly, on health and disease. The United Nations looks at the number of refugees and displaced persons, and at poverty. Increasingly, a few powerful nonprofit organizations do similar work, the most notable being the Bill & Melinda Gates Foundation, whose endowment is larger than the GDP of many countries.

What we have then is a world where thousands of highly skilled, educated economists and statisticians collect and process substantial amounts of data on behalf of hundreds of governments and tens of thousands of companies and nongovernmental organizations, yet almost no one analyzes the global economy as a system. Even the International Monetary Fund, which regularly supplies forecasts about world economic growth, depends on the national data assembled by each country in order to arrive at a global picture. Take the GDP figures of 190 nations, add them up, weight them based on size, and then divide. That is oversimplified, but the fact remains that the only statistics on the workings of the economic system internationally are the product of national data.

To be fair, even after years of discussion about globalization and "the world is flat," not everyone believes that there is such a thing as a global economic system. The world is divided into sovereign nations that can still raise or lower barriers to trade and capital, even if the trend of the past decades has been to lower and remove those barriers. Except for a few ultrawealthy people and multinational companies, money and profits are kept in local currencies and deposited in a bank that is incorporated in the same country that the business is headquartered or the individual lives. When people talk about their concerns and hopes for "the economy," they invariably mean their own national economy. Even though regional variations within one country can be as great as differences between one national economy and another, most of us conceive of an economy as coincidental to the state.

Finally, very few institutions and very few people—not even academics whose job is to push the boundaries of knowledge— deal well with radical change, inflection points, anomalies, and the unknown. History is littered with examples of revolutionary changes, in science, in technology, in governments, and in social systems and mores. Sometimes, these happen suddenly, with eureka moments, like winged flight at Kitty Hawk or mobs storming a palace. Often they happen and no one notices until later, whether in a garage in Silicon Valley or at a desk in some study where a manuscript goes unread until after the author has died. But societies and institutions don't much like change and will go to great lengths to avoid confronting the consequences. The financial world likes predictability; governments prefer the status quo; and individuals cling to routine. That is human nature.

On the flip side, there are always voices eager and ready to announce a new era and a new paradigm, and more than not, they are wrong, premature, or crazy. The end of the business cycle, risk-free investments, the waning of religion—all have been proclaimed and been false dawns. Until old frameworks and concepts are shown to be unequivocally wrong or broken, they don't tend to be abandoned. And so the state remains the basic unit; traditional ideas of what it means to have a balanced economy and familiar theories of what does and does not produce stability and security hold sway even as their very foundations are eroded by the endless currents of change that course through history; and the new systems gestate beneath our collective consciousness.

All of these myriad factors explain how it is possible for China and the United States to have converged over the past 20 years with hardly anyone noticing. No one is paid to notice; no one has developed theoretical frameworks that would predict it; and almost everyone still thinks of China and the United States as two distinct countries with two sovereign national economies.

In addition, while the process may have begun in 1989, not until after December 2001 did it accelerate to the point where it could be considered a distinct system. In the absence of any theories or data to trace its origins and evolution, it isn't surprising that this system could have evolved beneath the collective radar. The United States was consumed with the war on terror and focused primarily on Afghanistan and Iraq, as well as on North Korea and Iran. The European Union was also focused on those issues, and on its own continued internal challenges, the question of Turkey's entry into the EU, and the integration and opportunities of Eastern Europe. China was important, but not that important. Individual companies saw it as a key market for growth, but that didn't translate into an awareness of converging economies. If you were an executive of Caterpillar or General Motors, you viewed China as the next great growth opportunity, but it was over there, not here.

And then, in 2002, as the Internet bubble in the United States was bursting and companies were paring back on spending and trimming excessive inventories, as the telecommunications sector was collapsing under the weight of massive investments in fiber optics, and as economists were worrying about deflation, slack consumer demand, and the long-term challenges of growth, China began to accelerate more quickly than anyone had thought possible.

Soon enough, that garnered attention, though not without considerable skepticism about its viability. China's economic activity was said to be too concentrated in the state sector, too dependent on spending by the government, and too linked to the export of low-cost goods. That couldn't be sustained, it was said, and it was too unbalanced to provide a solid foundation for the future. Meanwhile, the U.S. economy began to improve, but without the commensurate increase in inflation and wages that had always accompanied economic growth. Some, most notably the then chairman of the Federal Reserve, Alan Greenspan, wondered about the conundrum of low global interest rates and minimal inflation combined with high growth. And as some scratched their heads about why certain things that had always happened were happening no longer, the Chinese and U.S. economies were becoming ever more entwined—quietly, and invisibly.

Still Waters, Running Deep

I T WAS NOT AN easy year. After recovering from the shock of the World Trade Center attack, the United States in 2002 confronted the downside of the New Economy euphoria and the consequences of living in the illusion that war was no more; that the collapse of the Soviet Union and the end of the Cold War also meant the end of history and the passing of ideology; and that the United States would enter a prolonged period of global dominance. September 11, 2001, proved that ideology was alive and well and capable of doing great harm, that history may have paused but was by no means at an end, and that the era of global American hegemony might be over almost as quickly as it had begun.

Already in the 1990s, Chinese leaders recognized that the United States would be their greatest external challenge. That didn't necessarily mean a threat or a competitor, but rather that as China's economy expanded and progressed along the path set by Deng and his heirs, it would inevitably confront the question of how to manage the relationship with the United States. There was no way that China could become more open without more interaction with America, some of which Chinese leaders in both government and business dearly wanted and some of which they would have preferred to avoid. They wanted investment in their economy, and they wanted to learn from U.S. and global businesses. They did not wish to be dictated to, and any hint of that triggered hot buttons of anger and distrust that China would once again be taken advantage of by a dishonorable and avaricious West.

Having flirted for more than a decade, China and the United States became more intimately entangled after December 2001. Trade statistics give some indication of the magnitude of the changes after China joined the WTO. Total trade between the two countries increased from almost $150 billion in 2002 to nearly $400 billion in 2007, close to $450 billion in 2008, and only marginally less in the first part of 2009 as the global financial system nearly imploded. Before 2001, trade had been growing steadily but not exponentially. After 2001, Chinese exports to the United States made up the bulk of those figures, but China's imports from the United States actually grew more quickly, albeit from a lower base. In 2002 the United States exported $22 billion of goods to China and imported $125 billion; in 2007 it exported $65 billion and imported $320 billion; in 2008, nearly $90 billion in exports and $350 billion in imports including Hong Kong. The United States represented about 20 percent of China's total trade with the world, and closer to 30 percent once U.S.–Hong Kong trade is included. Hong Kong trade, including exports to and imports from mainland China, are still calculated separately, even though the city-state reverted to Chinese control in 1997.

With some countries, such as Japan and Taiwan, China has imported significantly more than it has exported, and with others, such as Germany, the trade has been more evenly divided between imports and exports. China has needed high-end industrial equipment that it could not or did not make, including turbines, generators, high-grade steel, airplanes, locomotives, and a host of technology products. Because the United States itself had become less of a manufacturing nation and more of a service economy, it produced less of what China needed and consumed more of what China made.

These numbers give some sense of the scale of the relationship, but they can also mislead. They convey the unequivocal reality that the two countries have become each other's largest and most important trading partner. Yet that too is not quite as it seems. The one aspect of the China-U.S. relationship that is generally understood and recognized is that China sells to the United States goods that it produces at a lower cost than if those same products were made in the United States. But it also has become the largest market for U.S. corporations, which is a direct result of the early efforts of companies such as Yum, Avon, and FedEx. The story of China as a low-cost producer has dominated our collective consciousness; the story of China as an avid consumer has received far less attention. But it is the latter, not the former, that will matter most for the world in the years to come.

Until 2007, China had a trade *deficit* with the rest of the world even as it ran ever-higher trade surpluses with the United States. Until 2007, China imported more from Europe than it exported, and it has continuously run deficits with major partners such as Australia, Japan, and Korea. The United States through 2008 consumed one-third of all of China's exports, making it by far the largest buyer of Chinese goods. But while that would seem to support the point that China produces and the U.S. buys, here too there is the devilish problem of statistics.

Imports and exports are calculated by government agencies and international trade groups based on what enters or exits a country's ports. Agencies go to great lengths to identify the country of origin and to distinguish that from the country that the goods may have been shipped from or the nationality of the ship. So while Greek shipping lines carry a lot of goods, that doesn't lead to inflated trade figures between the United States and Greece or between Greece and the world. Then there is the challenge that one product can in fact have been made in multiple countries. A cell phone might have components from Singapore, a chipset from Taiwan, an LCD screen from Japan, plastics from Malaysia—all of which are shipped to a Chinese factory and then assembled. Even something as simple as a T-shirt could be made from cotton produced in the United States, with yarn spun in one factory in China, and the shirts then cut and sown at a different factory, only to be shipped back to the United States for silk screening.[1] The World Trade Organization has tried to create formulas that allow products to be ascribed to one country of origin, but such formulas simplify a reality that is anything but.

The way figures are created misses the crucial fact that many of the goods that one country imports from another may exist only because a company in the country that is doing the importing paid for them to be made somewhere else. If, for instance, General Electric assembles an appliance in a Chinese factory that it owns, that appliance may not be classified as a Chinese import when it arrives at the port of Long Beach, California, on its way to a warehouse for Gracious Homes. But if it sources the production of that appliance and its parts to a Chinese-owned factory or company on the mainland, when that refrigerator shows up in Newark, New Jersey, it is likely to be classified as an import. Categories of "import" versus "export" still reflect an earlier age when each state—at least in theory—was an economic unit with its own internal market and internal production geared to internal consumption. National figures act as if a nation's borders are physical barriers, with bright and shining lines separating an "us" from a "them."

A substantial portion of China's trade with the world since the beginning of the millennium has been generated by foreign firms sourcing products in China in order to sell them somewhere else, and not because Chinese factory owners figured out what foreigners want and decided to produce low-cost versions. Often, what is imported aren't finished goods but rather components for assembly in U.S. manufacturing plants, which has allowed those plants to operate more cost efficiently and thus stay open in the United States and even expand production.

In addition, it's been estimated that more than 50 percent of China's exports were paid for by foreign firms and were the result of foreign investment in China that led to the construction of the factories that produced those goods. Those same foreign firms are also responsible for more than half of China's imports. The GE plant or the Caterpillar plant or the Archer Daniels Midland soybean processing facility in China may have imported power equipment or industrial equipment in order to be built in the first place, and it may have imported those goods from Japan, or Germany, or the United States. The earnings from the activities of that factory in China contribute to the overall earnings of the company—if that company is incorporated in the United States or has shares trading on the New York Stock Exchange, the income and profit from business in China can add to U.S. tax revenues or to the share price even though the outsourcing of the factory may have led to less employment for workers in the United States.[2] Higher share prices may benefit the wealthy, but they also can boost the value of worker pension plans.

Then there are the sales made by that subsidiary factory in China itself, whether a John Deere combine, a Motorola cell phone, or an earthmover manufactured by Caterpillar composed of parts made in a factory in Mississippi, steel rolled in Korea, and assembled in the Pearl River Delta. Those sales in China directly augment the bottom line of those companies, just as the sales of fried chicken in Shanghai help Yum! Brands.

But they are invisible in the export and import figures, unless of course that Deere combine is first exported to Hong Kong and then reimported into China. Because Hong Kong is a transportation hub with rail links, shipping lines, and toll roads connecting it to multiple cities on the mainland, it is often more cost effective to ship goods to Hong Kong and then on to other destinations on the mainland. When that happens, however, the same product is counted twice, once as an import and once as an export, and both times as a Chinese product, when it isn't any of those things at all.

Trade is at the heart of this relationship, yet the trade of goods is only one aspect. There is also the exchange of ideas, which has been at least as important as the exchange of actual products. Trade has also been the most sensitive issue in the United States and in Europe, and is linked to anxieties about loss of jobs, loss of economic security, and ultimately loss of sovereignty. These concerns predate the China-U.S. relationship and can be traced to the very origins of the state. Empires of the past attempted to monopolize trade as a source of strength and power. European nations of the seventeenth and eighteenth centuries adopted mercantilist policies designed to prevent other states from accessing their trade routes. The attempt of the British government to constrain the ability of the American colonies to trade with France and Spain was one reason for the rising animus that led to the American Revolution. Even the nineteenth-century British Empire, where modern notions of free trade took root, had preferential laws for its own trade with India and other colonies and prevented goods from those colonies from flowing to other states without passing through England first.

The belief that trade is linked to both power and sovereignty is therefore entwined with nationalism and woven into economic theory. A nation's trade account is taken as a sign of its health or a symptom of its weakness. Trade surpluses are seen as a source of strength; trade deficits, as a sign of imbalances that if not corrected will erode a country's relative position in the world. As the volume of U.S.-China trade has exploded since 2001, the scale of imports versus exports (or exports versus imports if you're taking the perspective of China) has been interpreted as a danger sign for the United States, draining it at the expense of China. The intricacies of who is making what for whom and where get lost in a set of statistics that were designed when that was easy to determine. Instead we are left with a facile and misleading belief—shared so widely that it is almost universal—that the relationship between China and the United States has primarily been one of Americans buying, Chinese factories making, and the power balance shifting from the West to the East.

The understanding about trade may be false, but that sense of a shifting balance of power is true. Trade is not the reason. In the 1980s, and especially after the passage of the North American Free Trade Agreement in 1993, U.S. trade with Mexico soared, as lower-cost goods made in Mexican factories deluged the United States. That led to a wave of anxiety about the competitiveness of U.S. manufacturing. But it stopped with that. Few people expected that Mexico would soon surpass the United States or even rival its preeminence in the global economy. While the challenge of low-cost manufacturing struck a deep chord among American unions, Mexican trade did not raise alarms of American decline. With the collapse of the Mexican peso in 1994, the United States government came to the rescue, which was a vivid reminder (if one was needed) that the power dynamic between the two countries had not fundamentally changed just because patterns of trade and manufacturing had.

If China's only strength was its ability to manufacture low-cost goods, it would simply be Mexico with more people. Plenty of countries over the past decades have been able to undercut the manufacturing base of the developed world because of lower wages—including Japan in the 1960s, Taiwan in the 1970s, Korea in the 1980s, and Eastern Europe in the 1990s. The "comparative advantage" theory that goods will be made where they can be made more efficiently has held true in a world of fewer trade barriers. While developed countries tend to focus on the disruptions that result—the downward wage pressures and factory closures—less noticed is the advantage that those goods create. Walmart would not be able to sell $100 DVD players if they were made in the United States or Germany.

Of course, not all cost savings are due to comparative advantage, and many jobs have been lost not to the Mexicos and Chinas of the world but to the computer and to the Internet. The entry of China into the WTO in December 2001 coincided not only with the aftermath of 9/11 and the U.S. invasion of Afghanistan but with the continued downturn in the U.S. economy. The 2001 recession was primarily an "inventory" recession. Companies, and especially telecommunications companies, had ramped up production of high-technology equipment in the anticipation of continued robust demand. But after the massive spending to prepare for the feared collapse of computers worldwide because of the Y2K glitch that was supposed to crash operating systems—and did not—on January 1, 2000, companies began to pare back. It was a familiar pattern, and in retrospect should have been evident. Companies always reduce spending on new technologies after the first wave of adoption. Having bought all those networks and installed high-speed connections in the late 1990s, companies needed to take some time to digest and learn how to best use the new systems.

The result was a sharp contraction of business spending in the United States and to a lesser degree in Western Europe, combined with a plunge in stock values that continued until the major indices bottomed in October 2002. But during this time, to the surprise of most analysts, the unemployment rate remained relatively low and labor productivity soared.

The fact that productivity went up even as economic activity dropped off was not what traditional models and past patterns would have dictated. True, by 2002, the U.S. economy started growing again, though most people still perceived it to be weak throughout the year. Though the U.S. registered more than 5 percent growth in the first three months of 2002, popular sentiment said that the economy was still in recession. This began a trend that has only deepened: namely, the disconnect between big-picture economic data and how people in general feel about "the economy." For instance, people had been feeling increasingly uneasy and pessimistic about economic trends in the developed world even before the stock market crash of 2008 and the global downturn of 2008 and 2009. But for much of this period, one surprising and startling constant has been the surge in productivity.

GDP and productivity are supposed to go hand in hand, up and down together. Instead, since 2001, they have often gone in different directions. Why? In part, the explanation lies with technology. As businesses integrated the information technology of the New Economy boom, they were able to get more productivity out of each worker. Some of that is easy to fathom: if robots are making parts for cars, that means fewer workers are needed. If productivity is a measure of output per worker, and fewer workers are making more cars, then productivity goes up even as employment might go down. This extends to less tangible things like customer service: with software that tracks customer histories and preferences at the touch of a button, each customer service rep can handle more customers and take care of more issues in less time, which also leads to increased productivity.

The changes wrought by technology get less notice than the changes created by changing trade. One reason is that customer management software is less visible than a factory in China making toys. It's also true that a politician campaigning against hardships in her district has an easier time blaming China or Mexico than a Dell computer or a Cisco router. Hence a sign in Hickory, North Carolina, during a heated campaign for Congress in October 2002. "Gotta Job?" the sign read. "Mine Went to Mexico—Then China."[3] It wouldn't have had the same effect if it had said, "Mine Went to the Internet."

The year 2002 marked the beginning of a series of unexplained developments in the economy, when the official statistics ceased to square with either popular perceptions or academic theories. Not only did productivity soar, but inflation plummeted even as growth picked up. That was another example of something that wasn't supposed to happen. Historically more growth was almost always accompanied by rising inflation as demand picked up ahead of the ability of companies to meet it. Labor as well tended to benefit since more growth and better business conditions translated into higher wages, which also fueled inflation. But in 2002, inflation plummeted to almost 1.5 percent while wage growth went nowhere, except for benefits tied to health care, which went up. The final oddity was that the U.S. Federal Reserve aggressively cut interest rates from late 2001 through most of 2002, until the Fed Funds rate stood at 1.25 percent. But global interest rates on the U.S. 10-year Treasury note—set by the market and not by the central bank—barely changed, coming down below 4 percent but essentially staying in a band between 4 percent and 5 percent. Traditionally, for much of the twentieth century, when the Fed acted, market rates reacted. By 2002, that was no longer the case.

In 2002, China's purchases of U.S. Treasuries started to shape rates, but almost no one noticed or thought to connect the dots.

During the previous decade, China had begun to buy U.S. debt, but in 2000 it held less than $100 billion. Then, as its exports grew and its market changed dramatically after 2001, its foreign reserves grew even faster, to the point where it held nearly $700 billion in 2006, close to $1 trillion in 2007, and surpassing $2 trillion by 2009.[4] Initially, however, that trend got little attention, even in China itself, and its effects on global and U.S. interest rates were barely considered. When they were, it was usually assumed that China was just another buyer and that rates would move as they had always moved. Neither China specialists in the U.S. nor economists believed otherwise, at least judging by the absence of much debate or discussion. China experts weren't overly interested in economics; economists weren't overly sensitive to what was going on in China; in China, officials were more focused on their domestic economy than on the international system; and no one, anywhere, was specifically responsible for assessing a system that few believed even existed.

As a result, by 2003, the U.S. economy had become a mystery to most of the people charged with explaining it. Several years later, in February 2005, that was perfectly captured by Alan Greenspan in testimony to Congress when he confessed to confusion about the "interest rate conundrum" of long-term rates staying flat even as central bank rates fluctuated widely.

That conundrum has only become more prevalent since, and China and technology are the causes—along with the inability of people and institutions to adjust their models and orthodoxies. The statisticians kept measuring what they could measure and therefore kept missing the radical shifts that had occurred. Life moved more quickly than our collective ability to measure it and explain it.

The relentless focus on trade is one cause of the myopia, but so too is the inability to accept the full dimension of the transformations within China itself. Many experts on China were slow to give full credence to the changes that accelerated throughout the 1990s and then exploded in the 2000s. The headline GDP growth figures should have been a clue, but China grew an average of more than 9 percent throughout the 1990s without most experts predicting the scope of its impact on the world after 2001. As the earlier example of Mexico hinted at, figures alone don't tell a full story. Japan throughout the 1990s was mired in recession and a deep banking crisis yet remained the second largest economy in the world. Its footprint on the global system, however, was considerably less than the sheer size of its economy would have indicated. After a few years in the late 1980s when the world began to fear a resurgent Japanese empire, Japan had receded as a global force even as it remained statistically large. Meanwhile, the Cayman Islands hardly rated in global consciousness, but they became a primary locale for the registration of hedge funds, whose trillion-plus dollars in capital at the turn of the twenty-first century was already starting to set the tone for global equity and debt markets.

It wasn't just Americans and Europeans who missed the inflection points. The shifts were only partly appreciated in China itself. In 2002 much of the focus within China was the momentous changing of the guard from Jiang Zemin and Zhu Rongji to Hu Jintao and Wen Jiabao. The Communist Party of China may have been an autocracy, but it was also deeply wary that the individuals governing the party and the country might amass too much personal power. The experience of the dictatorship of Mao led to a determination by party elders that for the party to maintain its control and lead China out of poverty, no one person could become too powerful. The party and the nation came first; the ambitions of individuals would be subordinated to the common good. That explained both the intolerance for individual dissent and the unequivocal refusal to allow even the supreme leader to serve indefinitely in office. While Jiang did not cede power all at once, and was eased out of his multiple roles completely only in 2004, the transition was remarkably smooth and orderly. Even so, the politics of the succession consumed considerable time and energy in official circles for parts of 2002, which meant that issues such as macroeconomic policy and China's evolving role in the world at large were often left on automatic pilot.

For the millions who were not in the inner circles of the party but who instead were occupied with the daily bustle of building a new China, politics mattered less than commerce. Many of those who were actively involved in business cared little for the inner workings of the Communist Party. Regardless of who ran which ministry, the party establishment was firmly committed to the path of economic modernization and liberalization. If you were a banker, an industrialist, or an entrepreneur, the names of the individuals in power were not overly consequential. It helped to have prior connections, but you still had to go to Beijing and engage in the elaborate dance of banquets and meetings to move the system in a favorable direction. True, the heads of the state-owned enterprises watched carefully and lobbied quietly. A new vice chairman at a key agency could have a significant impact on those companies, including removing and appointing new CEOs. But here too, it was more an issue of personal careers than national direction. The reforms pursued by Zhu Rongji in areas such as banking and finance had only intensified the disruptions to the old system and increased the pace of reform.

Chinese opponents of entry into the World Trade Organization remained skeptical of the intentions of Washington and the Western world. The growing strains of rampant materialism in China's cities also became a source of concern and criticism. The gap between the egalitarian ideology of the Communist Party and the Mercedes-driving, gated-community-living, fine-

French-wine-collecting, Swiss-watch-wearing nouveau riche attracted both envy and disgust. Millions of Chinese aspired to the new lifestyles, but millions as well found the unbridled materialism culturally anathema and a sign of decline rather than ascent. For every person who couldn't wait to read the new issue of *TimeOut Beijing* and hit the hippest bars in Shanghai's trendy Xintiandi area, there were others who lamented the hypocrisy of party officials and the blatant disregard for the social welfare of hundreds of millions of Chinese who did not share in the urban bonanza.

Though the opponents of China's entry into the WTO lost that particular battle, they continued to sound the alarm about globalization. Because these intellectuals didn't directly challenge the authority or the supremacy of the Communist Party, they were able to write, speak, and teach with a surprising degree of freedom and candor. In fact, because they donned the mantle of Chinese nationalism, they could effectively hamstring the ability of party officials to muzzle them. The same forces that erupted after the U.S. bombing of the Belgrade embassy remained deeply entrenched on college campuses, which constituted a Chinese nationalist-conservative equivalent of the left-leaning American professoriate. These voices harped on the old feeling that the United States and its companies sought closer relations with China only because they wanted dominion and to "hold China down." One of the most prominent critics, Wang Hui of Tsinghua University, believed that China's growth was more ephemeral than it appeared, and based on a shaky foundation. By rushing to serve Western companies and copy them, China was demonstrating its own hollowness and the bankruptcy of its governing vision.[5] Wang Hui also warned that the rush to integrate with the West was leading to a globalized labor system that benefited only large corporations rather than the workers. Unless the Chinese state checked those tendencies, he warned, the quest for a good and just society would remain elusive.

So while the structural shifts accelerated after China's entry into the WTO, the cognitive shifts took longer. It wasn't just data that remained state focused, it was people's minds. China, because its government had made such a self-conscious decision to change course in the 1980s, was attuned to the fact that the global system was morphing more than the data suggested. Its leaders, from business to academia to government, hungered for change and made it a priority to analyze and study both the shifting internal dynamics of their own society and the changing dynamics of the world at large. The United States, on the other hand, having woken up to the reality of globalization in the late 1990s, turned away from its ramifications after 9/11 and reverted to state-centered notions of the world and of its own power.

These are obviously generalizations, and exceptions would not be hard to find. But the United States was the dominant global power. It spent more on its military than its next 10 competitors combined (China included); its economy of $12 trillion in 2002 was nearly a third of all global output, and it accounted for nearly 40 percent of global economic growth. It had been attacked by a small group of terrorists and in response had launched one war and was preparing to begin another. Policies such as the Patriot Act passed in the wake of 9/11 demanded transparency from international companies that wished to do business in the United States, as had laws passed in the wake of the collapse of Enron and WorldCom, particularly the Sarbanes-Oxley Act, which added additional requirements on companies. In short, the United States reasserted its role as a global hegemon. In that sense, it was at cross-purposes with a borderless world where the state mattered less.

That led, predictably, to growing discomfort in the United States with the pace and extent of China's rise after 2001. Earlier concerns about China as a low-cost producer proved to be dry runs for the deepening unease after 2001. Wall Street economists began to note what was taking place. They took a closer look at the anomalies and tentatively started to explore the possible links—largely invisible in the traditional models—between China's growth and what was happening to the domestic economies of the United States, Europe, Japan, and throughout the world.

At Morgan Stanley, for instance, the rather dour and bearish chief economist Stephen Roach issued regular notes to clients throughout the latter half of 2002 highlighting the importance of China to the United States and the global system. "China is the closet thing to an oasis in an otherwise struggling global economy," he wrote just a few days before the U.S. stock markets crashed to the lowest level in years. At the time, China was "only" growing 8.1 percent a year, which was then seen as rather extraordinary. (In 2008 when China's economy "slowed" to 9 percent growth in the third quarter, it was taken—erroneously—as a sign of impending problems.) Roach went on to list the various attributes of China's growth: a commitment to the reform of state-owned companies; more domestic consumption of goods; more industrial output. "The world," he said, "is no longer immune to the unintended ramifications of China's stunning success. Mounting deflationary risks are an important case in point." Because China was flooding the developed world with low-cost goods, and doing so while the U.S. economy was struggling to recover from the stock market collapse and the recession of 2001, there was a risk of long-term deflation that could crimp growth going forward. He warned that China's restrictive currency policy, with the exchange set by the government and the currency not allowed to float, could have negative consequences for global markets, but he offered no clear fix for that potential problem.

A few months later, Roach penned another note calling for a

halt to the rise in anti-Chinese sentiment in the United States. As the trade deficit yawned wider, more voices in the U.S. began to speak of China in ominous terms. Roach countered that China was not at fault. The cause of the trade deficit was "a pathetically low [American] savings rate . . . In that critical context, it's hard to blame China for America's penchant to live beyond its means." He concluded, prophetically, by highlighting that the real impact of China's rise lay in the future: "China's major global impact will shift to the demand side of the macro equation. In particular, I look for the Chinese to begin drawing down their outsize 40 percent national savings rate and become more and more enamored of Western-style consumption propensities, as well as Western-made goods. It's not showing up in the official data flow just yet, but . . . I am beginning to detect early signs of the emergence of the Chinese consumer. China-bashing runs the risk of interrupting this critical process at precisely the point where the world needs a stable China more than ever. China bashing must be resisted at all costs."

Roach was an early voice calling for greater attention to the unexpected consequences of China's rise. Even he, however, for all his acumen and prescience, remained locked in a framework of how "their" economy affects "ours." By the end of 2003, he was warning that the trajectory of China's growth, dependent as it was on state spending on infrastructure, wasn't balanced and that its economy would have to slow in order to redress those imbalances. He also sounded the alarm about the precarious state of China's banks. In spite of the reform efforts of outgoing premier Zhu, banks were still saddled with immense levels of nonperforming loans. Money had been advanced to factories and residential construction without much thought about feasibility and the ability of people to pay the money back. That, warned Roach, was a looming threat to China's continued prosperity.

Those concerns were shared widely, yet they never proved

valid. Unlike the U.S. banking system, which collapsed because of loans to subprime borrowers who couldn't afford their mortgages, China's banking system existed in a vacuum and the state absorbed the bulk of bad loans. Roach saw that China was breaking molds and yet fully expected that it would start to behave normally. He saw that it was more integrated with the U.S. than most people thought, yet he didn't recognize that it was because the banking system was so unintegrated that it wouldn't behave as expected. More on that shortly, but in 2002, the one thing that was globally integrated—more or less—was finance. China was managing to become integrated in everything except finance, which further confounded expected outcomes. Not fully appreciating that, Roach and others believed that as it was drawn more tightly into the global system, China would begin to have banking problems in the manner that traditional models would predict. In short, China was seen—even by those astute enough to notice—as a temporary exception to the rule, not as a sign that the rules might be changing.

There was a final aspect of China, at least as important as the structural shifts and data points but more difficult to quantify: culture. Chimerica isn't just a fusion of economies; it's also a fusion of culture.

I first stepped off a plane in Shanghai in 2002. By the standards of China experts, I was a novice. I spoke no Chinese (and still do not), and while I had book knowledge of China's long and storied history, my understanding of what had taken place over the past decades paled in comparison to former academic colleagues who had spent years studying and in comparison to business executives who may not have read much but knew how to navigate an ever-morphing modern China.[6] So when I started wandering around on a wet, misty night, I was about as green and ignorant as someone about to start an investment fund could or should have been.

I had been in dozens of countries and never experienced such a vibrant hum of a society on the move. The streets buzzed with an electrical charge of change, down to that *Blade Runner*–ish feel of the river with barges lit by neon and the old colonial Bund bathed in lights while the bulbous tower loomed on the Pudong side. Those first impressions solidified in subsequent trips over the next five years as I toured factories both high tech and low tech, and visited other cities, both old and new. It sounds a bit golly-gee, but visceral impressions can be a powerful gauge of what's going on. More than a century ago, when European visitors stepped off their boats and onto the docks of New York City, they often confessed to an immediate sense that something was different, something unlike the Old World from which they'd just come. They were struck by the hustle and the clatter and the sheer busyness and bustle they encountered, and those feelings were only confirmed when they actually started to speak with people. Even early in the nineteenth century, the young Frenchman Alexis de Tocqueville had made similar observations about the "American spirit," but in his day it was mostly frontier bravado, and energy that was still focused on conquering the land. By the end of the century, the land had been conquered, the cities were growing, and industry was booming.

As the United States began to emerge on the global stage, it too was a place where anything seemed possible and where the focus rested on the future, not the past. Having spent time in America toward the end of the nineteenth century, Lord James Bryce, in his magisterial *The American Commonwealth*, could not help but be swept up even as he recognized the pitfalls. "America excites an admiration which must be felt upon the spot to be understood. The hopefulness of her people communicates itself to one who moves among them, and makes him perceive that the graver faults of politics may be far less dangerous there than they would be in Europe. A hundred times in writing this book have I been disheartened by the facts I was stating; a hundred times has the recollection of the abounding strength and vitality of the nation chased away these tremors."

Substitute China for America, and much the same could be written today. China pulses with a similar sense of possibility, of limitless tomorrows combined with hot passions about contemporary problems. There are similar frustrations with political corruption and similar dismay at the manifold evidence of human failings. This is especially true of the cities, with their rapid, messy, filthy, and yet spectacular transformation. China has become America's twin, younger, different in its way, but more alike than not, arousing envy, respect, fear, and hope.

On that first visit to Shanghai, as I met with lawyers in a new office tower in the business district off the Nanjing Road, I accidentally got off on the wrong floor. It looked like any other office building in any other part of the world, and where I thought I was supposed to be was a plain door with a metallic sign that said simply "Huawei." The name meant nothing to me, but that alone said something profound—not just about my ignorance, but about the next stage of China's growth and the next step toward Chimerica. And when I went out that evening, it was hard not to notice the immense billboards lit up along commercial streets, with the smiling giant face of China's newest import to the United States: the gargantuan seven-foot-six Yao Ming, then in his rookie year playing center for the Houston Rockets of the National Basketball Association. He'd just been signed as a sponsor for the world's largest maker of athletic shoes. The Rockets wanted a good player, but Nike was more ambitious. It wanted Yao to usher in a new era for Chinese consumers, with Nike in the vanguard. Between the obscure yet powerful Huawei Technologies and the anything-but-obscure Nike, China was about to move well beyond the reforms of Deng and his successors and into a whole new world of commerce. And American companies were there, arms open and leading the way.

CHAPTER 9

Wow, Yao

H UAWEI AND YAO MING were the yin and yang of
the new China. Huawei was founded in 1988 to provide
switching equipment for telecommunications. It spent the first
half of the 1990s struggling with its product line and competing unsuccessfully against the acumen and technology of multinational behemoths like Siemens, Cisco, and Ericsson. But it
was able to sell its low-cost wares in smaller inland cities and
provinces. Then, at some point in the mid-1990s, the company
apparently landed contracts with the Chinese military establishment (the company's founder, Ren Zhengfei, was a former
People's Liberation Army engineer) and went from an obscure,
small high-tech venture to an obscure, large high-tech venture
with deep but opaque connections to the state, tens of thousands
of employees, a multifaceted product line, and sales throughout
the world.

To help manage such rapid growth, Huawei hired IBM, which
itself was then in the midst of a transformation from a main-
frame computer company with a crack sales force to a global
consultancy working with companies to craft bespoke solutions and strategies for the new world of transnational business.
Huawei also formed ventures with Texas Instruments, Lucent
Technologies, and Motorola. By the late 1990s, its revenue in
China and overseas had topped $1 billion. Little about Huawei

is unambiguous, however. The company's founder and chairman, Ren, has never spoken with the press. Huawei is prominent both in China and in the international telecommunications equipment business, but its culture of secrecy arouses fear and suspicion. The extent of its connection with the Chinese military establishment is not clearly known, and the company has denied that there is any relationship at all. Its technology is of consistently high quality and yet is cheaper than what most of its competitors produce, including its one main Chinese rival, ZTE Corporation. Huawei has, in short, become a major force without anyone understanding how it works.

The same could be said of China's rapid evolution over the past two decades. Most of the deliberations of the Communist Party remain and may forever be hidden; corporate leaders are not all as reclusive as Huawei's Ren, but none communicates frequently or freely in public; and the inside story of most deals and policy discussions has never been and likely never will be told. There is no Bob Woodward of the Chinese media; no one writes memoirs that tell all; business books discuss how-to strategy and at times offer hagiographic biographies but no inside scoops. Huawei's progress has been sudden and mysterious but only marginally more so than the rest of what has happened in China of late.

After hiring IBM, Huawei dramatically increased its international sales. IBM itself had refocused its business toward the global market and away from its dependence on the United States, and a similar approach made sense for Huawei. As the global demand for wireless and Internet communications equipment grew exponentially, Huawei carved out a space as the low-cost alternative, especially to Cisco Communications. Cisco equipment has enabled the modern Internet age, and its routers and switches have been integral to the expansion of communications globally. But its product line was expensive, and for countries in the developing world, the money simply wasn't there. Huawei was able to provide similar products at a fraction of the cost. Its thousands of engineers in China, highly educated and trained, were paid top dollar by Chinese standards but a pittance compared to an American executive living in Silicon Valley. Its salespeople also earned top dollar by local standards but nowhere near what their counterparts in England, France, or Germany made. Huawei could, in short, make similar products, sell them for less money, and generate immense profits, which it then plowed back into research and development. The result was that international sales of Huawei equipment went from about $250 million in 2001 to nearly $2.5 billion in 2004. Revenues in Africa, Central Asia, Russia, and the Middle East helped jump-start its international presence, but then it began to win contracts from established multinationals that operated in those markets and throughout the world. These included marquee names like British Telecom and, not surprisingly, IBM.[1]

In 2003 Huawei formed a joint venture with 3Com Corporation, a U.S. maker of telecommunications equipment that had been a major force in the 1990s but had been severely challenged by the collapse of spending on telecommunications equipment after 2000. The purpose of the joint venture was to reinvigorate 3Com and give Huawei access to the lucrative U.S. market. That was a red flag to the market leader, Cisco. As the venture was being negotiated, Cisco filed suit in the United States against Huawei, claiming that Huawei's products weren't just low-priced substitutes but in fact low-priced copies made from illegally pirated software and a host of other infringements on Cisco's intellectual property.

In the negotiations surrounding China's entry into the WTO, the issue of intellectual property was never far from the surface. Western companies had long complained that while China's market was hugely attractive, it came with a cost. Though there were laws on the books making it illegal to steal intellectual property, in practice it was common for factories to produce pirated goods. Movie and record companies complained of the rampant copying and selling of pirated movies and compact discs, a fact that most Western visitors to Beijing were well aware of as they strolled through open-air markets where it was possible to buy a DVD of a first-run movie that was still playing in theaters in the United States and Europe. But that was only one component of a larger issue. Companies ranging from Microsoft to Oracle to video game makers faced the chronic challenge of what to do about pirated software, and any company sourcing goods in China had to worry that once its product line was made, the factory owner would turn around and make the same goods under a different label and sell them locally.

Intellectual property is the primary source of value for many companies. For Qualcomm, for instance, the bulk of its revenue comes from royalties that it collects on technology that it has patented for wireless cell phone communications. Over the past decade, it has moved away from actually making phones, chips, and devices, and toward research, development, and licensing its designs. The same might be said for any number of technology and communications companies, and these depend on legal systems that enforce their patents and the contracts that guarantee them payment when their designs are used.

But even with the provisions embedded in the WTO protecting intellectual property, companies operating in China routinely found that their products had been copied. Often, when these companies brought their complaints to local courts, the courts either sided with the Chinese entity accused of infringing or took so long to adjudicate the dispute that by the time a decision was rendered, the infringing company had spent years illegally selling pirated products. Many Chinese technology companies act as "original equipment manufacturers" for multinationals and assemble the various components that then got sold as, say, a Dell computer. Rather than blatantly stealing the blueprints, these companies often reverse engineered the product. Reverse engineering is not uncommon for software companies in the U.S. and Europe, some of which have been notorious for taking a competitor's product and then replicating it without technically copying it. While Cisco accused Huawei of stealing its intellectual property, it is probably more accurate to say that Huawei engineers took Cisco's products, disassembled them, studied them, and then figured out a way to create similar products on their own.

It's also true that Huawei may have done precisely what it claimed: namely, that it had brilliant engineers and that Chinese companies and acumen were just as capable of producing sophisticated high-tech equipment as Europeans and Americans and that to suggest otherwise was insulting and racist. And in the case of Huawei and Cisco, the timing of the case raised the question of whether Cisco was in fact worried about its intellectual property or more concerned about the prospect of Huawei in alliance with 3Com competing against Cisco in the United States and Europe, undercutting its market share with lower-cost products that worked just as well.

By the end of 2003, Cisco dropped its suit and settled with Huawei, and Huawei assumed a more dominant role in its joint venture with the fast-fading 3Com. The details of the settlement weren't disclosed, but it was assumed that Huawei agreed to pay Cisco a modest royalty on certain products, though not those sold in China itself. Huawei's growth continued unabated, and it solidified its position as a global player. And then, three years later, after it sold its portion of the joint venture back to 3Com, it attempted to buy all of 3Com for $2 billion. By then, the dimensions of China's emergence were increasingly apparent in the United States and were rousing considerable opposition. In fewer than 20 years, Huawei went from a tiny, provincial Chinese company to a global titan that was seen as a threat to the continued dominance of the United States. And it did so because of an alchemical combination of its own ingenuity and the know-how of an American company.[2]

Issues of intellectual property were not confined to high-tech companies. On the other end of the spectrum, textile and apparel makers also faced the challenge of Chinese factories copying merchandise and selling it on the side. The question for foreign companies in those industries doing business in China was how to make sure that their business remained viable in the face of continued infringement and copying of their products. And that is where the story of Nike and Yao Ming comes in.

Like many athletic wear companies, Nike began its push into China in the 1990s, after having established itself throughout Asia the decade before. Initially, it looked to China much as it had looked to other regions of Asia: as a place to make its sneakers at low cost. But conditions in factories in Indonesia, Vietnam, and elsewhere had led to widespread outcry that Nike, known for its somewhat New Age-y image as a kinder and gentler organization, was in fact a hypocritical company just as intent on its bottom line and willing to sacrifice just about anything to it. As it moved more of its operations to China, Nike was determined to avoid the labor rights issues that had dogged it elsewhere. It also wanted China to be more than a place where it could make shoes cheaply; it wanted China to be the next great market for its merchandise.

But shoes are one of the easier things to copy. Many of the factories were not Nike-owned but contract manufacturers. They could easily take the specs for an Air Jordan sneaker, make however many thousands for Nike, and then turn around and make the identical shoes with a different label and sell them in China. That was a particularly problematic type of piracy.

Those DVDs of a movie selling in the alleys of Beijing might be of low quality and might even have been made by someone holding a video recorder in a movie theater. But the knockoff Nikes made in that Chinese factory weren't low-quality copies like some cheap fake Rolex sold on a street corner. They were, for all intents and purposes, Nike shoes, made from the same design, with the same material, just with a different label.[3]

So what was Nike to do? A similar challenge confronted its competitors in China, including New Balance, Adidas, and Reebok. Nike could take a factory owner to court, but even if it won the case, the next factory might do the same thing. It could pull out of China, but that meant forgoing the most compelling new consumer market in the world and leaving it to others to exploit. Nike chose a different course: the company would continue to crack down on fraud where and when it could, but instead of constantly playing defense, it would focus instead on building the Nike brand in China. The designs could be stolen, but the brand, well, that could be controlled.

The mystique of brand held as much allure in China as it did elsewhere, and perhaps more. As the purchasing power of the Chinese consumer grew, so did the hunger for brand names. Some of these were Chinese: computer maker Lenovo and appliance maker Haier both carved out niches as coveted domestic brands. But the most desirable products were made by foreign companies. Just as KFC had marketed itself as an emblem of the modern, Western good life, foreign companies selling to Chinese consumers lured them with the promise that buying their products was a ticket to the comforts, pleasures, and status of the modern world. For young buyers, they sold themselves as cool; to older buyers, as status symbols. And there was also the promise that brand-name Western goods were higher quality, lasted longer, and delivered more. For Nike, which prided itself on performance and scoffed that other shoe companies were all brand and little substance, the question was how to convince consumers that its shoes would allow them to reach higher, draw closer to their dreams, and outperform. Yao Ming, a larger-than-life basketball player about to make his debut in the United States, seemed to be the perfect solution.

In December 2002, the *Washington Post* reported on its front page that an average weeknight NBA game between the Houston Rockets and Cleveland Cavaliers, hardly a marquee matchup that year, attracted an audience of about 1 million people in the United States. In China, 17 million tuned in. They watched to see the rookie Yao play center for an American pro team. He had been signed to a four-year, $17 million deal by the Rockets, and the fact that an athlete groomed in the Communist Party system of producing world-class competitors had inked a lucrative deal with a capitalist sports league spoke volumes about how things had changed.

Yao had essentially been bred. Both his parents played basketball. His 6'2" mother, Fang Fengdi, perhaps the tallest woman in China, had been married to an even taller man. She had served as a Red Guard during the height of the Cultural Revolution and had been an ardent Maoist. She enthusiastically participated in the glorious plan of the local government to use her and her husband to produce a sports superstar. The Shanghai authorities who encouraged the match had gone back several generations to ensure that size was embedded in the bloodline. The result was Yao, a baby behemoth who just kept getting bigger.

Though Yao was raised in the insular cocoon of the Shanghai sports program, he was also the focus of a costly experiment. He was trained, fed, and clothed by a team of doctors, coaches, and then agents whose goal was to make him the first international Chinese sports superstar. That meant not just attention to his diet but to his wants, and like any basketball-playing teenager in the 1990s, he wanted a pair of Air Jordan sneakers. The problem was how to find a size 18 in China. His handlers couldn't, and instead had to find someone in the United States to ship them. That led Nike officials to send someone to check out Yao and offer him a chance to go to a Nike-sponsored camp in Paris intended to groom aspiring players. Recognizing that Yao had the potential to become a transnational star, Nike signed him to an endorsement deal while he was still playing for his local Shanghai team.

After he agreed to become a Houston Rocket, Yao moved with his entourage to the United States. He was barely 21 years old, and his mother went with him, bought a $500,000 home, and took over his care and feeding—literally. Meanwhile, his agents and marketing directors handled the requests that came his way. "We're being flooded with offers for endorsements, from multinationals, software firms, computer manufacturers, shoe companies, apparel companies. You name it, they all want it," said representative Zhang Mingji on behalf of Team Yao. As Yao entered his rookie year, his management team was busy diversifying his portfolio of sponsorships. The NBA also got into the act and used Yao to increase its presence in China. Thirty of the Rockets' games were broadcast on Chinese national television during the 2002–03 season, attracting an audience significantly larger than the games drew in the United States.[4] While the NBA had been trying to gain traction in China for years, it made a quantum leap when Yao joined the league.

The efforts of Nike to focus on its brand in China were directly related to the ongoing challenge of protecting its intellectual property through traditional means. The only sure way to preserve and expand its customer base in China was to enhance the brand. If people only bought the shoes—as opposed to the image—then the products could always be undermined by knockoffs and piracy. If owning the brand, the real brand, was the caché, then the company would be less vulnerable—though if exact replicas were sold, that would still erode the company's market share. Chinese consumers, much like American consumers, are among the most brand conscious in the world. That is a difficult statement to quantify, but marketing mavens have long noted the propensity of Chinese consumers to look either for the lowest-priced goods and find the best deals or to go to the higher end and buy products that make a statement about status, taste, and wealth.

The young men and women who constituted the core of the new urban consumers were especially brand conscious. The typical female reader of a popular Chinese fashion-lifestyle magazine might have "at least one Louis Vuitton handbag, one pair of Gucci shoes and at least seven lipsticks by . . . Estée Lauder and Lancôme. Male readers . . . are likely to be found around town in an Armani suit and Hermes tie, and they'll offer you a light with their Zippos." When the magazine surveyed its readers about their buying trends, they claimed that "they were willing to pay substantially more for an international brand." This indulgence in the material world has suffused urban culture in China since the turn of the new millennium. If the focus of Chinese consumers in the 1990s was snazzy appliances and the trappings of the modern Western home, the past years have seen a notable shift toward goods and services, fancy clothes, chic bars and restaurants, and accessories.[5]

Granted, this type of consumption was affordable only for a relatively small segment of China, mainly the urban elites who were directly reaping the benefits of the accelerating economy. They may have made up only 10 percent of the overall population, maybe less, but even that meant at least 100 million people, with appetites similar to their counterparts worldwide and, increasingly, with the purchasing power to meet those desires. Per capita income was still barely $1,000 a year, though considerably higher when adjusted for purchasing power. Economists use purchasing power parity to adjust for different costs of living, and given that even the most expensive parts of China were significantly cheaper than almost anywhere in the United States or Europe, its purchasing-power-adjusted income in the early 2000s was somewhere between $4,000 and $5,000 a year. That still was far short of per capita income in the United States of more than $35,000 per year, and similar figures throughout the European Union.

Most economists assume that when a household has an annual income of at least $5,000 or its purchasing-power equivalent, it begins to behave like a "middle-class" family. The pattern is familiar: at that income level, people start to spend on things that middle-class families buy everywhere, from computers to televisions to cell phones and clothing, dining out, and eventually a car as well. They can afford more than the necessities of life. The $5,000 figure in China is misleading because it averages hundreds of millions of rural poor with several hundred million more urban affluent. But the figure does at least convey the reality that in the first years of the twenty-first century, China crossed a significant line. Because of its size, a large portion of its people remained impoverished and not integrated into the global economy at all, while a smaller portion but a numerically large group was becoming affluent enough to be considered real consumers.

Whether the abandonment of egalitarian Communist ideology for the Habitrail of consumerism is a positive development remains an open question. Wanting more stuff may be the fodder for corporate growth, but it may or may not be a long-term key to a stable society. China in the past two decades hasn't been static; it's been in intensive flux, yet its commitment to rapid growth has assumed its own logic and provided a goal and focus. In addition, it's not as if it took effort to get the Chinese people to consume. In spite of decades of Maoism, they were consumer savants.

The propensity to consume is central to understanding the hows and whys of Chimerica. As we saw with Avon's success in the 1990s, awakening China's consumer passions was not particularly difficult. But in the 1990s, mass consumerism was constrained by low incomes, even as those incomes were on the rise. That was why the first success stories of Western companies in China were those that sold lower-end goods, desirable because they were foreign but still affordable. For most of the Chinese middle class in the 1990s, Avon and Kentucky Fried Chicken were luxury goods. Ten years later, the range of products expanded dramatically.

By 2003, as it became clear that China would be a force to be reckoned with, many hands went up to say, wait a minute, this is simply a repeat of what happened with Japan in the mid-1980s. Japan surged in those years, and its wealth and appetite for all things Western aroused both notice and suspicion among the established players. No sooner had China begun to attract more scrutiny in the press and in public imagination than the comparison to Japan began. For a brief moment in the late 1980s, there was palpable concern in the United States that Japan was about to surpass America and become the world's dominant economic force. When the Japanese purchased iconic properties such as Rockefeller Center and Pebble Beach golf course—not to mention the flood of Japanese cars and electronics that dominated the American market—alarms went off warning that soon the United States would have to cede its global mantle. Japanese companies seemed to be more efficient and more able to compete, and Japanese banks muscled aside their less well-capitalized American competitors. But then, almost as quickly as Japan had surged, it sank. Inflated property values and the weight of bad loans brought down its banks, and slow government responses kept the Japanese economy stuck in a downward spiral of no growth and deflation for much of the 1990s and into the first years of the twenty-first century.

In the fall of 2003, as I worked to launch an investment fund focused on U.S. and Chinese companies that were central to China's growth, I discussed the idea with potential investors and laid out the rationale for why China presented a unique set of opportunities. Time and again, the parable of Japan was raised as a cautionary tale. Why, people wanted to know, would China prove to be any different than Japan? The answer was simple: China has a culture of consumption; Japan does not.

To say that isn't to suggest that Japanese consumers don't hunger for things. Of course they do, and any visitor to Tokyo marvels at the high-end stores, the luxury goods, and the teen and youth culture of games, manga comics, and gizmos. But a vibrant consumer culture is both a strength and a pathology. Consumer cultures place the acquisition of goods at the top of the social agenda, and you can tell where a culture is on the spectrum by one simple thing: gambling. Japan, for all its consumption, was and is a socially conservative society with a high savings rate and a disinclination to gamble. Brands are in part successful in Japan because they feed into that conservatism and respect for hierarchy, with luxury brands appealing because they represent "the best." China also has had a high savings rate, approaching 50 percent in recent years, but that is because until the 1990s, there was almost nothing to spend on. Even now, if you have disposable income in China, there are few ways to invest, with no bond market to speak of, and a stock market widely and correctly regarded as a casino. That said, casinos are quite popular.

In fact, the only country in the world that rivals the United States as a haven for gambling is China. Okay, Monaco should be added to the list, and maybe the Bahamas, but tiny alcoves hardly compare to countries with the populations of China and the United States. At the turn of the millennium, gambling in China was confined to the island of Macau, a one-time Portuguese colony an hour by hydrofoil from Hong Kong. Macau had a seedy, exotic reputation as a haven for gangsters and gamblers, who favored dice and card games in cavernous halls filled with shouting sweaty men and cigarette fumes. It was like an earlier version of Las Vegas or Atlantic City, before they got cleaned up and family friendly. But it also attracted "whales" from the mainland and from Hong Kong, who were willing to risk millions on a few hands of baccarat. For years, the most prominent Las Vegas casinos wooed those high-flyers with promises of comped villas and private jets, until American casino companies had the idea of building their own outposts in Macau.

That led to a mad dash to construct new hotels and gaming pits. Steve Wynn, who had led the 1990s transformation of Las Vegas, competed against Sheldon Adelson of Las Vegas Sands to be the first American casino operator to tap the lucrative Chinese market. Wynn's eponymous casino faced off against Adelson's Venetian, and both competed with hotels erected by Wynn's old company, MGM Mirage, headed by Kirk Kerkorian, and with local Hong Kong operators who renovated and expanded their operations. The local operators, and none more than Hong Kong billionaire Stanley Ho, had the advantage of easier access to the mainland market. Their junket salesmen had deep connections in Shanghai and the Pearl River Delta region, and had long lured the traditional wealth of Hong Kong. But the new entrants were able to attract well-heeled customers who wanted the cachet of an American brand-name operator. More competition translated into more business. Macau passed Las Vegas as the world's largest gaming spot in 2006, with revenues just shy of $7 billion, and while both markets suffered in the downturn of 2008–09, Macau suffered less.

Gambling as a proxy for consumption isn't a scientific gauge, but the link is hard to deny. Those companies like Yum and Avon that had invested such time and effort in the 1990s did so because they were convinced that China would become a consumer engine at some point in the years ahead. By the first decade of the twenty-first century, those convictions began to pay off. While each year may have been long, and at times the prospects must have seemed bleak, China's consumer power grew more rapidly than even bullish analysts predicted, although consumer spending as a percentage of overall economic activity still contributed less than spending by the government. In the late 1990s, optimists were saying that within 20 years, China would reach a critical mass of income and become a substantial global market. It took less than half that time, and the pace has continued to accelerate.

The opponents of China's entry into the WTO did not view that progression as a positive, nor did many in either China or the United States who questioned the sustainability of the bottomless appetites of modern consumer culture. Others in China continued to criticize the crass materialism as the soulless pursuit of a lost nation. Underneath the giddiness about the surge in goodies that so many more could buy, about the malls and shopping centers and cool new cell phones, many in China—young and old—confessed to cultural confusion, to a sense that while there was more stuff, there was less meaning.

Beginning in 2003, as Internet connections became more available in China and Internet cafes sprang up, online video games became popular, especially the so-called multiuser games. Developers of these games, like developers anywhere, try to find the perfect formula of action and mystery to hook an audience composed largely of urban teens, college students, and young men with disposable income from their parents. One of the more popular games, developed by NetEase, was called Fantasy Westward Journey. Adapted from the Chinese epic classic

Journey to the West, the game took players on a mythic quest in a preindustrial world of knights and villages and dragons. Some players became addicted, playing for 60 or 70 hours a week, a syndrome that had already attracted attention and criticism elsewhere in Asia when the games were introduced. When I visited one of the Internet cafes in Shanghai, just off a busy, noisy street, there was an eerie stillness as a hundred people wearing headsets sat staring at screens, largely in silence, sipping sodas. The only noise came from the clicking of buttons, and the images that unfolded on the screens were of a world without pollution, where goals and values were clear, where there was land to explore and clean air to breathe. Ennui isn't particular to China, but the contrast between the movement of the culture and the subject matter of the games is striking and disturbing.

And yet, nothing has halted the pace of change. The games, the whispers of complaint—those aren't harbingers of any immediate change in trajectory; they're escape valves, ones that bear uncomfortable similarities to the *Matrix* movies or to earlier Aldous Huxley–like visions of dystopian brave new worlds. If anything, companies have noticed the concerns and the ennui and created products to cater to them. The subject of the games, the magazines that discuss the ills of modern urban life, and other distractions have partly masked the hollowing of the egalitarian ideology of Communism and filled the cultural void. That is the wonder of consumer capitalism, and why it is so difficult to counter.

The rise of the Chinese consumer led Nike to intensify its marketing and sales efforts in China, first with Yao Ming and then by focusing on the 2008 Olympics. In fact, Nike allowed Yao to sign deals with rival Reebok and instead turned to other means to attract attention and market share. The potential was that deep. It was why companies like Cisco and Nike plunged into China knowing full well the risks to their intellectual property and the high odds that it would be stolen and infringed. Even with the losses attributable to flimsy protections of intellectual property, the possible gains were too large to forego. It was why Motorola and Intel and Procter & Gamble and General Electric and Emerson Electric and Archer Daniels Midland and hundreds of other multinationals invested billions in China—not to make low-cost goods and sell them in the United States but to make them and sell them in China.

Even as the bottom line of many of these companies began to reflect the China phenomenon, the commentary and popular perception in the United States was that China mattered solely because it was a low-cost producer and an exporter. Beginning in 2003 and picking up pace in 2004, China started to attract more attention in U.S. newspapers and the media in general. At first the coverage was negative and focused on the outbreak of the SARS virus in the spring of 2003 in Hong Kong, which spooked not just markets but health officials worldwide about the prospects of a global epidemic. Images of families fleeing Hong Kong wearing face masks did not depict China in the best light and, in fact, reinforced long-held views that China was more of a threat than an opportunity.

But SARS proved not to be the crisis that some feared. In 2004, stories about China proliferated in the *Wall Street Journal*, *Fortune*, *BusinessWeek*, the *Economist*, and the *Financial Times*, and focused on China as the next new thing. Many pieces were notable for their hyperbole more than their sagacity, and in the rush to announce that China was the new "It" country, they oversimplified. Yet, they identified the trend more accurately than many of the experts who remained skeptical about the viability of China's path. The media seized hold of the degree to which China's rise was intimately connected to the United States and how the story wasn't just about a new superpower but about the old one as well. They understood, implicitly, that the China story was also a U.S. story, and that it would define globalization for years to come.

The media grasped that an article on Huawei wasn't just about a Chinese technology company. It was about Cisco, about competitors to American economic might, and about the future of global commerce. The secrecy of Huawei, the discomfort caused by its connections to the Chinese military, and the fear that it would be an unstoppable force were part of the reason that China was not just a curiosity but a concern. Never mind that Cisco itself did ample work for the U.S. Defense Department and for the National Security Agency, and other highly classified work for the U.S. military and intelligence establishment. It seemed more ominous in the American imagination when it was *their* high-tech company helping *their* military. The Chinese, for their part, had reason to fear and suspect U.S. intentions, both over Taiwan and toward China in general.

Yet fear and suspicion were balanced by the manifold rewards that China offered, including for American companies such as IBM. At the end of 2004, IBM sold its personal computer division to China's Lenovo in a deal that generated less outcry but no less astonishment than Huawei's shadowy competition with Cisco. And, of course, IBM was instrumental in helping Huawei become a global player, but during these years, IBM was undergoing its own metamorphosis. As it divested itself of a low-margin business that represented its past (personal computers), IBM was investing time and energy in building a franchise as a vital source of expertise for companies like Huawei that hungered to make the leap to international prominence. IBM's CEO, Samuel Palmisano, articulated a vision for IBM as a company that wasn't beholden to any one country for its growth and that instead defined itself as a global business. For Big Blue, which for much of the twentieth century epitomized the organization man and the strength of the American economy, the

1990s were a difficult time. IBM seemed like a lumbering giant in the face of nimble New Economy competitors. Yet within a decade, it was transformed, and China was one reason why.

The internal contradictions of China were evident, and encapsulated in Yao Ming alone: a product of Communist state-planning who ended up being a potent symbol of Chinese capitalism; an endorsement machine who managed to embody both nationalist dreams and the avaricious ambitions of his considerable coterie of advisors, handlers, and one very determined mother. Somehow Yao has been able to carry those contradictions comfortably, as has his legion of fans. It would be too much to say that as Yao goes, so goes Chimerica, but it's as good a metaphor as any.

As China mania picked up in the West, however, so did China skepticism. In the view of economists and investors, China's development was imbalanced and unsustainable. For all the consumer activity, much of the economy was fueled by state spending. The accepted view was that unless the economy became less reliant on capital spending by the state, growth would collapse. That orthodoxy proved to be as faulty as the equally strong belief that trade between the United States and China was unfairly benefitting China at the expense of America.

The tenor of the discussions in 2003 and 2004, therefore, was that China was an incredible story but also heading for a major correction. The economy was too skewed to the state and too dependent on foreign trade and investment capital, with insufficient consumer demand, not enough rule of law, and, above all, an archaic banking system about to collapse under the weight of nonperforming loans. The 2004 U.S. presidential election turned China into a looming menace, a proxy for economic anxiety and continued job loss in the U.S. manufacturing sector. Meanwhile, prominent voices began to warn that higher inflation in the United States was imminent and that interest rates were about to go up around the world, both of which would lead to lower growth.

These assumptions proved almost completely wrong. Inflation stayed low; interest rates did not rise; and growth remained strong. The models were outdated, the data incomplete, and the worst mistake of all was the assumption that China's financial system could not handle the changes. There were problems, for sure, ones that the Chinese leadership focused on intensively, but the consequences were not what almost all informed voices predicted. We have looked at some of the ways that China became the growth engine for American companies. But at the same time, American companies became the reform engine for China's finances. Without that involvement, China's banks and many companies may have slid close to collapse. No model factored in the influence of global institutions on China's domestic economy, yet that proved the key to why things evolved as they did and not the way so many thought that they would.

CHAPTER 10

The Great Wall and the Gold Rush

C HINA'S ECONOMY IS IN trouble!" "It's too early to say whether China will have a hard landing!" "China anxiously seeks soft landing." These comments were par for the course in the middle of 2004. There was wide consensus that the furious pace of China's growth was unsustainable, precarious, and imbalanced. The best that could be hoped for was a soft landing, during which the economy slowed gradually but did not actually implode. The alternative was a hard landing, which would look more like a crash. Either way, a correction was both inevitable and necessary.[1]

China, however, didn't have a hard landing in 2004 or in 2005 or later. It didn't have a soft landing. It had no landing.

Once again, what was expected didn't happen. Traditional models and assumptions dictated a clear outcome, yet reality bore little resemblance. The reasons for the expectations of China's slowdown varied. Some believed that China's growth was too dependent on foreign investment. Others felt that the currency, with its exchange rate set to the dollar by the government, was undervalued. In exchange for China's goods, cash poured into the country, creating a buildup of the country's reserves that would be one ingredient leading to dangerous inflation and excess money supply. Still others pointed to what they believed was an unhealthy dependence on nonperforming bank loans and state spending. For all the consumption of the booming coastal cities, the economic system was still light on consumer activity as opposed to spending on large projects. There were even questions about China's infrastructure and ability to meet the power demands of urbanization and industrialization. China's GDP grew by nearly 10 percent in the first half of 2004, a good few percentage points above what the central government had predicted, and concerns about overheating weren't confined to foreign economists. Premier Wen Jiabao, as committed to creating a market economy and every bit as adept as his predecessor Zhu, spoke with unusual frankness to both foreign and domestic audiences about the need to reign in the excesses and the substantial risks if the growth were left unchecked by the government.

China had faced a small crisis in its banking system a decade earlier, which Zhu had dealt with forcefully. But with a much larger and more complicated system in 2003 and 2004, the concerns were magnified. China had begun to assume a significant position in the global economy, and so its possible travails attracted more notice and generated more anxiety worldwide about the ramifications. Though the United States remained the world's largest economy by far, and accounted for more than a quarter of global growth, its system was also suspect. Though the headline numbers looked solid enough, there was a sense that all was not as good as it appeared statistically. The U.S. trade deficit with China widened, and manufacturing employment lost jobs every month. Average incomes did not advance even as health care costs soared and corporations generated heady profits. The thought of China growing created one set of fears; the thought of it slowing raised another.

Few disagreed that the Chinese banking system was broken

and that unless it was fixed, it would constrain growth and ultimately halt it. The problem of China's state-run banks had been understood by Deng in the 1980s, by Jiang and Zhu in the 1990s, and remained an issue for Hu and Wen in the early years of their rule. China's banks under Mao were nothing more than appendages of the state that funneled money as directed by central and local authorities. In no way did they function as commercial enterprises with an eye to making money on loans, pricing risks, or charging for services. Over the years, the national banking structure had been altered. There was a central bank in the form of the People's Bank of China and four main lending banks that in theory focused on distinct areas such as agriculture, construction, commercial, and retail. The central bank set interest rates and printed money. The "big four" continued to do what they had always done, which bore little relationship to banking in the Western sense.

In spite of some structural changes, the core issues remained: China's banks were in bed with government and party officials. If an official in some province wanted money for a new factory or a bridge, he went to his friend at the bank and asked. The bank officer was undoubtedly a member of the party as well, perhaps a relative, and there was no question about providing the funds. There was also no question about asking for the money back or demanding interest payments. The same was true for the central government. The chairman of the People's Bank was a ranking member of the party, and the various branches were staffed by officers who saw their primary duty as serving the party and the state in whatever way their superiors dictated. If the party five-year plan set a goal of a certain number of new bridges or power plants, then there was no question of a bank refusing to grant a loan for those to be constructed. If a state-owned enterprise sought funds for that project and had the explicit support of the local party cadres, then the money would be provided regardless of the long-term economic viability.

There were also lower levels of institutionalized corruption. Local banks were staffed by officers connected by various ties with local businesses, whose funding requests were rarely turned down. The legacy of the command economy of the 1950s and 1960s was that there was still a mentality that simply building things was an accomplishment. Party cadres, businesspeople, and banks could inform the central government that they had proudly done their duty by constructing more housing complexes or aluminum smelters and had thereby generated that much more output. Even though the central government tried to shift attitudes and discourage production for its own sake, those habits remained.

This way of doing business gave rise to the widespread belief that China was hopelessly corrupt. Loans were given based on who you knew rather than on what you were doing. The economics of the project mattered only marginally. And once the loan was extended, it had a tendency to sit there, on the books, forever. The result—according to conventional wisdom—was an inefficient system weighed down by nonperforming loans and unproductive use of capital.

The issue of corruption is not clear-cut. Every developing system goes through periods where rules are murky or nonexistent. That was as true of China in the 1990s and beyond as it was of the United States in the nineteenth century, with its "wildcat" banks that would open one day and close the next. In the absence of clear laws and rules, people rely on connections and word of mouth. The reason family businesses thrive in those environments is that family members usually do not double-cross one another. They may not treat one another well, but they tend to honor contracts and commitments with one another because it is ultimately in their self-interest. Friends and in-laws also tend to form close business bonds. At the end of the day, corruption emerges where there is little trust that the state will enforce a contract between parties who are connected only by their business interests and not by family ties.

For China, that sense that things are done only through connections permeates much of the advice about doing business in the country. Foreigners are urged to focus on *guanxi*, which refers to that tight web of personal connections that must be cultivated in order to get anything done.[2] Throw out the old rule book, discard the familiar way of doing things, and plunge into the mysterious world of formal meetings with little substance, followed by banquets, ritual toasts, and weeks spent cultivating contacts. Then and only then will deals be concluded and a working relationship be established.

Certainly there are ways of doing things in China that are particular to China. But that isn't really saying anything. Every society has ways of doing things that are specific and not written down or codified in law. Americans and citizens of Western European countries may pride themselves on transparency and the rule of law, but try getting a land deal or a real estate development done in southern Florida or Las Vegas or California's Inland Empire without knowing who sits on the county's planning council or other relevant committees. They may grant you a license after months of wading through the regulations, or they might raise various zoning issues that would make the project impossible or impossibly expensive. Try selling a piece of property, renting an office, or opening a business in France. The blizzard of regulations, transparent but paralyzing, can bury even the most competent foreign business. Knowing the right people who can help you navigate the system is always essential everywhere.

Yet even if corruption in China was not quite what many Westerners claimed, China's banks did hold massive quantities of loans that had no chance of being repaid. The actual amount of those nonperforming loans was itself the source of controversy. Few people in any part of the world—including China—believed the public figures issued by the Chinese government, which sometimes claimed that nonperforming loans constituted only a small percent of the overall total. In part, the distrust of the official loan numbers stemmed from the fact that data were first released only in 1998. Another problem was that as the Chinese government grappled with bank reform, its first response was to transfer bad loans to new holding companies. That made it appear that the loans didn't exist, at least not on the banks' books.[3] Yet, that wasn't the rationale for transferring them. Under premiers Zhu and Wen, official China wasn't interested in pretending that a problem didn't exist. They both were pragmatists driven to create a strong and stable system, and they knew that manipulating the data was optics, not a solution. They simply did not view the problem in the same way traditional Western economists did.

They recognized that state-owned banks had hundreds of billions of dollars of bad loans. They also understood that easy credit, tight connections, and lack of discipline about the cost of capital had been a key element in the crash of Japan in the 1990s. At the same time, they recognized the ways in which China was different. To begin with, the government had very little debt. That was in contrast to most developed countries, including the United States. Whether China's bad loan number was $100 billion or $400 billion, it wasn't compounded by billions more in government debt. Yet there was a more fundamental difference in how Chinese officials viewed the problem.

The definition of nonperforming loans is almost self-explanatory: loans that generate no interest and eventually must be written off by the lender. A nonperforming loan is capital spent with no subsequent benefit to the institution that spent it. In the United States or Europe, a bank with a high level of nonperforming loans is a failure as a business. Think of the savings and loan crisis in the United States in the 1980s. Hundreds of billions of dollars in loans went to real estate developments that were busts. The lenders then went bankrupt, and the government was left to clean up the mess. The vast expansion of subprime mortgages in 2005 through 2007 triggered a credit meltdown in 2008. Dozens of banks went bankrupt and others would have had it not been for government bailouts in 2008 and 2009. Having misjudged the creditworthiness of the loans, financial institutions had sold those mortgages in bundled securities to buyers who overestimated the value as well. The cascade throughout the system was devastating.

Yet in China, the sheer size of nonperforming loans relative to the overall size of the economy is much greater than the size of the subprime market was to the U.S. or European Union economies. Even taking into consideration the fact that there aren't accurate numbers on the amounts, it is striking that the bad loans in China have not produced the crises that they did in Japan in the 1990s and in the United States and Europe in 2008.

The reason is simple—so simple, perhaps, that it has been overlooked or ignored. The fourteenth-century English theologian William of Occam wrote that when searching for answers and explanations, the simplest theory is usually right. The wisdom of "Occam's razor" seems unquestionable, but time and again, people discard simple explanations in favor of complex ones. Nonperforming loans haven't brought China to a halt, because they aren't really nonperforming loans.

Loans can only be truly nonperforming if someone calls the loan and if there is a consequence for the lender. An additional condition is that the loan has to be understood as a pure financial instrument in the first place. For much of the past 20 years, those conditions did not apply to money advanced by Chinese banks to state-owned businesses. In fact, absent a culture that treated loans as financial products meant to generate return, the loans were basically vehicles for funding the modernization of the state that Deng set in motion in the 1980s. They were, in essence, checks backed by the government to fund the transformation of China and modernize the economy. While there was also a hope and expectation that loans would generate interest payments and perhaps be repaid, that wasn't as important as getting things done.

It's not that all Chinese officials and bank officers were indifferent. But they perceived the situation in China differently than those outside China. They were not as concerned about the ratio of good loans to bad loans, or about likelihood of repayment. They were faced with an old system that had no pricing of risk, no cost of capital, no assessment of return on investments, and no performance mandates for bank officials other than keeping local and national party bosses happy. One reason that Chinese leaders beginning with Deng and continuing with Hu have been so adamant about not allowing China's currency to trade freely and float like any other currency is that they knew for certain that opening up China's financial system to global capital and global financial institutions would lead to a deluge and a collapse at least as severe as what happened in the old Soviet Union in the early 1990s. And with far more people and a more complicated society, they legitimately feared that the result would be far worse, with not only the collapse of the state, but famine, violence, and anarchy. That had happened in China earlier in the twentieth century, and so the fear cannot be dismissed as self-serving paranoia. Chinese officials treated the currency and the closed banking system as a modern-day Great Wall—a vital barrier keeping the perils of the outside world at bay.

As the process of reform continued, however, the Chinese leadership recognized that the system could not remain a closed loop forever. The whole thrust of Deng's reforms was to open China to the world in order to create a vigorous economic system that would pull people out of poverty and maintain both stability and the legitimacy of the party in the process. That opening began with new enterprises that were encouraged to attract outside investment and allowed to trade. It also included allowing foreign companies more room to operate in China. It did not include opening up a banking system that in Western terms wasn't a banking system at all.

In order to join the WTO, China had to agree to permit foreign banks to do business in China within a five-year period. Before 2006, when that period would expire, Chinese banks would have to reform enough to make it feasible for institutions such as Citigroup, Morgan Stanley, and Deutsche Bank to set up branches and engage in lending activity. That explains why Zhu began the first wave of bank reform in the 1990s, and why his successors were so focused on changing the way domestic banks functioned. They knew that once there was foreign competition, Chinese banks would be at a disadvantage. Global financial institutions had systems for pricing capital, for assessing the creditworthiness of customers, and for making sure that risk was taken into account. They were structured to make profit and to use their deposits for that purpose. Of course, the events of 2008 demonstrated that too many of those models were deeply flawed, but even so, the core discipline of running banks as a business was rigorous compared to how things had been done in China.

One of the failings of domestic Chinese banks was that they were not attractive for individual deposits. Without paying much in interest and with a reputation for corruption, banks were seen as a necessary evil, and many people kept all or a large portion of their savings in cash in their homes. The banks also made little effort to attract capital from individuals or small businesses, and instead relied on periodic infusions from the state. That would have to change if domestic banks were to be at all competitive with foreign financial companies.

But here, as with the entire Chinese system, the reform imperative had to be weighed against stability. If you were a high-ranking official, you couldn't just snap your fingers and command banks to price risk and lend to private entrepreneurs. You couldn't order them not to lend money to state enterprises or not to provide funding for local projects, no matter how economically questionable. The old system of patronage and dole may have been wasteful and inefficient, but it was a system. Until a new one existed to take its place, it would continue because it had to.

Take the analogy of the old bridge. If a city has an old, creaky bridge that is in danger of collapse, it is faced with a quandary. It can tear down the bridge and build a new one, but that might take years and cause as many disruptions as it solves. It can spend on maintenance every year to prop it up, delaying the inevitable. Or it can build a new bridge next to it, prop up the old one until the new one is complete, and then reroute the traffic once the new one is ready for use. That was what Chinese officials confronted with its banks.

There was a final need that the old system filled, and that was to channel money to projects deemed vital by the central government in its five-year plans. While the long-term goal was to end the command economy, China has remained a state-driven economy with a clear long-term strategy. Urbanization, modernization, and phasing out antiquated industry and moribund agriculture were orchestrated by the central party. Banks had a vital role in funneling state money to those airports, roads, public transportation projects, power plants and grids, rail links, and steel mills.

Here as elsewhere, China played a game of three-dimensional chess. Officials both maintained aspects of the old system while encouraging and demanding reform. They allowed foreign competition to act as a spur and a model to domestic institutions while maintaining sufficient protections for those institutions so that they weren't driven out of business before they could compete. Government officials also allowed for inefficiencies and some corruption as a trade-off for short-term stability. And they had, unlike so many other developing countries, two advantages. They had money, and they had global financial institutions willing to invest time and energy even with the constraints of a closed economy. Everywhere else in the world, Western banks had said to emerging economies, "Do these things first, and then we will provide capital and expertise." In China, they provided capital and expertise first, on the expectations that reforms would follow. And they did so because in a growth-constrained world at the beginning of the twenty-first century, China offered one of the only potential opportunities. It was almost virgin territory for global finance, the last unconquered market, and every major institution in the world wanted in.

Meanwhile, the Chinese kept underwriting the losses caused by nonperforming loans. At the beginning of 2004, the government injected $45 billion into the system in order to recapitalize the banks. At the same time, Beijing continued to license foreign institutions to do business in China. That included allowing major firms to invest in China's closed stock market (which had until then been open only to Chinese nationals and Chinese companies) and to purchase ownership stakes in select banks. The Western perspective on the $45 billion recapitalization was summed up by one foreign bank: "A drastic overhaul in credit underwriting and corporate governance reform will be essential to improve the quality and profitability of . . . China's banks, in addition to the recapitalization exercise." Or to paraphrase in plain English: "The bleeding may have been stopped, but the patient will die without more drastic action."[4]

That was not how Chinese authorities viewed the situation, however. Unlike foreign banks, no one was actually holding Chinese financial institutions to account. Because capital could flow into China but could not as easily flow out, the same rules didn't apply in China as they did almost everywhere else in the world. Yes, if China had been completely porous to global capital and integrated into the global financial system, then the level of bad loans and lack of discipline would have caused a massive wave of write-downs, losses, and bank failures, as well as a drying up of capital. That did not happen, or even come close to happening. The central government wasn't about to call the loans, and it remained the primary source of funding.

The ultimate goal was to have Chinese banks act like their global peers—in time. But that time would come only when they were ready, when the training wheels came off and they were forced to sink or swim based on their own effectiveness. Until then, the hybrid system, the old bridge–new bridge system, would continue.

There have been and still are only two countries in the world that can function according to their own rules and not according to rules that are set for them: China and the United States. The evolution of China's financial system is testament to that. It is in the realm of finance that Chimerica first began to exist as more than a description. The United States, even with the implosion of the Wall Street credit system in 2008, is still able to run large deficits because the dollar is the global currency of last resort, and the U.S. government can lend itself money. No other country has that latitude, because no other country has the dollar as its domestic currency. China has what would otherwise be a dysfunctional banking system and can still draw foreign investors by the droves—investors who demand little and actually lobbied the government to be allowed to invest in those dysfunctional banks solely because they saw the long-term potential as unparalleled, irreplaceable, and utterly necessary to their own long-term health. Meanwhile, investment flows both ways; China's central bank buys U.S. bonds with the surplus it has generated from trade.

The unique path charted by China's leaders as well as foreign investment in China's banks kept not only China's financial infrastructure intact but the United States—and by extension the global system—as well. That system nearly collapsed at the end of 2008. The fact that it didn't is due in no small measure to the fusions of the two economies.

The flow of U.S. and foreign funds into China's banking sector was a dramatic departure from how global financial institutions have behaved elsewhere in the world. It allowed China to reform its financial system by drawing on the expertise and the capital of the world at large and of Wall Street in particular. The central government signaled that it wanted more discipline by bank officials and branch managers, and that it wanted loan officers and executives to consider the long-term viability of the borrower and the future cash flow of the project. It also urged banks to broaden their offerings to the growing middle class, including credit cards, auto loans, and home loans, and to make it attractive for them to deposit their funds. The government then worked to set up a viable asset management industry and to invigorate a moribund stock market.

At the very end of 2003, the Chinese government announced that the constitution would be amended to guarantee private property rights. While property markets and private businesses had been lively, until this change, the actual legal status was poorly defined. Lack of clear property rights had been one more headwind, along with the widespread conviction among both Chinese and foreign businesses that there were rules passed by officials but no consistent rule of law. The passage of the property act marked yet another step along the way toward the free-market hybrid that China was crafting, and it led to a burst of property speculation in the major cities. In order to offset the mania for apartments and the endless flipping of new condo units, the government then turned its attention to the stock market.

Here as well, the role of foreign financial institutions was key. A functioning equity market is one way to allocate capital more efficiently—or so the theory goes. Stock markets also provide companies with additional sources of funding, provided not by banks per se but by shareholders. The Chinese government sanctioned two stock markets in the early 1990s, one in Shanghai and one in Shenzhen. Shanghai became the primary market, with more than a thousand listed companies. Only Chinese nationals could invest, and for a time, the market boomed. But then it swooned, trading dried up, and the market stagnated until 2004.

China's stock market bore little resemblance to markets elsewhere in the world. Almost all of the listed companies were state owned. They sold only a small percentage of their shares, reporting standards were almost nonexistent, and no one pretended that the companies were run for the benefit of the shareholders. The government created the stock market as a way of injecting capital into dying state companies, and while there may have been dreams of a dynamic trading exchange that allocated capital to successful companies and penalized those that were inefficient, there wasn't a financial infrastructure that would have made that possible. Companies bought one another's shares and then held them. On any given day, it was possible for no shares of even large companies to trade. Once the capital had been raised, it disappeared down the same black hole of inefficiency that characterized most of what state-owned enterprises did. As of 2002, China's stock market had a total valuation of about $600 billion, which was quite small by global standards; only $150 billion of that ever traded, and the rest was locked up in shares that never switched hands.

After 2001, the government worked closely with foreign asset managers and sought the advice of market regulators around the world in order to kick-start the market. Some of the better Chinese companies had been trading in Hong Kong, and that had exposed them to global capital flows and the discipline that forced on management. As new private companies started to form, they looked to list not in China but in Hong Kong, and then after 2002, in New York.

As I began to manage the fund in 2003, rarely a week went by without a Wall Street bank bringing a Chinese company on a road show to raise money for an initial public offering. By 2004, what had been a steady flow became a deluge, as more than 50 Chinese companies were listed in New York in that year alone. The investment banks that were handling the offerings were the usual suspects, though Goldman Sachs, Morgan Stanley, and Credit Suisse were more heavily represented. Investment bankers from these houses had spent the prior five years in offices in Shanghai shuttling back and forth to Beijing to work with regulators to allow for more foreign listings and also to revamp China's financial markets. Many of those bankers had also spent years in Hong Kong and knew the region; some had done a stint in London, Frankfurt, or New York. Their goal was to tap the potential of both a new wave of young Chinese entrepreneurs and to manage the public offerings of some of the more attractive Chinese state companies. The result was a funky mix of high-tech Internet ventures and staid banks and insurance companies.

On the cool side were companies like Shanda, NetEase, and Ninetowns. All of them provided a mix of online games, Internet portals, and cell phone messaging services. They were much like their New Economy precursors in the bubble era in the United States, and their IPOs were just as wildly successful. They were, by and large, led by thirty-something CEOs with boyish looks who had been either game developers, crack programmers, or astute marketers. Some of the games were copied from Korea; others were Chinese originals. They combined an online gaming culture popular in Japan and Korea with the start-up culture of Silicon Valley, and they were then expertly packaged by Wall Street investment bankers and served up to U.S. investors. On its first day, for instance, a company called Ctrip.com nearly doubled, even though there was nothing especially dot-com about its business model. It consolidated hotel rooms for business travelers in China and used vast call centers to help with bookings. One day, when there were enough personal computer users, it planned to extend its services online, but the marketing advantage of adding the *.com* was irresistible.

Yet while these companies bore a strong resemblance to their New Economy cousins, there was one major difference. They had substantial earnings, and in the more sober investing climate of the early years of the twenty-first century, they traded at reasonable prices relative to their revenues and growth. While some of the stocks did well and others didn't, the companies themselves were on the whole of higher quality than similar ones in the United States a decade earlier. But more to the point of our story of convergence is that these were domestic Chinese companies brought to the U.S. capital markets by Wall Street investment bankers looking for the next great growth story. Many of the companies were already partly owned by the private equity arms of the investment banks that had funded them at early stages. Then, as they went public, American hedge funds and asset managers further underwrote them. Here again, China developed a new entrepreneurial culture using American capital and expertise.

If these offerings looked like China's version of Silicon Valley, and if the prices paid sometimes seemed out of whack, that was nothing compared to the enthusiasm for Chinese financial companies. Beginning in 2003, a slew of major Chinese financial companies listed their shares in Hong Kong and New York, including China Life Insurance Company, the Industrial and Commercial Bank of China, China Merchants Bank, Ping An Insurance Company, and the Bank of China. The ICBC was the biggest public offering in the world since the 1990s, and Goldman Sachs alone agreed to purchase a 6 percent stake for $2.5 billion. When the company went public and its shares soared, Goldman's investment doubled. Morgan Stanley made 12 percent of its profits in 2006—more than $1 billion—from fees underwriting Chinese companies, including a lucrative offering for China's version of eBay, called Alibaba.com.[5] If the 1990s had been the beginning of a lucrative new market for Main Street USA going to China, the early 2000s was the gold rush for Wall Street.

The same investment banks whose research departments were churning out reports on the perilous state of China's financial system were simultaneously pouring billions of dollars into China's banks and insurers and collecting billions in fees from servicing them. Chinese companies were turning to global financial markets, and the more innovative start-ups were eschewing domestic bank financing altogether and looking instead to U.S. capital markets and stock exchanges. Chinese authorities were using both the expertise of Wall Street and the infusion of capital to build a new financial system literally on top of the old one. China's stock markets were given a regulator not just with the authority but the political backing to go after companies who submitted fraudulent financial statements, and the banking community was tasked with improving the way it assessed loans and priced capital. After 2004, the Shanghai stock market started to zoom ahead, as did Chinese companies trading in New York and Hong Kong, largely because investors finally had confidence that the system would function with set rules and more transparency.

None of this is to suggest that China's financial system was transformed overnight. One informed observer described the system as one where "Tony Soprano rides the Chinese dragon." State-owned companies may have listed their shares, but in no way could it be said they were run for the good of the shareholders. Even getting them to answer the phone and respond to investor concerns could be a challenge. And yet the combination of incremental reform combined with unparalleled opportunity meant that huge sums of money flowed into the system from the United States, even as Chinese institutions were in turn buying U.S. Treasury bonds in order to manage the trade deficit. It's often said that money is fungible. For Chimerica, that meant that as it flowed to China from Wall Street in one form, it then also flowed back to Wall Street and Main Street in another.[6]

Capital flows and business transactions were distinct and separate components of the financial relationship between China, the United States, and the world. But the weaving together of the financial systems changed the trajectory of both economies in ways that the models did not predict. China never did have that landing, hard or soft, and the United States never did have that rise in inflation and interest rates that its steady growth was supposed to create. Even as the United States was awash in easy credit and the booming housing market, inflation of goods was nowhere to be seen. Later, in 2006 and 2007, there would be inflation of vital raw materials, but not of finished goods. China was absorbing foreign capital, restructuring its financial system, and providing a suite of goods to the United States. It also bought U.S. debt, and the net result was to export low costs. China didn't slow, and the United States never encountered the headwinds that were expected.

As we now know, other headwinds proved to be catastrophic, as the easy credit tied to the U.S. housing market led Wall Street to structure products and derivatives that were in turn bought by the world's institutions, including Chinese banks. Just as Main Street companies in the 1990s faced with New Economy powerhouses went to China to find growth, Wall Street firms in the 2000s confronted the lack of organic growth in the developed world and used the housing market and China to compensate. Between the two, Wall Street was able to generate turbocharged profits. But where the housing-backed mortgages and derivatives were built on sand, the business in China was rock solid.

Even if the banking system was shaky, the growth it was supporting—in the form of infrastructure, buildings to house workers at factories, and new businesses—was real. Even if some of the activity was unnecessary, based not on need or future potential but on who-you-know networks, it was better for China to err on the side of excess than paucity. As long as the old system continued to exist side by side with the new, there would be vanity projects erected by local business leaders and officials who wanted their cities to be just as shiny and modern and rich as Shanghai or Beijing. That was a cost of China's development model.

Traditional Western analysts focused intently on the liabilities of the model. Too much capital spending on projects that do not yield return, and too little consumption, they said. They pointed to the fact that as China's growth accelerated in the 2000s, consumption actually decreased as a percentage of GDP, even as it increased in the United States. But the analysis wasn't quite right. Chinese spending went up substantially in these years, and only decreased as a percentage of the overall economy because the pace at which it grew wasn't as rapid as spending by the state on infrastructure. That spending, however, was a necessary precondition for the middle-class, consumer-oriented economy that Chinese leaders were striving to create. Every Western company recognized that China was successfully establishing the necessary conditions for a market. As a result, while there had been a steady flow of investment in China in the 1990s, it became a flood in the early 2000s.

Public sentiment was changing as well. When I thought about launching a fund in 2002, one concern was whether anyone would understand the China story in the United States, or whether it would be seen as too exotic, too risky, too other. By 2004, as China became the "it" story in the business press and magazines, everyone I spoke with recognized that China's rise was real and that it had significant implications for the future of the United States and the world. They wanted assurances about the rule of law and about transparency and about whether political tensions, environmental issues, and the shadowy role of the Communist Party would be impediments in the years ahead. But no one needed convincing that China had come of age and that it was about to alter how the world would look in the twenty-first century.

As for the United States, even with 9/11, few questioned whether America would continue to enjoy a long period of global hegemony. Then China stepped onto the global stage—right into the middle of a spotlight shining on the United States and its ongoing soliloquy about the world and how it should be. To say that feathers were ruffled would be an understatement.

CHAPTER 11

Benedict Arnold
Goes to Mississippi

O N A COLD DAY in Virginia stumping for the upcoming Democratic primary, Senator John Kerry thundered against the outsourcing of jobs that had become the scourge of the American workingman. "We will repeal every single benefit, every single loophole, every single reward for any Benedict Arnold CEO or corporation that takes American jobs overseas and sticks you with the bill." The Benedict Arnold line resonated with many voters, and Kerry garnered his party's nomination for president. Throughout the 2004 campaign, he continued to hammer away at corporations that shipped American jobs overseas, and though he rarely mentioned China by name, he didn't need to. Every newspaper that carried his remarks—and that meant every news outlet in the country—connected the dots. Jobs were lost, and China was the cause.

The relentless attack on Benedict Arnold CEOs worked because it tapped into a widespread insecurity that global trade was advancing at the expense of the average American, and that corporations and Wall Street were getting rich while the middle class and Main Street were falling further behind. Kerry later clarified that he wasn't attacking all outsourcing of jobs or global trade per se, only those companies whose executives took advantage of tax loopholes to close U.S. plants, eliminate U.S. jobs, and hire people overseas to do the same work for less. He recognized that lost jobs were one part of an equation, and that lower-cost goods that many American consumers craved were another. Still, he kept on that particular warpath until his defeat in the general election that November.

Like the Seattle protests against the WTO in 1999, the rhetoric of the 2004 presidential campaign mined a rich vein of populist discontent with the way the world was going. Some of that was almost as old as the republic. Populist anger at Wall Street and the sense that eastern fat cats were robbing the people of the fruits of their labor were prominent features of the political and social landscape for much of the last half of the nineteenth century, and popped up again during the New Deal and during the new wave of progressive politics in the 1970s. What was different about 2004, however, is that the old attack on Wall Street and greedy corporations fused with a new anxiety about China. The rumblings about Mexico and NAFTA a decade earlier were a dress rehearsal for the animosity about the rise of China. For all the fears about Mexico undercutting the American worker, no one thought that Mexico would use that low-cost advantage to supplant the United States as the world's leading power. China was something else entirely.

The primary threat was what many termed "the China price." Because wages were so much lower in China, anything that could be made in the United States or Europe could be made in China for 30, 40, or 50 percent less. In fact, China could undercut almost any place in the world, including formally low-cost venues such as Taiwan and even more recent low-cost centers like Mexico. It wasn't just that China could utilize a labor force of young men and especially women in their 20s, who were migrating from the countryside to industrial centers in the coastal provinces. It was that the infrastructure that China built in the

1990s made it easier to get goods from China to others points throughout the world. Cheap labor was the obvious source of China's strength, but expensive modern infrastructure was what actually elevated it into a different league.[1]

The most visible consequence of the China price was that the trade deficit between China and the United States continued to expand. The size of the deficit ($125 billion in 2003), and the widely shared belief that the erosion of U.S. manufacturing jobs was the direct result of the rise of China, led to calls in Washington for China to revalue its currency. The exchange rate between the dollar and the Chinese yuan was set by the Chinese government; the currency did not float freely. The peg against the dollar had been determined many years before, and as China's manufacturing exports grew, so did criticisms of the currency. The charge was that China was deliberately keeping its currency undervalued relative to the dollar in order to maintain its competitive advantage and flood the developed world with cheap goods. The demand that followed was predictable: China had to revalue its currency or suffer restrictions on its exports.

In an election year, there is usually an inverse relationship between rhetoric and reality. The former becomes increasingly shrill, while the latter becomes evermore static. Congress rarely passes meaningful laws, though sometimes in late summer, it will quickly enact a piece of legislation designed to inoculate legislators against what they feel might be a critical issue on Election Day. For the most part, however, politicians declare positions and take stances knowing full well that words are cheap and anything one says in the course of a campaign is, in the end, just words. During 2004, there were constant condemnations of China as a threat to American jobs, and there were repeated calls on China to revalue its currency or suffer the consequences. While Republicans tended to defend the advantages of free trade, both Democrats and Republicans were critical of China's exchange rate policy and accused the Chinese of manipulating the currency in a way that hurt American companies and consumers. The demands that China allow its currency to appreciate were appealing to many voters, but in spite of the apparent popular resonance, none of them was ever acted on.

In the face of American pressure, Chinese government and business leaders had two primary responses: they reminded critics that while China did indeed have a huge trade surplus with the United States, it was running a trade deficit with the rest of the world, including with Japan, South Korea, and much of the European Union; and they said that the blame for the imbalance didn't lie with what China made and how, but with what Americans consumers wanted and at what price. Unlike American politicians who used public forums to denounce what they termed China's unfair and anticompetitive policies, Chinese officials usually made their case through more discreet channels. Of course, the public nature of the U.S. denunciations did raise hackles in Beijing. While Chinese officials were willing to discuss areas of disagreement in private, they viewed American public criticism as both bad form and arrogance. If the primary goal of U.S. policy had been to get China to reconsider its policies, public denunciations would have been the last tool selected. In truth, the denunciations of China in the United States were aimed more at a domestic American audience than at China itself.

Chinese officials also countered that China's economy, its gaudy growth numbers notwithstanding, was a fragile system. The country was still poor on a per capita basis, and there was a yawning gulf between the urban areas of the coast and much of the agrarian interior. The advantages that a cheap currency gave China were not optional. If labor suddenly became more expensive or the currency rose, there would be a risk of inflation and a lack of competitiveness that might derail the domestic economy and cause widespread instability. In addition, given the tenuous state of China's banks, a sudden revaluation of the currency could cause Chinese export companies to generate lower profits, and that in turn could cause a wave of defaults on loans, which was something that the financial system didn't need and possibly couldn't handle. Chinese officials had an additional concern about currency speculation inside China and the black market for dollars. While a revaluation per se wouldn't address that problem, any sudden shift or rumor of such a shift could precipitate a wave of under-the-counter activity as various parties attempted to position themselves. Because currency was part of the financial Great Wall that the government believed was essential to the country's growth and stability, black market speculation was perceived in a harshly negative light.[2]

In both public pronouncements and private discussion, U.S. authorities rarely placed themselves in the shoes of the Chinese officials whom they were speaking with, and the same was true for Chinese officials listening to Americans. American politicians and critics of China assumed that the currency peg was a cynical manipulation by China to take advantage of the United States, while Chinese authorities viewed U.S. pressure and criticism as yet another indication that China would not be allowed to take its rightful place as one of the leading nations of the world. Chinese officials also couldn't fathom why the Americans were so concerned. From their perspective, China was still a poor country, and the United States was the richest nation in the world. The playing field wasn't close to even, so why were the Americans acting as if China were a threat?

No doubt, China and outsourcing proved a convenient bogeyman for election-year politics in the United States. Occasionally someone would raise a hand to remind people that the China threat was overstated. "Much of our deficit with China is the transfer of previous deficits with Korea and Taiwan," said Clyde Prestowitz of the Economic Strategy Institute. "Most of what China sends to us we stopped making back in the 1970s and 1980s." The emergence of China may have come "at some cost to American jobs but at a bigger cost to countries that compete directly with China, such as its Asian neighbors and Mexico." Yet these comments were drowned out by the stories of once-vibrant American factories shutting down, of thousands thrown out of work because some avaricious business owner decided to follow the bottom line, destroy a community, and relocate production across the Pacific.[3]

Another culprit responsible for the erosion of manufacturing jobs in the United States was information technology. As companies confronted a slower growth in the developed world, they aggressively pursued new markets such as China and greater efficiencies that would allow them to enhance their profitability. Computers, customer management software systems, and faster communications links allowed companies to do more with fewer people. Just-in-time manufacturing, which had been perfected by innovative organizations like Dell, meant that companies could keep very lean inventories and gather parts from a supply chain that stretched around the world. If parts were cheaper when sourced to Malaysia or China, then they were made there. But without information technologies that made it possible for companies to coordinate different parts and different suppliers around the world, much of the outsourcing would have been impossible. Only with complicated logistics software and systems that made sure that precisely calibrated parts would arrive from multiple countries at the same time in one factory could these global supply chains function effectively. Even as job creation was weaker than many would have liked and wage growth was minimal, productivity gains remained impressive, with around 4 percent growth in late 2003 and into 2004. Productivity was a perfect proxy for the gains generated by information technology. It wasn't just low-cost labor that changed where and how goods are made: the forces unleashed by the 1990s New Economy played a central role as well.

But focusing on those trends would have diluted the political argument. It was much easier to rail against China and Benedict Arnold CEOs than to examine the nexus of technology and the ubiquitous desire for cheaper goods and services that were just as much a part of the mix. China also made a better target than India. While India was indeed siphoning certain types of American service jobs, its global footprint was much smaller. Call centers throughout the United States were being closed and relocated to India, which had the advantage of an English education system. But democratic India had more barriers to global commerce than Communist China. There were multiple restrictions on how much business foreign companies could do in India, especially retail companies, and the sorry state of national infrastructure, especially transportation, made it unfeasible for global corporations to relocate manufacturing there. Call center and software programming jobs were vital to parts of the United States, but in the national consciousness, the loss of those jobs didn't strike the same chords as the continued decline of U.S. manufacturing employment. In self-image, the United States had been built on the backs of the steelworkers and the autoworkers, not the "yes, can I help you?" anonymous voices on the other end of a warrantee call.

The debate over outsourcing was hopelessly muddied by ideology. Anyone suggesting that the issue of jobs was complex and not a simple equation of a job gained in a Chinese factory equalling a job lost for an American worker risked being deemed a conservative free marketer in hock to moneyed interests. Those who questioned the untrammeled march to free trade were seen as protectionists and throwbacks who didn't recognize how the world had changed. Reality, as usual, was more nuanced and confusing than political slogans or ideology. Some jobs were lost, others were long gone. Millions of people benefited from lower-cost goods, even while companies benefited more.

If there was any doubt about the messiness of reality, the case of the China bra wars should have put those to rest. The Republican Party in the United States was the standard bearer of the advantages of unlimited free trade, but only to a point. In late 2003, looking ahead to the election, President Bush placed a punitive tariff on imported Chinese bras, asserting that Chinese manufacturers had an unfair advantage and were harming U.S. textile workers, especially in Republican strongholds like North Carolina and South Carolina. The "boudoir tax," as one wry publication termed it, was padded with noble rhetoric about protecting American workers.[4] There was only one small problem: there were almost no American bra manufacturers left.

Yes, North Carolina alone lost more than 100,000 textile jobs after 2001, but that was because manufacturing had relocated to Central America. China was positioned to undercut those areas. In addition, while the Bush tariffs did help his electoral fortunes in certain states, it also earned him the enmity of companies like Wal-Mart and Playtex, which had arranged sourcing deals with Chinese manufacturers at very advantageous prices. The new tariffs threatened to increase their costs of obtaining the bras, which they would not be able to pass on to the consumer. In that sense, the tariffs neither protected U.S. jobs nor helped U.S. companies. The tariffs also indirectly jeopardized Japan and Germany, not the intended targets. China had been buying textile factory equipment in anticipation of 2005, when global tariffs would come down in accordance with a previously negotiated WTO schedule. Those factories were being built on the assumption that demand would increase as tariffs came down, but Bush's tariffs threatened to alter the progression, which in turn led to a pause in China's orders for Japanese and German equipment.

These unforeseen and unintended consequences were a startling indication that the fusion of China and America would decrease the power of the U.S. government. It would, in fact, decrease the power of all central governments, including Beijing. As the economic ties became more layered and complicated, the traditional tools of economic coercion became two-edged swords. As companies created new global supply chains, moves of governments to protect workers could have the unintended consequence of also hurting workers. If Playtex found its cost of goods going up faster than its ability to raise prices, it would face pressures to cut costs. As a U.S. company, it may have shifted production abroad, but it still had a considerable sales and marketing group in America. If profits were squeezed, Playtex might begin to lay off people. The same was true for countless others. As companies and supply chains went global, governments remained national. Governments continued to think of the world in binary terms: my country, their country; our goods, their goods. Companies had a different perspective, as did capital.

And there is no question that companies were reaping the rewards of China's growth. Those who had been in China for years started to see accelerating profits, and those who were new to the scene were able to get up and running much more quickly because of the efforts of the early movers. Kentucky Fried Chicken did well in China in the 1990s, but by 2004, China became the primary driver of growth for Yum! Brands even though the number of outlets there accounted for less than 5 percent of the total global base. In China, KFC was cutting-edge, dynamic, and hugely profitable, and the company was expanding at a rate of more than 25 percent a year, opening new outlets in strongholds like Shanghai and moving into the interior cities at a rapid clip.

Nike diversified from Yao to local icons such as the hurdler Liu Xiang and began to expand its presence throughout the country. Along with KFC, Nike became one of the most recognized and respected brands in the country, voted the Middle Kingdom's "coolest" in one independent survey. Its factories, which once produced shoes primarily for export to Europe and the United States, were busy making shoes and apparel for sale to the Chinese, with special styles and signature footwear marketed purely to a Chinese audience. In 2004 Nike in China was opening, on average, 1.5 new stores a day and had sales of $300 million a year. The company cultivated its image by turning to the Internet for advertising, and started embedding ads in the middle of those hugely popular video games. It sold a promise of individuality to a young, urban market that was looking for new identities in a fast-changing world. And not only was Nike's business booming, but margins were expanding even with prices for its products nowhere near what they were in the United States or Europe. Nike founder Phil Knight had once famously told his executives, "There are two billion feet out there. Go get them." After many years of laying the groundwork, more of those feet were wearing Nikes every year.[5]

Few companies captured the peculiar nature of the China-U.S. relationship better than Wal-Mart, the massive discount retailer that consumed swaths of Middle America, disrupting small businesses as commercial life relocated to big box structures and strip malls on the outskirts of town. Few stores have been as reviled as Wal-Mart even as it achieved stunning success, offering tens of millions of people low-cost versions of the middle-class goods and services that had seemingly become part of their birthright. When those new DVD players were priced at $200 or $400, they were out of reach for many in the lower middle class. Then Wal-Mart found a way to sell them for under $100 and they were ubiquitous. The trade-off was a transient labor force that was paid minimum wage with almost no benefits. The other trade-off was that in order to sell items so cheaply, they had to be made even more cheaply, which meant evermore sourcing to China. Wal-Mart in the 1980s was known for its rigid commitment to American suppliers and had even used as a marketing slogan "Buy American." Yet its model by the 1990s demanded continually lower prices, which many suppliers in the developed world could not match without lower labor costs. It is not an exaggeration to say that without China, and without Chimerica, the modern phenomenon of Wal-Mart would have been impossible.

It's been estimated that in the first years of the twenty-first century, as much as 15 percent of all U.S. imports from China were goods for sale at Wal-Mart stores, worth a total of $18 billion in 2004 alone. If Wal-Mart were a country, it would have been China's sixth largest export market. The Wal-Mart effect also touched hundreds of companies that supplied the company, as well as any retail competitor. It wrung efficiencies wherever it could, and made a deep commitment to information technologies that included using sophisticated inventory systems to cut down on any excess ordering and to respond to demand in what was close to real time.

Like Nike, however, Wal-Mart also had a strategy to expand into China and become a retail presence on the mainland. It opened its first stores in the mid-1990s, including a Sam's Club in Shenzhen, which had about as much name-brand recognition as a Deng's Outlet would have had in Wichita, Kansas. All of its stores were joint ventures with local Chinese businesses, and by 2005 it had opened nearly 60 branches. It wasn't the first Western mass-market retailer; the French company Carrefour was in China and had a considerable headstart, as did the UK giant

Tesco. And Wal-Mart faced a unique challenge from China's fastest-growing supermarket chain, a domestic company conveniently called Wumart. In China, Wal-Mart replicated its model of large stores offering thousands of products, but the product mix was different, with more space devoted to groceries and foodstuffs than in the U.S. Some of the stores had KFC outlets just nearby or attached, which the company thought would help attract customers who weren't already familiar with the brand.[6]

Wal-Mart in the United States evoked a panoply of emotions, including wonder at the range of inexpensive products, revulsion at the soulless anonymity, discomfort with the coarse attitude toward workers' rights and health care, and dismay over the disappearance of a small-town America. In China, however, the reaction was different. If a new Wal-Mart in Chongqing threatened to drive mom-and-pop proprietors out of business, it was seen as a price of progress rather than a loss to be mourned. The groceries at Wal-Mart promised to be free of diseases, and the selection was unparalleled, including toads, eels, and spicy chicken feet. At one store opening, the lines snaked around the block, and by the end of the first day, 120,000 enthusiastic customers had shopped. China had more than 100 cities with a population of 1 million or more, and Wal-Mart saw the country as a green field for future expansion, an opportunity to generate more organic growth than it could possibly generate in the United States or other countries where its market share was already approaching saturation point.

Like Nike, Wal-Mart faced pressure in the United States to ensure that its suppliers in China adhered to certain labor standards. Nike had faced that uproar years before when it was revealed that its factories in Asia employed child labor. Nike was also more vulnerable because it portrayed itself as a progressive company, whereas Wal-Mart made little secret of its disdain for unions and workers' rights. Still, Wal-Mart's sourcing in China was a lightning rod for criticism of its callous attitude, its lax enforcement of labor standards, and the loss of American jobs. U.S. suppliers that had Wal-Mart as a large customer had trouble competing against Chinese equivalents. Famous brands like Mr. Coffee coffeemakers, owned by Sunbeam, almost ceased production in the United States in response to pressure from Wal-Mart and others to cut wholesale prices so that the coffeemakers could be sold for the astonishingly low retail prices that Wal-Mart offered. During the 2004 election, when Wal-Mart became the poster child for lost jobs, the company promised to be more vigilant about labor standards at the many Chinese factories that served as its suppliers. Those efforts were mixed. Even when the company did crack down on excessive hours at a Chinese factory, the operators sometimes evaded the problem by setting up another unregistered factory nearby. Wal-Mart executives saw one, but not the other. But it was the shadow factory that allowed the supplier to meet the demand at the price set by Wal-Mart.[7]

Wal-Mart, of course, operated in other parts of the world as well, and had a larger presence by far in Mexico than it did in China. But the unusual combination of sourcing opportunities and market potential made China different for the company and for the structure of the relationship between the two countries. In fact, the erratic tariffs thrown up by the Bush administration, as well as the export subsidies that the Chinese government used to bolster Chinese products, masked the degree to which companies as distinct as Wal-Mart and Nike were functioning in a world that saw little differentiation between the national borders of China and the United States and instead operated in a global market that was anchored by and determined by the Chimerica supply chain.

Some economists noted that by 2004, the global economy was being fueled primarily by Chinese production and American consumption. According to the International Monetary Fund, more than half of the world's economic growth was generated by the two alone, with the percentage increasing with each passing month. Chinese exports were a global phenomenon, and the United States was the consumer of last resort for products around the world. The crisis that began in 2008 showed that the American consumer could not forever absorb the excess products of the planet, nor could Wall Street firms endlessly generate growth from credit constructed on the flimsy foundations of the U.S. housing market. In 2004, however, the global engine was powered by the twin pillars of China and the United States.

Yet even here, where some of the dynamics were understood, U.S. consumption and Chinese production told only part of the story. Statistically, those were the most evident components of global economic activity. But we have seen how statistics and models could measure and explain only what they were set up to measure and explain. They could not, and did not, account for something unprecedented.

There had been low-cost producers before China emerged, and the U.S. consumer had been a global engine since the middle of the twentieth century. Other countries had bought U.S. debt, and other emerging markets had provided growth for multinational companies. But the China-U.S. system involved everything simultaneously. China combined a large domestic market with a huge export machine. It attracted immense sums of foreign investment capital, and with its currency nonconvertible, it accumulated ever-larger reserves. It sold goods to the United States, and then, with its large pool of savings and profits, lent the Americans the money to buy those goods. With the income gained from producing those goods combined with the spending by the government to build cities and a national infrastructure, China developed a new middle class with income and desires, which U.S. and multinational companies then pursued as the only possible long-term alternative to the American consumer.

No one aspect of the relationship was sufficient to meld the two economies. It wasn't foreign direct investment alone, or low-cost production, or an emerging Chinese middle class, or the purchase of U.S. Treasuries, or the currency, or any other single factor. It was the unique combination of all of them. Any one facet would simply have meant a dynamic bilateral relationship between China and the United States. All of them together led to a superfusion that turned the two economies into one unit.

The unprecedented flow of goods and money meant that widely accepted models of earnings growth, interest rates, and wages did not function as predicted. Even as the economies of the developed world managed decent growth, there was no goods inflation and no wage increase for most workers. That wasn't supposed to happen. Yet wage stagnation had more modest consequences than in the past. Many people could still afford the goods and services they wanted—and homes—because the price point was kept low by the China price and because China's purchase of U.S. debt kept interest rates in check. Some of that system collapsed in 2008, but, as we shall see, not because of Chimerica and not as much as it would have without the interdependence of China and America.

Captains of capital saw immense profits, some built on the illusion of derivatives and credit, and more derived from the very real foundation of Chimerica. By 2004, more than 100 of the S&P 500 companies—which represented many of the largest companies in the United States—were getting between 20 percent and 40 percent of their profits from outside the United States. Within a few years, more than 400 of the 500 would be able to say that, a whopping 40 percent or more of all profits coming from outside the United States. And while the U.S., the European Union, and Japan, which collectively accounted for almost three-quarters of global output, managed less than 3 percent growth, companies exposed to China routinely managed to generate earnings growth of 20 percent, 30 percent, or even more. Some of that was due to greater efficiency and more productivity, but much was also pure revenue growth fueled by China.

The China effect involved more than China and more than the United States. Countries ranging from Brazil to Australia to South Korea to Japan saw their economies invigorated because of demand coming from the Chinese. As China's industrial build-out picked up pace and moved to include the cities of the interior and of provinces that had been left behind in the initial wave, China's demand for raw materials soared. Soon that would lead to rising prices around the world and cause a new wave of alarm that China was exporting inflation to everyone else, but initially the price increase for copper, iron ore, nickel, oil, and steel were more modest. Still, countries that exported raw materials, as well as countries that sold high-end equipment to China, did well as China did well.

The global growth driven by China was one reason that certain companies were able to transcend the anemic growth of their countries. Yet, it wasn't just China driven, but Chimerica driven. China's exports to the United States generated some of the income needed for purchases of high-end equipment and industrial commodities. The $150 billion a year or thereabouts that flowed into China from the pockets of U.S. consumers via Wal-Mart, Nike, Home Depot, Motorola, Intel, and throughout the entire supply chain was in turn used to build maglev trains connecting Shanghai's new airport to downtown and the world's highest railroad to Tibet. Money flowed from Main Street USA to new power plants and ports in Dalian and Tianjin, and into the pockets of millions of new urban residents in China who then spent that money on Nike sneakers, Wal-Mart spicy chicken feet, Tesco soap, and Procter & Gamble's Oil of Olay. That money also funded meals at McDonald's purchased by middle-class Chinese on their way home to watch televisions made from glass produced by Corning and assembled by Chinese brand names like TCL Corporation.

These companies thrived because they were able to tap multiple markets without the burdens that affect nations and government. Companies, large and small, can focus on markets that are growing and invest in them while cutting back on ones that are stagnant. Increasingly, companies aren't responsible for the health care of their workers, and they can play one country's tax regime against another to pay as little tax as possible on the revenues they earn. The anxiety of the 2004 presidential election may have been wrong in some of its claims but correct about the overall trend: it was good to be capital, not good to be labor. Companies and capital were enjoying mobility and flexibility; labor wasn't nearly as mobile or nearly as nimble.

Those trends had been gathering momentum for decades, but without the meshing of China and America, the consequences might have been considerably worse for labor and workers in the United States. Take the case of Caterpillar. Few things are more iconic than a trucker cap with *CAT* emblazoned on it. The company personifies the man-over-nature spirit that drove the conquest of the West and the transformation of North America into an industrial powerhouse. With its earth-moving equipment and trucks, backhoes, Dumpsters, road graders, excavators, haulers, loaders, and diesel engines, Caterpillar makes the vehicles that enable humans to alter the earth, to mine and mold it, destroy it and re-create it. They are not an environmentalist's dream, but they are an integral part of the business of extracting raw materials and then using them to build things. By the late 1970s and early 1980s, Caterpillar had seen the days of explosive growth in the United States wane, and it looked abroad for new markets. With few competitors (Komatsu and Hitachi in Japan being two of the only other companies with its range and quality), Caterpillar machines became as vital to mining in Australia and clearing in Brazil as they were to construction in the United States. Caterpillar's only liability—and it was significant—was that its prices were high.

And then there was China. As of the mid-1990s, China looked to be a good but not great market for Caterpillar. The cities were growing, but much of the work could be done with simple equipment. The coal industry in China was often small scale as well. The first customer for Caterpillar was the Chinese government, which didn't require a credit system to fund those purchases. The first factory on the mainland opened in 1994, but even 10 years later, it had only produced a total of 5,000 machines. As growth picked up, however, demand increased for the full suite of equipment. In 2004 that factory made another 5,000 units, and the pace quickened in 2005 and approached $1 billion in sales. Caterpillar also began to license designs to local manufacturers and allow some transfer of its technology in order to boost its presence. Like other companies, it was willing to give up some of the long-term potential of its intellectual property in order to boost market share in the short term.[8]

Caterpillar saw its business in China take off yet was unable to capitalize on it fully. Being a cautious, conservatively run organization, it was slow to revamp its production lines. Its factories tended to be of the older, fixed-line type rather than fitted with more flexible production lines. That made it more costly and more challenging to adjust to variable orders. The company also was cautious in its estimates for future demand, and looked carefully at the historical connection between national and global growth rates and how much of its equipment would be bought. Because of the nature of its business, Caterpillar tended to be closely tied to GDP growth, and it used the analysis of groups like the International Monetary Fund and the World Bank as well as its own internal economic forecasts to plan ahead.

As we have seen, however, China's growth was more robust than expected. Its appetite for the machines that Caterpillar made so well proved to be greater than the company had anticipated, as did demand from countries that were extracting raw materials for sale to China. After 2004, China became the largest consumer of the world's industrial commodities, including iron ore, nickel, zinc, cement, copper, and aluminum. Even with an economy that was less than 15 percent the size of the United States and the European Union combined, it was responsible for almost all the growth in consumption of materials, a development that almost no one foresaw—including the companies whose business it was to extract those raw materials. Caterpillar was no exception, but its rather conservative culture and production methods, as well as the way that it locked in supplies to manufacture its machines, meant that even as demand soared, it couldn't keep up, and its margins suffered.

While the company may not have made as much money as it could have, it still saw a huge increase in revenue and profits. That remained true even as the U.S. and European housing and construction markets began to sag in 2006 and then collapsed after 2007. As anxiety increased in the United States that China was siphoning jobs, demand from China didn't just help Caterpillar rake in billions; it kept workers employed in a factory in Oxford, Mississippi.

The Oxford plant made high-pressure couplings for use in Caterpillar machines. It was, in fact, the only factory in the world that made them. The company had elected to centralize the production of these small vital parts in one place and then ship them wherever they were needed, whether that was a factory in Wuxi, China, or Brazil, or elsewhere in the United States. As demand shrunk in the developed world and stayed strong in China, the Oxford plant continued to hum along. The local economy was anemic and getting weaker, but the factory wasn't tethered to the local economy of Mississippi any more than Caterpillar was brought down by an increasingly adrift U.S. economy. The only thing that derailed the plant was a tornado in February 2008 that did severe damage and took the factory temporarily off-line. What the global economy couldn't derail, Mother Nature did.[9]

Oxford, Mississippi, was one of hundreds of small and large communities whose factories continued to exist in the United States because of global markets and the pull of China. The changing patterns of commerce destroyed many businesses, but created some as well. The former made dramatic headlines and fueled political movements, while the latter—the Oxford Mississippis of the world—were just life as usual and attracted less attention.

The political rhetoric of 2004 and beyond accentuated the sense that economies are still defined by the nation, and heightened the sense of us versus them. The Chinese government, for its part, interpreted the diatribes as a signal that its increasing affluence and hunger for goods and commodities would generate friction with the United States and that it needed to take steps to lessen its dependency on the American market. They remained locked into a nation-state framework as well, and internal debates reflected the same tension of us versus them. Our people are poor, the Chinese reasoned, while the Americans are rich. If the United States is complaining about currency and jobs, it is because their politicians don't want to deal with their internal social and economic problems, not because of China. And so it went.

Even as the economies became more entwined, the mindset remained the same. Economists continued to publish reports predicting what lay ahead for China and the United States, along with every other country in the world. Everyone gave lip service to the world being flat, and there was wide consensus that businesses and capital flows were now global. Yet few attempted to game out the ways in which new systems might create unexpected outcomes. When the data surprised, that was written off as anomalous or as a temporary phenomenon or an imbalance. No matter how much China consumed, China continued to be viewed primarily as a low-cost producer. No matter how much profit China created in the United States, potential threats from China were given pride of place in most discussions. It shouldn't have been surprising, therefore, that after the U.S. election, the relationship between the two entered a tense period.

In some ways, the tensions represented the rearguard action of the nation against the relentless tide pulling the two economies together. Few may have fully grasped what was happening, but governments and cultures have a sixth sense for threats. The data may not have demonstrated what was happening in full, but you could feel that *something* was happening, that it was unlike anything that had happened before, and that it would upend the familiar and replace it with the new. The years between 2004 and the present haven't seen a coronation or a celebration of Chimerica. If anything, they have witnessed a reaction against it. The fusion may have been amorphous, but people knew one thing for sure: they didn't like it. And when one of China's premier state-owned companies attempted to buy a jewel in the American crown, all of those lingering fears and accumulated anxieties erupted and threatened to bury Chimerica under heaps of xenophobic ash.

CHAPTER 12

A Not-So-
Harmonious Rise

I N THE SPRING OF 2005, the Chinese state-owned company CNOOC made a bid for Unocal Corporation, one of
the largest energy companies operating in Central Asia. The acronyms were the only thing that was dull about what followed.

CNOOC stood for the China National Offshore Oil Company, which had been created in 1982 to oversee just what its
name suggested. Unocal was the multibillion-dollar Union Oil
Company of California, which had been founded in 1890 and by
the late twentieth century was a major player in the Alaskan oil
fields and in a project to construct a natural gas pipeline across
central Asia that would traverse both Afghanistan and Pakistan.

The announcement that CNOOC intended to buy the company for upward of $18 billion set off a firestorm in Wash-
ington. Congressional leaders blasted the deal. The tone was
one of frenzied alarm. Democrats and Republicans, in a rare
demonstration of bipartisan hyperbole, were equally outraged.
Typical of the responses was Congressman Richard Pombo
(R-California), who urged the Bush administration to block
the deal, warning that it could have "disastrous consequences
for our economic and national security." Not to be outdone,
Senator Ron Wyden (D-Oregon) told Treasury Secretary John

Snow that it was imperative to review the deal closely. "I don't think being a free trader is synonymous with being a sucker and patsy," he declared.

The proposed purchase unleashed concerns that had been building for years. The campaign rhetoric had made allusions to China, but those were secondary to denunciations of outsourcing by American companies. The possibility that a Chinese state-entity might acquire a U.S. energy company produced an uproar on Capitol Hill that echoed the Red Scares of decades past. Unocal did have connections to the U.S. government, and the company's activities in Afghanistan both under the Taliban regime and after the U.S. invasion in late 2001 were shrouded in national secrecy. The concern that a Chinese acquisition would give the Beijing government access to past secrets wasn't entirely unfounded, but at heart, the reactions spoke volumes about the anxiety over China's rise.

It also spoke to a new determination on the part of the Chinese government to use its financial reserves to secure energy supplies. The country had been an oil exporter in the 1970s, when its industrial footprint was comparatively light, and it had begun to import oil in the 1990s as its own fields dried up and its demand increased. Though the overwhelming majority of the country's electricity needs were met by coal, as the road network expanded and trucks and cars proliferated, the need for oil grew accordingly. As Chinese leaders looked into the twenty-first century, they saw ever more need for both oil and raw materials, and they interpreted the hostile rhetoric in the United States as an indication that if China did not secure its own access to those supplies, it would be vulnerable to American and world pressure in the future.

Much of the American criticism of the proposed deal was directed at the intimate links between CNOOC, the Communist Party, and the central government in Beijing. Opponents said that they didn't trust the motives of the government or the company, and that China would act in its own self-interest. If that meant preventing the United States or the European Union from accessing oil and gas reserves that one of its national companies controlled, then it would do that. Meanwhile, there was another bidder for Unocal—Chevron—which had the advantage of being American and having better lobbyists in Washington. There were also allegations that China didn't "play fair," either in trade or in its dealings with U.S. companies, and that therefore the United States could hardly be obligated to treat CNOOC's bid as just another corporate transaction. Senator Byron Dorgan of North Dakota argued that "there are policy questions that have to be answered. When a Chinese government-controlled company tries to buy an American oil company, is it a free-market transaction? The answer is no."

The bid also provided another opportunity to draw attention to China's currency reserves and to the yawning gap between imports and exports between the two countries. A new bill was introduced in Congress by Democratic senator Charles Schumer of New York and Republican Lindsey Graham of South Carolina demanding that China revalue its currency sharply or else face a punitive 27.5 percent tariff on all exports to the United States. While the bill was more for bluster than actual passage, it was an effective shot across the bow, a purposeful warning that powerful voices in the United States government viewed the trade imbalance as China's fault, as harmful to American economic health, and as a source of tension. The furor over Unocal removed whatever ambiguity there might have been and announced to the world that relations had now entered a new phase. Rather than celebrating and cheering China's transition from Maoism to the market, it would now be viewed with more skepticism and more distrust.

Faced with a hostile Congress, CNOOC withdrew its bid,

and Chevron acquired Unocal. To some degree, passions had been skillfully manipulated by Chevron, but its lobbyists alone couldn't have whipped up that level of intensity had it not been nascent. For their part, the Chinese were understandably annoyed and taken aback at the reaction. "The unprecedented political opposition . . . was regrettable and unjustified," CNOOC said in a public statement. "This political environment has made it very difficult for us to accurately assess our chance of success, creating a level of uncertainty that presents an unacceptable risk to our ability to secure this transaction."[1]

The company might also have said, but of course did not, that no one plays fair when it comes to international trade, America included. Hidden costs, license and visa restrictions, veiled or not-so-veiled subsidies, tax breaks for exports—all are standard practice. And every country, especially emerging ones, looks to secure vital raw materials that are integral to its growth. The Europeans did that throughout the nineteenth century, and the United States did as well in Latin America and the Middle East. There was nothing odd or untoward about China perceiving a need to guarantee access to the gas, fuel, and commodities that it required in order to proceed along the path that Deng had set.

In addition, CNOOC was responding to the changed landscape created by the U.S. invasion of Iraq, which had been an area of interest for Chinese expansion. While CNOOC's chairman repeatedly said that the desire to buy Unocal was purely commercial, that didn't mean that strategic considerations couldn't be satisfied simultaneously.

Even before the CNOOC imbroglio, Chinese leaders were beginning to reflect on how they would engage the wider world as they emerged from the slumber of the twentieth century. There were heated internal debates within the Communist Party about how to describe what was happening. Initially, the official line was to speak of "China's peaceful rise" whenever the topic of China and the world came up in public forums, either in China or abroad. But after some reflection, the leadership decided that even that phrase might be too unsettling to foreign audiences, given that the implication of "rising" might set off alarms. After more consideration, President Hu described the process as "peaceful development." While *peaceful rise* continued to be used, it was often with the caveat that China was focused on internal development and not yet at a stage where it could impact the external world substantially.[2]

China's self-image and how it was perceived were not in sync. It thought of itself as an emerging poor nation struggling for respect and a seat at the table. It had fought for years, literally, to gain its seat at the United Nations Security Council that had been occupied by Taiwan for much of the Cold War, and now it was demanding to be heard and respected. But when China looked at the United States, it saw a dominant power with a military whose capacity dwarfed the People's Liberation Army and an economy many times its size and far more sophisticated. The continued American criticisms of China over currency, over its stance on Taiwan, its human rights record, and its ambitions were interpreted not as valid concerns but as excuses to keep China in its place as a second-tier nation.

True, Chinese officials also understood that some of the American rhetoric was political theater aimed at domestic constituents. Even the CNOOC rejection was not quite as absolute as it seemed. The company continued to do close business with rival Chevron in developing and exploiting fields in western Australia, and the company chairman, Fu Chengyu, became something of a celebrity in the media for his ease with English and his frank discussions of the challenges ahead. And while the oil bid was stymied by the astute lobbying of Chevron, only a few months before, another rising Chinese company had successfully acquired a major American competitor.

For years, the Chinese start-up Lenovo had been producing workmanlike personal computers that had a large following in China and an increasing presence in other parts of the world. The company had begun life as a research unit of a state-owned technology institute in 1984. Its scientists were ambitious young men who wanted to make computers. By the early 1990s, they were animated by a pie-in-the-sky vision: "China should have its own IBM. It should have its own multinational companies." By the dawn of the twenty-first century, Lenovo was selling 2 million desktop computers and 120,000 laptops. One of the key aspects of the emergence of the Chinese middle class was the proliferation of cell phones and personal computers. Cell phones were adopted first, with as many as 200 million users by 2002 and double that within five years. Home computers followed, though adoption was slow relative to the use of computers in Internet cafes. China home computer and Internet connections became truly widespread only after 2004.

Most Western computer makers had long since ceased to manufacture components. Dell, Hewlett-Packard, Compaq, and IBM sourced a large percentage of their hardware to original-equipment manufacturers in Asia. For IBM, which had pioneered the personal computer as well as the heavy-duty mainframes that were a fixture of corporate America in the 1960s and 1970s, the personal computer business had become a struggling division. It was losing as much as $500 million a year, as nimble rivals like Dell gained market share and proved more adept at just-in-time assembly and online marketing. The result was that IBM decided to sell its PC division. The surprise was that it was sold to a Chinese company that many Americans had never heard of, and the agreement was announced in October 2004.

It wasn't a particularly big deal in dollar amount, valued at

$1.75 billion. Under the terms, Lenovo would continue to make IBM ThinkPads for five years. The negotiations had been fairly smooth, given that IBM was intent on selling and Lenovo was equally intent on buying. IBM had initiated the merger talks, which Lenovo managers later admitted that they never would have considered on their own. They may have dreamt about becoming a global brand, but buying IBM's computer division seemed to them as much of a pipe dream as a local supermarket chain buying Wal-Mart. Lenovo had a robust business, growing quickly, but it was still only a quarter the size of IBM's PC division when the deal was forged. When news broke, there were some raised eyebrows in Washington amid concerns that Lenovo might access technology that had been used for weapons and military systems. Some IBM employees wondered if their pensions would now be redeemed in yuan. Yet those concerns didn't reach the fever pitch that later characterized the Unocal uproar, and the merger was approved. In China, the deal was described as "a snake eats an elephant" fable come true. Lenovo's chairman called it "astonishing."

The two companies agreed to have two research centers, one in Raleigh, North Carolina, and one in Shenzhen, with corporate headquarters in New York. Lenovo, which had succeeded because of low-cost innovations rather than innovative research, acquired a world-class research and development operation, and the new entity became the world's third largest personal computer company. In subsequent years, and contrary to expectations that the two together would be less than the sum of their parts, the company developed cutting-edge ultrathin laptops and was mentioned in the same league as Apple for its streamlined designs and functionality. It was, not surprisingly, dominant in China, and controlled a third of the market—a market second only to the United States for personal computers in 2007 with 27 million sold.[3]

It's fair to say, however, that the hostile reaction to the proposed Unocal acquisition affected the Chinese leadership more deeply than the benign response to the Lenovo deal. The very unpredictability of American reactions troubled the Chinese government, and the pending punitive tariffs in response to the failure of China to revalue its currency were taken as proof that no matter what China called its transition—"peaceful rise" or "peaceful development"—the U.S. government would stand in the way. European countries were just as hesitant about allowing foreign buyers to purchase companies that were perceived as vital to national interests, whether in defense, energy, or finance. But the European Union wasn't seen by China as the driver of the global system; the United States was, and its strong presence in the Middle East and ties with the major oil-producing nations was viewed as a potentially devastating constraint on China's future growth.

In response, Hu Jintao worked tirelessly to build ties with countries that were scorned by the United States, and especially those that had substantial natural resources. The result was an informal league of countries that had either alienated America or just weren't seen as strategically important by Washington. During the Cold War, there was an Eastern bloc and a Western bloc. This new informal Chinese imperium was the geopolitical equivalent of the Island of Lost Toys. Zimbabwe, Bolivia, Venezuela, Nigeria, Angola, Sudan. Between 2001 and 2006, China's total trade with Africa—evenly balanced between imports and exports—surged from $10 billion to nearly $60 billion, which made Africa as a whole China's third largest trading partner after the United States and the European Union. Most of Africa's exports to China, not surprisingly, consisted of oil, food, minerals, and metals. Chinese businesses, spurred and supported by Beijing, worked with Angolan oil refineries and drillers, Zambian copper mines, South African manganese prospectors, Gabonese iron ore merchants, and timber companies throughout the continent. China poured upward of $7 billion into projects in Africa in direct investments and many billions more in setting up subsidiaries of companies like PetroChina, most notably and controversially in Sudan. As the international community became more concerned about the role of the Sudanese government in the ongoing conflict and genocide in the Sudanese province of Darfur, China was charged with complicity because of contracts between its oil companies and Sudan's government as well as because of arms deals that it had approved. Eventually, faced with increasing pressure to use its leverage in Sudan, the Chinese government began to cooperate with United Nations efforts to halt the violence in Darfur, though that proved largely unsuccessful.

China's unwillingness to intervene was consistent with its overall policy of live and let live. Time and again, Chinese diplomats drew a distinction between its approach to international affairs and America's. Where the United States often attempted to dictate to its allies and adversaries, China approached relations with other countries in terms of mutual interests. It did not feel that it had the right to interfere with other governments or cultures. Of course, it also rarely had the power to interfere. It could not exert its will militarily, and given the increasing unpopularity of the United States and the Bush administration, the Chinese leadership astutely recognized that China could gain more by taking a hands-off approach. It could go to any country that was embroiled in a conflict with the United States and say, "Hey, we will never presume to tell you how to run your country or try to impose our sense of what's right and wrong. We are here as your friends. Let's work together." President Hu described China's efforts in Africa as part of an overall strategy to achieve a "win-win" outcome that would lead to more rapid development in Africa and provide China access to essential commodities.

This was a big development for China, as was its diplomacy in Latin America. Hu initiated warm and friendly dialogues with the presidents of Bolivia and Venezuela, both of whom were quite vocal in their criticisms of the Bush administration and in their declamations that China represented a new alternative to either being with the United States or against it. For China, it helped that both Bolivia and Venezuela are rich in oil and natural gas, though getting that gas to China would be an expensive proposition even in liquefied form. But Hu had at least two goals, one symbolic and one long term. The symbolism of a Chinese premier flying around the world being embraced as a hero and a friend was itself an achievement, a sign that China would be a central part of the global system. Even if the countries that did the embracing were often poorer nations with strained or weak relationships with Washington, that could be used to China's advantage. The Chinese could claim that they too were a poor emerging nation and were helping others have a voice in a world order too dominated by the United States. And they could, at the same time, develop links to resource-rich countries that promised to provide China with a lasting supply of agricultural and industrial commodities.[4]

Hu's goodwill tours of the backwaters of the world were part of the shifting dynamics between China and the United States. Hailed as a hero and visionary in the developing world, Hu had a much more lukewarm reaction when he visited the United States in the late summer of 2005. In fact, President Bush would not even throw Hu a state dinner. The Bush administration was disturbed by China's glacial movement on currency revaluation, on its ambivalence in pressuring North Korea to renounce its plan to acquire a nuclear weapon, and on a host of trade issues. There was also growing public angst about the rise in gasoline prices, which was just beginning to impact consumer spending in the United States.

China's exertions to forge close relations with resource suppliers went hand in hand with the rapid increase in global prices for key industrial commodities. After 2004, the price of oil rose sharply, zooming past $50 a barrel and heading to its eventual peak of $145 a barrel in the summer of 2008. China became the world's largest consumer of copper, which led to a doubling, then tripling, and then quadrupling of copper prices. That made housing construction in the U.S. more costly, as copper was the primary ingredient for piping. China's appetite for steel was equally voracious, and while it was a major producer of low-end steel, it imported higher-end products from Japan and Korea. Its demand for steel—needed for the thousands of miles of rail tracks, those tens of thousands of new buildings, and its fast-growing auto industry—made it the world's most significant consumer of iron ore. The glut of China's low-end steel production combined with its massive imports of sophisticated high-end output put upward pressure on iron ore and the price of high-end steel. That made everything from automobiles to construction more expensive in the United States.

While China's consumption of oil was a third that of the United States (about 6 million barrels a day by 2006 compared with 20 million barrels a day for the United States), its rate of imports had taken the world by surprise, as did its consumption of raw materials. The global supply of oil and metals was the result of decisions made by extraction companies in the 1990s, which had assessed world growth rates and the correlation between those and energy and resource use. Given that it can take 10 years or longer to bring new mines or oil fields into service, especially with stringent environmental regulations throughout the world, companies involved in those industries need to plan decades in advance. That is why multinationals such as Shell Oil spend millions of dollars a year on scenario-planning exercises. They need to be right about long-term trends in order to decide how much to spend on exploration and on bringing new supplies on line.

The demand for oil and metals tended to be closely linked to statistics such as GDP growth, or so those companies believed. The problem was that no models had assumed that China would suddenly start to grow as quickly as it did when it did. The result was a supply shock. China needed more than world supply could provide. Oil was actually the least of the problems, as there is more elasticity in oil production, although refining capacity is always an issue. Nonetheless, China's unexpected rise was at the heart of the sharp increase in the price of global commodities, and after 2005, those price spikes began to hit the pocketbooks of consumers in the United States and throughout the world. If China was already distrusted as a threat to American jobs, now it was seen as a threat to the cost of living.

As U.S. attitudes toward China turned increasingly suspicious, China contemplated alternatives to the close economic embrace. But for all of its charm offensive in Asia, Africa, and Latin America, China's ties to the rest of the world paled in comparison to its increasing entanglement with America. For China to proceed along its path, there was no alternative to a closer embrace with the United States, its government, its consumers, and its companies. American companies were a source of innovation and investment in China's domestic economy; its consumers were the most avid buyers of China's output; and the dollar provided the peg for the Chinese government to value its own currency as surely as gold had been the backstop for all currencies prior to the middle of the twentieth century. The negative political rhetoric in the United States and the occasional statements in China that it could go its own way regardless of attitudes in Washington did nothing to slow the movement of business and capital, any more than the antitrade sentiment of the late 1990s altered the trajectory then. In fact, while the public tenor in the United States was negative toward China, corporations were tripping over themselves to get in on the action.

From industrial companies to retail, from services to luxury goods, China became the focus for businesses around the world. It was a gold rush of global proportions. Shanghai, Beijing, Shenzhen, and Hong Kong were the magnets. Western businessmen commuted to these cities as the next frontier. Deals were quick, entry was easy, and results were swift. On the Bund in Shanghai, luxury stores made the riverfront strip seem like any comparable destination in any first-tier city in the world, akin to Rodeo Drive, Fifth Avenue, the Via Veneto, Rue de Rivoli, and Bond Street. Beijing began to tear itself down only to build itself up in preparation for the 2008 Olympics, while formerly sleepy cities like Chongqing, Changsha, Tianjin, and Dalian entered their own phase of supercharged growth. Dalian and Tianjin alone poured billions into new port facilities, to allow the massive container ships, the iron ore freighters, and the oil tankers to enter and leave the country with the swift efficiency made possible by new cranes, terminals, and logistics systems.

The Boeing Company took one look at China's plans for airport construction and realized that the skies over Asia were where it would find the next wave of commercial aviation, not in the tired, often bankrupt, union-laden airlines of the United States. Looking ahead—and given the lead times for designing and manufacturing a commercial airplane, Boeing always looked more than a decade ahead—China was poised to buy thousands of airplanes at a cost of nearly $300 billion over the next 12 years. Industrial companies like Danaher and Eaton faced backlogs in China and scrambled to meet the demand for hydraulic systems that powered both equipment and factories. Asset management companies salivated at the prospect of Chinese mutual funds and bond funds as China's markets became more regulated and as the newly wealthy looked for advisors to help them grow their estates. Las Vegas gambling impresarios began to see their expectations for Macau come true and committed billions more to future expansion. KFC maintained its stellar growth, and parent company Yum! Brands started rolling out Pizza Hut to a Chinese public that had been uninterested in and unfamiliar with pizza. Like KFC, Pizza Hut was positioned as a high-end night out for families, and even though few Chinese diners confessed to liking pizza, they were satisfied with the experience as "a slice" of modern life. Motorola briefly rivaled European cell phone leaders Nokia and Ericsson with its strong sales on the mainland, while Microsoft and Intel poured money into large-scale research and development projects. IBM, which had hoped for first-mover advantage in China, was soon battling competitors ranging from India's low-cost Infosys Technologies to established U.S. consulting firms such as Accenture, all of which hungered for the lucrative market of helping multinationals rationalize their businesses and harmonize their China franchise with the rest of the global supply chain. These were serious endeavors by sober companies, but that wasn't all. In late 2004 Hooters opened its first restaurant in Shanghai, where it brought the delights of scantily clad, buxom women serving chicken wings to a populace that had been sorely lacking such outlets.

United Technologies Corporation, one of the larger industrial conglomerates, saw so-so growth in the United States and Europe but stunning demand in China. Its Otis Elevator division outfitted the skyscrapers multiplying with geometric frequency, and its Carrier division provided the centralized heating and cooling systems to make those buildings habitable. Its plant outside of Shanghai operated on 24/7 swing shifts in order to meet the demand, even as its prices increased along with the precious copper piping that was the key ingredient to the refrigeration systems. Procter & Gamble already had a billion-dollar brand with Oil of Olay, and it looked to replicate that success with other products, ranging from Pampers disposable diapers, to household cleaning, to Gillette razor blades. Avon saw its revenues in China grow more than 40 percent a year, as women in China spent more disposable income on skin care and even as competitors such as Estée Lauder also established their franchise. Brands familiar to Western consumers thrived in China, with Coca-Cola, Colgate toothpaste, Tiffany silver, Coach bags, Wrigley chewing gum, Kraft snacks, along with hundreds of others finding their niche.

The Communist Party frequently spoke of its desire to create a "harmonious society," and it looked at Western companies as partners in building it. Just what that phrase meant, of course, was anyone's guess. It was a political slogan that had some resonance, but at base, it was a statement on the part of the government that growth must continue in order to ensure that stability was maintained. As Hu Jintao said in April 2006, it meant "a society of democracy and rule of law, fairness and justice, integrity, fraternity, vitality, stability, order, and harmony between man and nature; it is a society where there is unity between the material and the spirit . . ." It would be hard to find a larger assortment of homilies, though a Western leader would not speak of "the material and the spirit," and an American politician would be more likely to mention God. Nonetheless, the aspiration isn't without substance. It is easy to label Hu hypocritical, especially on the rule of law, yet the gap between his rhetoric and how the party and the government behaved was no greater than can be found in many other societies. Leaders often give voice to the ideal, even when their own behavior flies in its face. In private sessions and occasional veiled remarks in public, Hu also spoke of the imperative that the fruits of China's growth be more widely shared between rich and poor, urban and rural, and he worked to make sure that growth and modernization weren't limited to the provinces of the coast. But in order to maintain the momentum, the capital and efforts of Western business were as vital as they had been in the 1990s.

At least one Western conglomerate viewed the harmonious-society slogan as useful for its purposes. General Electric, under the initiative of its CEO, Jeffrey Immelt, committed the company to develop products and services that would be more environmentally sound and would in time reduce the amount of greenhouse gases produced by its equipment. Calling these efforts "ecomagination," GE saw particular potential in China. The central government was beginning to grapple with the destructive consequences of its hypercharged industrial growth. Some of that growth had directly benefited GE, and several of its divisions had reached $1 billion in revenue in China, including train locomotives and power turbines for electricity plants. Having helped China's "dirty" growth, GE wanted to be integral to the next wave of green, sustainable growth, which meant providing nascent cleaner coal technologies and equipment for hydropower, among other things.

The company had $6 billion in China sales in 2006, and top GE executives began to work with Chinese officials at both national and local levels to urge the adoption of more energy-efficient equipment. The push was both idealistic and pragmatic. Immelt demanded an emphasis on sustainability and greener products, but he also demanded revenue and aggressive growth targets. By urging the adoption of next-generation technologies, the company was pursuing a green agenda that also meant future sales of cutting-edge equipment.

GE sales and marketing arms integrated the harmonious-society mantra and all but equated buying GE products with following the mandate of the government. Upgrading coal-power equipment, which was the primary source of China's urban pollution and greenhouse gas emissions, was central to that strategy, but GE also sold wind turbines and water purification and desalination systems for municipalities. Of course, its expansion came with hidden costs. Its international competitors such as Siemens and Mitsubishi also wanted the businesses, and one way that Chinese buyers upped the ante was to demand blueprints and intellectual property sharing as part of the deals. Companies that were more willing to share designs with their Chinese counterparts won more business than those that didn't. GE had to weigh its immediate desire for more sales with the long-term question of whether it would have to give away too much in the process. In many cases, it decided to share more than it would have liked, betting that its own ability to spend on research and innovate its way to the next generation of competitive products would outweigh whatever it lost by giving Chinese producers the knowledge to make current products without needing GE's expertise.[5]

And then there was China as a Hail Mary pass for desperate companies. The auto industry had been a bellwether for the industrial might and innovation of the United States during the heart of the American century, but by the late 1990s, it was struggling. The dip in fuel prices had led to the explosion of sales of SUVs, but even with those going strong, the Big Three automakers of Detroit were saddled with high costs, powerful unions, and products that had intermittent and limited appeal relative to the quality cars produced by foreign companies. Yet, in China, the largest of the ailing Big Three, General Motors, was a company transformed.

Until the end of the 1990s, China was bicycle land. Those pictures of thousands of bicyclers filling the streets were almost a cliché, and used as stock footage for news stories and movie backdrops. But with urbanization and the new consumer culture came a lust for cars and a need for trucks; cars to get people where they wanted to go, and trucks to transport what those people wanted to buy to the stores that wanted to sell them. As late as 2003, there were fewer than 2 million passengers cars sold in China, compared to nearly 10 million in the United States. Cars were still expensive luxury items in China, which meant that they cost double the price that similar vehicles commanded in the Western world. Yet there was a palpable sense that the appetite for cars would soon explode, just as it had for other goods that were part and parcel of life in the capitalist world. Surveys pointed to a large pent-up demand; young Chinese viewed buying a car as one of the ultimate signs of status and success. With a market still so immature and the desire so evidently there, carmakers throughout the world rushed to get a piece of the action.

That meant that just about every auto manufacturer in the world set up joint ventures in China, from Volkswagen to Nissan, Hyundai to Peugeot, Audi to General Motors. Like the United States in the 1920s and 1930s, China's car market was fragmented, and there were dozens of small manufacturers. But as with all things in China, the growth was incomparable. By 2007, China was the second largest market for cars in the world, and sales of passenger cars topped five million units. The leader was Volkswagen, but right behind was GM—a company that was soon to see its sales plummet in the United States, that was brought to bankruptcy after decades of sclerotic complacency, but experienced a too-little, too-late moment of rebirth on the other side of the Great Wall.

Beginning in 1997, GM invested more than $1.5 billion in joint-venture factories outside of Shanghai. At first that investment seemed a colossal waste, but by 2005, it was looking like the wisest thing the company had done in years. By 2007, China represented 11 percent of GM global sales, at more than one million vehicles, and GM was neck and neck with Toyota and

Volkswagen in terms of overall share of a China market that was growing nearly 25 percent a year. Even as sales slowed in 2008, growth was still in the double digits, which presented a stark contrast with evaporating sales in the United States and shrinking business in Europe. While GM faced the same issues that GE did in terms of piracy of intellectual property, it was driven by its immediate need for sales more than by strategic concerns about what the loss of its intellectual property might mean in the future. It had found an island of prosperity in a world that was no longer tilting its way. Placing faith in its capacity to generate new products more quickly and efficiently than Chinese competitors, GM aggressively pursued the China market to offset its decline elsewhere. It was too little, too late, but it offered the glimmer of what might have been if the company had felt more urgency to innovate and evolve in the United States.[6]

The rampant success of U.S. and multinational companies in China was in inverse proportion to the rising tide of negativity about China in American public opinion. The fact that the benefits of the relationship seemed to accrue almost entirely to corporations that were getting richer while so many millions of Americans were barely treading water did not endear people to the rise of China, peaceful or harmonious though it may have been. The fact that China was becoming as brand happy as Western consumers also wasn't seen by many on the left as progress, but rather as a sign of soulless capitalism claiming another victim.

The animosity crossed party and ideological lines. Conservatives and Republicans voiced discomfort with increased Chinese military spending, the rhetorical aggression toward Taiwan, and the continued preeminence of the Communist Party. Liberals and Democrats tended to focus on labor conditions in Chinese factories, the country's flawed record on human rights, and unfair trade practices that undermined the continued viability of U.S. labor unions. While Congress stopped short of passing its threatened punitive tariff bill, representatives continued to speak of China in ominous terms, particularly after the Democrats made considerable gains in the 2006 elections and retook control of the Senate.

The appointment of Henry Paulson as Treasury secretary in mid-2006 promised a renewed effort to establish a constructive, ongoing discussion with China on issues of mutual concern. As head of Goldman Sachs, Paulson had been central to his company's push into underwriting and other activities in China. He had made numerous trips and saw China as a potential partner for the future. One of the first things he did as secretary was to create a formal "U.S.-China Strategic Economic Dialogue," to be conducted semi-annually between him and his counterpart, China's Vice Premier Wu Yi, who, among other things, was the highest-ranking woman in the politburo. After Bush and Hu made the formal announcement of the dialogue, Paulson stated that in his view "the relationship between the U.S. and China is the most important bilateral economic relationship in the world today." Regular engagement was the only way to work through disputes, and would provide an outlet for American officials to communicate the ways in which they felt that the "Chinese don't play fair when it comes to trade and economics." For their part, the Chinese leadership viewed the formal dialogue as recognition by the world's leading power that China couldn't be dictated to and that it had at last earned the treatment accorded to equals, even if there was rivalry and tension.

Yet the very creation of this regular channel of engagement took on partisan overtones in Washington. Republicans, pro-business and avid free traders, could be painted as indifferent to the working-class Americans struggling to keep up with rising expenses and stagnant wages. To the degree that China could be blamed both for soaring energy costs and declining wages, and to the extent that the Bush administration and Congressional Republicans could be held responsible, a closer embrace of China was easily portrayed as part of the problem for the United States and not part of the solution.

Here too, popular attitudes were more nuanced than what was conveyed in the media or in politics. For every angry Lou Dobbs railing against "the China price" and unfair competition, there was a businessman like the wedding dress designer I met on a plane to Hong Kong, who sent his designs by e-mail to a small factory of skilled seamstresses in the Pearl River Delta region and was able to use the lower costs and quick turnaround time to open more mall outlets in several states in the Midwest. Or the novelty item seller who went to China once a year to buy merchandise and who could maintain his business only because of the opportunities that China offered. And the hundreds of companies small and large that became clients of Li & Fung, which had begun life as a merchant trader in Hong Kong in 1906 and grew to be a soup-to-nuts, one-stop solution for sourcing. You could bring Li & Fung a drawing on a napkin of a product you wanted to make, and it would find suppliers of the raw materials, arrange shipment to a factory it had identified, negotiate the price, coordinate logistics from the factory to the port, handle customs duties, and make plans to deliver the finished goods to Long Beach, California, along with freight forwarding to a warehouse anywhere in the United States or any other part of the world.

In all respects, however, the ambivalent relationship between China and the United States was almost universally described in terms of the interaction between two nations. In early 2007, Niall Ferguson, an academic whose career spanned both England and the United States, penned an opinion piece in the *Wall Street Journal* cowritten by Moritz Schularick titled "Chimerica." In it they argued that seeing China and the United States as two countries missed the bigger picture. Think of the United States and the People's Republic not as two countries, but as one: "Chimerica. It's quite a place: just 13 percent of the world's land surface, but a quarter of its population and fully a third of its economic output. What's more, Chimerica has accounted for around 60 percent of global growth in the past five years. Their relationship isn't necessarily unbalanced; more like symbiotic. East Chimericans are savers; West Chimericans are spenders. East Chimericans do manufactures; West Chimericans do services. East Chimericans export; West Chimericans import. East Chimericans pile up reserves; West Chimericans obligingly run deficits, producing the dollar-denominated bonds that the East Chimericans crave. As in all good marriages, the differences between the two halves of Chimerica are complementary."

But as astute as Ferguson and Schularick were, their perspective remained marginal. They also oversimplified, though given the constraints of penning an op-ed, that is not easily avoidable. Chimerica is more dimensional than savers in one place and spenders in the other, more than one exporting and the other importing. The stories told in these pages so far have shown a much more complicated, more complete entanglement of what had been two independent economies into one messy system. Yet whether described in reductive terms or with more nuance, the idea that these two were forming one symbiotic system struck most people in both countries as fanciful at best and absurd at worst. Borders were still borders, and the mental ones were even more imposing than the physical ones.

The result was that even as the symbiosis of Chimerica deepened and became more multifaceted with each passing day, the nation-state continued to exert a dominant pull on the collective consciousness of both Chinese and American citizens. Global bodies such as the United Nations were still composed of states, and even the European Union was built on the principle that its component parts retained many of the powers that the state always had. If anything, as the material reality of Chimerica increased, so too did the resistance to it. Or perhaps it is more accurate to say that in both China and the United States in 2007 and to the present, expression of dislike and distrust of the other became more common. Given that few people actually knew that Chimerica existed, the discomfort had to be channeled through familiar pathways, and that meant nationalism and politics.

Nationalism and politics both were on increased display as China prepared to host the Olympics in 2008, which was supposed to be its official coming-out party and the symbolic moment when it took its rightful place among the leading nations of the world. Instead it became an event fraught with anxiety and tension, both in Beijing and in the United States. Taking place in the midst of an unfolding economic crisis, the Games brought to the surface tensions that had lacked only a clear catalyst. And as difficult as the Olympics were, they served as an oasis of calm given the meltdown of the global financial system a few weeks after the Games ended. As it turned out, the Games marked the culmination of one phase of Chimerica; what followed after demonstrated just how real it actually was and how that strange fusion of economies that had occurred over the past 20 years may have been the only thing capable of keeping the global economy from plunging into the abyss.

CHAPTER 13

The (In)Glorious Olympics

ALL COUNTRIES THAT HOST the Olympics treat the event as both an honor and an opportunity to show off. In the years leading up to the event, national governments spend billions of dollars sprucing up the host city, improving transportation infrastructure, building stadiums and dormitories, and often opening a new airport to welcome the athletes of the world. Some countries are more organized than others—South Korea in 1988 made substantial improvements to Seoul and was ready well in time; in Greece in 2004, the paint was barely dry in Athens the morning after the opening ceremony. But what China did to Beijing made these earlier efforts seem like window dressing.

Estimates vary, but the total amount spent on preparations certainly topped $40 billion. Anyone who visited Beijing in the years before the Olympics was struck by the proliferation of cranes and construction sites and the wholesale destruction of the old twisting alleys of the *hutongs* to make way for hulking new buildings. Some of these—like the Rem Koolhaas–designed national television headquarters, with its middle section suspended between two massive towers, defying both common sense and gravity—were cutting-edge and innovative;

others were just newer versions of the massive Maoist edifices that had guarded the wide avenues of the city since the 1960s. Old Beijing, that world of hidden alleys, cul-de-sacs, and small, almost self-sufficient communities nestled in the midst of a cold, often inhospitable city, had survived the wars, invasions, revolutions, and pogroms of the twentieth century, but it would not survive the Olympic Games of 2008.

For both the Communist Party and the new wealthy elites, old Beijing represented the unwanted past. When the nations of the world arrived for two weeks of competition in August 2008, the Chinese leadership wanted to celebrate the new face of China. They wanted to demonstrate just how far the country had come since Tiananmen and how fast it was capable of moving forward. The message to the outside world was that China had arrived, but there was also a message to the Chinese people that the government was beginning to fulfill the promise of the 1949 revolution that all of China could be prosperous. All countries take pride in hosting the Games, but China in 2008 went to a different level.

To be sure, some of the preparations were a bit Potemkin village. Guided by slogans like "One World One Dream," and "New China, New Beijing, New Olympics," the government revamped the city. A half million trees were planted around the Olympic venues to create a feeling of a harmonious development. Factories on the perimeter of the city, especially coal-fired ones, were shut off weeks in advance to make sure that the air was the right shade of blue. Taxi drivers were given English lessons to speak a language they still couldn't understand, even though half the cars in Beijing were barred from the roads to cut down on emissions. Public nuisances like spitting, slurping, and spray painting were banned. Tens of thousands of volunteers stood ready with a smile to guide visitors to their destinations, and tens of thousands of police stood ready to maintain order. In China, it was the former that attracted attention; for Americans and Europeans, it was the latter.

When the Games were awarded to Beijing by the International Olympic Committee in 2001, it was with the expectation that hosting would further integrate China into the global community and would lead to more political reform and greater openness. After being awarded the Olympics in 1988, South Korea had moved toward more participatory democracy, and many in the international community hoped that holding the Games in Beijing would have a similarly palliative effect on China. Yet there was something condescending about the tenor of discussions surrounding China, as if the country were an errant, misbehaving child that had to be brought into the fold. Said one prominent publication, "China's leaders want the Games as a way of legitimizing their rule. They want the WTO membership to cement reforms and to show that the country is taking its proper place on the world stage. But the Games . . . will force an openness that China's leaders cannot begin to imagine."[1] Other comments boldly predicted that the more China was integrated into the international system, the more difficult it would be for the Beijing regime to stifle political expression and run roughshod over individual rights. It didn't quite work out that way.

In the months before the Games, it became apparent that President Hu was as committed to the absolute centrality of the Communist Party as he was to the economic modernization begun by Deng. The party's Eleventh Five-Year Plan announced in 2006 committed the government to more spending on infrastructure, more banking reform, more attention to the rural-urban divide, more focus on education, and more emphasis on the environment and the deleterious consequences of industrial growth. Democracy and freedom of expression were not part of the package. There was a nod to more openness to the world at large and continued emphasis on a harmonious society. But the government remained far more committed to its path of economic modernization than it did to political liberalization.

As Beijing focused on internal development, the outside world became ever more critical of the Chinese government and the nature of its political system. It wasn't just the United States that led the charge to focus attention on the perceived failings and outrages; activists and human rights groups in the European Union and throughout the world used the upcoming Games as an opportunity to focus global public opinion on China's shortcomings.

The drumbeat of criticism grew louder a year before the Games began, with several high-profile product safety cases in the summer of 2007. Mattel, which sourced almost all of its toys in China, was forced to recall millions of toys that had either defective magnets or lead paint. At the same time, pets in the United States were killed or harmed by contaminated shipments of pet food from China. Several car accidents in the United States were traced to faulty tires made in Chinese factories. Congress was already preparing a bill that would penalize China for manipulating its currency in a manner that created unfair trade practices, and the defective tires along with tainted food and toys—which happened to affect the more vulnerable segments of the U.S. population—were seen as proof that China's rise, far from being peaceful, was potentially malignant.

Standards in China were certainly less rigorous than they should have been. But consumer concerns over product safety predated concerns about China. In the 1960s, Ralph Nader established himself as a consumer advocate by exposing safety issues of U.S. made cars. In 1990 there was a global recall of Perrier water (made in France) because of fears of benzene contamination. In 1997 there was a wide-scale recall of halogen torchiere lamps because of an unfortunate tendency for the bulbs to explode. The outcry over dangerous tires made in China followed a much more egregious episode in the late 1990s: 88 deaths were attributed to defective Firestone tires, which led to the recall of 6.5 million in 2000.

In 2007 China was a major source of product defects, but the actual number of faulty products was, regrettably, normal—proportionate to how much it produced and comparable to the safety issues that have bedeviled manufacturers of all nationalities in past decades. Companies, not countries, bear ultimate responsibility for what they sell, and it said volumes that instead of a product safety issue, the episodes in 2007 became a China issue.

Chinese officials viewed the assault on Chinese quality control as one part legitimate and one part an expression of U.S. hostility. In response, they claimed that product safety was an issue for them too—for goods made in America. Zhao Baoqing, a trade official, attacked the quality of U.S. goods sold in China, and pointed to American-made cranes and generators as posing serious safety hazards. This was more than tit-for-tat. There were instances of product safety problems harming Chinese citizens that were the direct responsibility of American or Western companies. The CEO of Mattel initially placed the blame for the defective toys on lax regulations in China, then apologized for his remarks and promised to overhaul his company's safety inspections of its many vendors.

The uproar in late 2007, however, was only a dress rehearsal for the outbursts of 2008. Just as the Chinese were cleaning their red carpet for the Olympics, the rest of the world seemed to be turning against them. The issue of human rights had never been far from the surface when Western nations interacted with China, and the memory of the violent suppressions of the Tiananmen protests had faded but never evaporated. Both the national government and local governments in China could react harshly to signs of dissent, and the arrest of dissidents remained common. So too did arrests and imprisonment of peasants who questioned the edicts of local party officials. Mistreatment in prison was common, and trials were run according to opaque and sometimes whimsical procedures that rarely seemed fair to those without power and connections.

The Beijing government had also come under increased international scrutiny because of its relations with the government of Sudan, which had been complicit in the ongoing atrocities in the Sudanese province of Darfur. Celebrities such as Mia Farrow and Steven Spielberg called on China to put pressure on Sudan or face boycotts of the Olympics, and Spielberg withdrew as an artist director of the opening ceremonies in protest. Labeling the upcoming games "the genocide Olympics," international human rights organizations stepped up the criticisms of Beijing and threatened to mobilize a global movement against the upcoming Games. The final straw was the long-simmering sore point of Chinese rule over Tibet, which has assumed a large place in Western imagination because of the heroic stature of the Dalai Lama, the exiled leader of the Tibetan Buddhist community, an international herald of peace, and a constant reminder of the repressive aspects of Chinese rule.

In March 2008, monks and college students took to the streets in the Tibetan capital of Lhasa to demand more autonomy from Beijing. At first the police gave the crowds a wide berth, and Western journalists were allowed to report on the scene. Then the situation deteriorated. Calling the protestors "lawless mobsters," Chinese authorities reacted with predictable heavy-handedness. Police suppressed the crowds, killing dozens, inflicting injuries, and arresting many more. Journalists were banned. It was hardly the first time such violence had occurred in the province, but because of the upcoming Olympics, it received intensive media attention around the world. That was, in fact, the intent of the organizers of the demonstrations.

Hosting the Games always contained the risk that opponents of the Beijing regime would use the opportunity to embarrass the government or goad it into ham-handed responses that would generate international outcry. But Chinese officials had focused mostly on security in Beijing and on stifling any hint of opposition to the regime in the capital city. They seemed to be taken by surprise at the outburst in Tibet, which exposed their own myopia about the peculiar dynamics that the Games would create. The world expected the event to be part of the opening and liberalizing of China, while China expected the event to be a celebration of its achievements of the past decades and proof that the formula of state autocracy and market capitalism was succeeding. Those expectations, while not necessarily incompatible, set the stage for problems. The Tibet protests, and the response of Beijing, unleashed a wave of outrage against China that the Chinese government was ill prepared to handle.[2]

The most visible sign of that anger were the protests that erupted during the international torch relay. In Paris, the torch bearer was literally mobbed by angry crowds denouncing the Chinese government, some of whom used fire extinguishers to put out the flame. In San Francisco, police had to cordon off the route and then secretly change it and still have a security detail surrounding the runners in order to protect them. Faced with restive public opinion, Western leaders hinted that a boycott of the opening ceremonies or of the entire Games themselves was not out of the question. Gordon Brown, prime minister of the United Kingdom, announced that he would not attend the opening ceremonies, as did Angela Merkel of Germany. In the United States, senators Barack Obama and Hillary Clinton, in the midst of their fierce dual for the Democratic nomination, both urged President Bush to take a harder line against Beijing for its activities in Tibet and its continued support for the Khartoum government in Sudan.

The Chinese were appalled at the reaction. They felt humiliated by the public display of animosity and by the tarnishing of the Olympic torch relay, which they had thought was above politics. Instead of a triumphant procession, the relay became a dash of shame. Not just the government, but millions of Chinese citizens retreated into a defensive nationalism. How dare the rest of the world criticize China for its actions in Tibet, which was legally a province! In the eyes of official China, objecting to its actions in Lhasa would be like the world rising in protest against an American National Guard unit or regular police putting down a riot in Los Angeles. As for the accusations of human rights abuses, China replied that in the span of a few decades, hundreds of millions of people had been raised out of dire poverty and were now employed and living in decent apartments throughout the country. That was progress on human rights, and yet all the world could do was excoriate.

For years, Chinese officials had deflected human rights criticism by emphasizing poverty alleviation. In the words of a high-ranking official, "the struggle against poverty must remain at the forefront of the human rights agenda."[3] Many in the West scoffed that admirable though that was, it was beside the point in terms of human rights. But Chinese officials were more on the mark than not. The 1948 Universal Declaration of Human Rights (which is the basis for most of contemporary human rights policies) gave as much attention to economic rights as it did to legal rights. It enunciated the view that economic security—enough food, calories, shelter—was essential to the human spirit and to human rights. On that score, China could boast that it managed to raise more people out of poverty in a scant few decades than any society ever has and to give those people hope for the future. The focus on legalistic rights, on free expression, free press, and the ability to protest publicly and hold demonstrations, was to the Chinese government less important than building a stable society where the vast majority of people were materially secure. Relative to China's long and storied past, that would be an immense accomplishment and one that the government admitted was still unachieved. That, however, was their focus and not political reform or democracy per se.

The government also countered that with nearly three million members of the Communist Party of China, the party itself had a form of deliberative democracy, though one that unfolded in secret and away from public scrutiny. Leaders were elected at the local and national levels, and both the politburo and the senior leadership of the party were held to term limits that had already resulted in a peaceful handover from Jiang Zemin to Hu Jintao. It was not democracy in the liberal, Western sense but rather a form of consensus rule, where a small percentage of the population worked to determine policy. The irony is that while that seemed nonsensical to Western ears, it was akin to the Athenian democracy that is romanticized in the West. Classical Greek democracy enfranchised only a small percentage of the population, and left women, slaves, and peasants to obey the rule of the privileged citizens. While the deliberations in ancient Greece were more public than in Communist China today, the system then wasn't appreciably open or participatory. And no one can hold up fifth-century Athens as an exemplar of human rights, given that the concept was alien, and coercive tools such as torture, corporal punishment, and executions were accepted without question. Over the course of history, democracy has had many forms, and when the Chinese authorities use their version of the word, they do so in the belief that their system offers one evolving form of it.

But Western opinion largely rejected those arguments as

specious and beside the point. It would be difficult to find many voices in the United States or Europe who accept China's version of its human rights record. In fact, the statements above are more likely to be greeted with derision than serious consideration. That's why in the run-up to the Olympics and during the Games themselves, the crescendo of criticism of China found considerable traction on both the left and the right in the Western world. The defensiveness of Beijing, its blunt tactics and tone-deaf sense of public relations compounded the problem. Initially the Beijing authorities made provisions to unblock access to Internet sites for Westerners staying at select hotels and for the press corps. But when the Games began in August 2008, certain sites remained blocked. Western journalists and bloggers had already been drawing attention to Beijing's restrictions on the press and on access to content it found objectionable—which included any criticism of the government, any agitation for democratic reforms, and any number of infractions that were neither explicitly forbidden nor technically allowed. When these journalists found themselves unable to access certain pages on the Web, they used the blocks as an excuse to once again lambaste the Chinese authorities for the repressive nature of the regime. Chinese authorities then relented, but the damage had been done.[4]

That was only one of numerous issues that beset the Beijing Games. China initially promised that there would be a "protest zone" where groups could register and stage demonstrations, but even that haiku version of openness was sabotaged by the labyrinthine procedures to obtain permits. Ahead of the Games, China significantly tightened visa restrictions to the point where it became extremely difficult for casual visitors to come to the events. And the regime also denied visas to a range of people who it feared would disrupt the collegial spirit that it wanted to convey. The government then attempted to prevent television crews from broadcasting from the city itself and tried to keep them in the Olympic confines. Networks around the world objected strongly, and some restrictions were lifted. But in the court of international opinion, these measures backfired and stoked the already strong flames of negative sentiment.

While the Games themselves went off smoothly, there was one final issue that received unflattering attention: China's record on the environment. In the years before the Olympics, Beijing had become increasingly polluted, as had much of urban China. Because the primary source of electricity is coal, and because the vast majority of coal-fired plants have little in the way of pollution controls, air quality had decreased sharply in the past decade. In addition, thousands of factories, ranging from steel mills to aluminum smelters, automobile plants to chemical plants, textile mills to plastics factories, added to the environmental burden. Many cities have water systems designed for a fraction of the population, and have seen a significant increase in the numbers of cars, trucks, buses, and taxis, all belching fumes. Most of the rivers have become so polluted with sewage and industrial waste that they are toxic to any life. Beijing has its own special issues. As the surrounding region has been denuded of trees and converted from farmland, the land has become more susceptible to soil erosion, so that when the winds pick up from the deserts to the north, the city can be inundated with sand and debris, which further degrades the air quality. August, with its searing heat, is a particularly troublesome month. Beijing was deeply concerned that the air would be so bad that events would be postponed and the world would be treated to images of a grim, grimy, polluted city.[5]

As the international community became more attuned to the dangers of global warming and the urgent need to do something to contain the level of carbon emissions, the dangers of China's industrial path had become increasingly evident. Public opinion in the United States, which had been late to join the chorus of anxiety about climate change, had by 2008 turned decisively in favor of action. The Bush administration's intransigence about the Kyoto Accords to limit emissions was no longer in sync with public sentiment, and China's record on the environment was yet another reason for Americans to dislike the regime and its policies.

While China contributed less to greenhouse gas emissions than the United States, its per capita emissions had reached a critical stage. The central government recognized the problem and had begun to take steps to address it, because the resulting health and public safety issues threatened the country's growth trajectory. But even when Beijing made a decree, enforcing it at the local and provincial levels was challenging. Balancing rapid growth with more environmentally sound policies is not easy anywhere, and China's need to keep moving forward meant that even as the government made an aggressive commitment to spending on alternative energy, it continued to build coal plants at a rapid clip. The central government promised to invest as much as $200 billion on cleaning up the water and air, and on solar, wind, hydroelectric, and nuclear energy in order to decrease the dependence on coal energy and limit emissions. Even so, it will still become the world's largest contributor to greenhouse gases within the next 10 years, surpassing the current leader, the United States.

In the weeks before the Games, Beijing shut down many of the factories in the vicinity of Beijing. Officials also spent considerable time and money to attempt to clean the air. No one had ever tried to alleviate pollution so quickly and so drastically. The municipal authorities banned more than half the car traffic and thousands of trucks, replaced coal plants on the outskirts with natural gas facilities, and suspended construction on multiple projects. The first days of the Games were gray, filled with smog, but many of the events were indoors. That didn't prevent bad press, but at least it wasn't as dire as feared. The last week proved much clearer, and the track-and-field portion, as well as the marathon, went without a hitch. Still, experts concluded from the Beijing experience that it is much easier to generate pollution than it is to reverse it. Hardly a surprise, and hardly the lesson that Beijing wanted reinforced.

The aftermath of the Games brought a surge of nationalism in China. For hundreds of millions of Chinese, the Games were everything hoped for: an affirmation that the country was moving forward and capable of holding its own in the assembly of man. For many in the West, the Games were proof of the totalitarianism of the Chinese state and the degree to which the government was willing and able to manufacture its own reality in a disturbingly Orwellian fashion. The gap between how many in China perceived reality and how it was perceived by a substantial portion of the world had been wide during the isolationist height of Maoism. As China became capitalist in all but name, that gap barely narrowed.

To say that China's pride was wounded by the relentless focus on its shortcomings would be to miss just how disturbed millions of Chinese were. Message boards on Web sites like Sina.com and 360.com, popular among educated and affluent urban twentysomethings and thirtysomethings, angrily viewed Western attitudes as proof that China would not be accepted no matter how much it tried to accommodate input and criticism. They were appalled that Americans felt the right to denounce China's record on human rights, given that the United States was fresh from its own compromised record after the revelations of abuse in the Iraqi prison at Abu Ghraib and the legal limbo of the hundreds of prisoners at Guantanamo. They were also infuriated that Americans believed they had a right to judge China on environmental issues when the record of the United States on the same score left so much to be desired.

Even before the Olympics, there was a wide fissure separating how "we" see "them" and how "they" see "us." One evening in Beijing, I was having dinner with a senior American executive of a major multinational company with extensive business in China. His home base was Singapore, and at dinner with us were two of his Chinese managers who headed up the Beijing office. One of them had just moved back to China after five years in Singapore, and he raised a glass to celebrate being back. "It's so good to be home," he said with obvious pleasure, "so good to be in Beijing and be free." The American was taken aback. "What do you mean 'free'?" he said, his voice rising with annoyance. "Beijing isn't free. Singapore is. You know that." The Chinese executive replied evenly, "Singapore isn't free. I was always on edge. I didn't know when I could get a fine for some violation of a rule I didn't even know. Here, unless I stand in Tiananmen Square with a sign saying 'Down with the Government,' I can do want I want and say what I want and no one cares." The American manager didn't bother arguing with him. "That's just stupid," he said, and changed the subject.

During the Olympics, public opinion in the Western world was at best ambivalent about China, its government, and its role on the world stage. Both liberal and conservative blogs, for instance, were equally critical of Beijing: liberals for the hypocrisy of the regime and the cravenness of the international community in not holding the government accountable for its policies in Tibet, Sudan, and elsewhere; conservatives for the buildup of the Chinese military and the refusal of the Beijing regime to honor either intellectual property law or the independence of Taiwan. On the eve of the Olympics, according to a survey conducted by the Chicago Council on Global Affairs, three-quarters of Americans believed that China's economy would become as large as that of the United States; 42 percent felt that this would be a negative, and 41 percent saw China as the primary threat to America's vital interests. Tellingly, more than two-thirds were convinced that China was guilty of unfair trade practices. Attitudes were further clouded by the spike in energy prices, and of oil and gasoline in particular. While many Americans blamed big oil companies for $4-a-gallon gas, many also sensed that China's consumption of raw materials and energy was a key driver of the soaring costs that were directly impacting the daily lives of millions of people.

Inside China, however, most believed that the world as a whole had positive feelings about their country. In surveys conducted by the Pew Global Attitudes Project, nearly two-thirds felt that the United States was the country having the most negative impact on the world, while a third saw the United States as an enemy. Public opinion in China was overwhelmingly supportive of the government and positive about the trajectory of the state and of the society as a whole. In fact, the Chinese had become substantially more positive about their country and the economy between 2002 and 2008, with 86 percent satisfied with the direction of the country in 2008 versus 48 percent in 2002, and 82 percent satisfied with the economy versus 52 percent in 2002. More than three-quarters said they thought that free markets made people better off. At the same time, the majority of those surveyed were dissatisfied with their own household income and aspired to more. People also expressed concern about the gap between rich and poor and about the rising cost of living. Still, overall, of the 24 countries surveyed by Pew, China was by far the most optimistic and positive about its future.[6]

Public opinion surveys are only snapshots in time, and even then do not necessarily capture the mutable nature of people's views. How people respond to questions is highly dependent on the tenor of the news and on whatever events immediately precede the survey. Ask the same question about attitudes and feelings two months apart or even two weeks apart, and reactions can be diametrically different. The rising tide of negativity about China in the United States on the eve of the Olympics was undoubtedly due in part to the negative news items, focus on environmental concerns, and the protests surrounding the torch relay, which also help explain the rising tide of negativity about the United States in China. Still, these sentiments were more than passing emotions and spoke to the real gulf that had begun to widen in the opening years of the new millennium.

The rising distrust and suspicion, however, was in almost inverse proportion to the increased interdependence. As the economies of the two countries became more intertwined, public opinion became more nationalistic and tended to view the other with a wary eye. To some extent, that should have been expected. As integration of the European Union picked up pace in the 1990s, discontent with the union also increased. Support for the EU, according to Eurobarometer surveys, showed that less than half the population of the member states supported integration in 1997, with rising percentages saying it was actually a bad thing.[7] Public opinion tends to be conservative and reluctant to embrace change and the unknown, especially when confronted with the reality that change can be disruptive and even destructive of the status quo.

When the familiar is endangered by the unknown, people often react defensively. They cling to what they know and view what they don't as a threat. Throughout the 1990s and into the first years of this century, the Chinese and American economies became ever more symbiotic. Urban China was inundated with American brands and market principles, while American companies turned to China as a source of vitality lacking in the developed world. While few people were aware of the full dimensions of what was happening, they knew enough to understand that something was changing, and that with greater dependence came less autonomy, less sovereignty, and more vulnerability. Even as the economic systems were blending together, identities, bureaucracies, and culture remained defined by the nation-state.

The Olympics became an unintended synecdoche for the entire U.S.-China relationship. True, once the Games began, the focus shifted from politics and protests to gymnastics and track, but that was not necessarily a good thing in terms of subsequent attitudes. The ill will generated on both sides wasn't dissipated by the actual Games so much as frozen in place. It even manifested itself in the tempest-in-a-teapot uproar over whether the Chinese women gymnasts had been fraudulently allowed to compete with falsified birth records that showed them to be older than they were. For most Chinese, the probing questions and accusations about the gymnasts' age were one more sign of Western and American malevolence, and to Americans one more indication that China intended to compete globally by cheating.

After nearly 20 years, the U.S.-China relationship had evolved into a Chimerica that was profoundly shaping the economic systems of both countries and of the globe. With that came not less tension but more, though few spoke of impending war or even cold war. Those who did were so fringe that they were written off as cranks and kooks, and in that sense, at least, the relationship in the summer of 2008 was less contentious than it was in 1949 or 1989. Americans were on the whole cool about China rather than hot—either in affection or anger—and Chinese public opinion was both distrustful of America and yet optimistic about the future.

In retrospect, the summer of 2008 may have been the dying moments of the old world. The U.S. economy was beginning to crack under the strain of rising fuel costs, stagnant incomes, and the popping of the housing bubble that had propped up some consumer spending and, as it turned out, a mind-boggling percentage of Wall Street financial profits. In March 2008, Bear Stearns, one of the most venerable Wall Street investment houses, collapsed under the weight of its ill-conceived derivative business built on a foundation of toxic mortgages, and bankruptcy and liquidation were avoided only by a shotgun marriage with JPMorgan Chase arranged by the government. Bear had been actively involved in soliciting funds from China, and one prominent Chinese institution was contemplating a multibillion-dollar stake just before Bear went under.

The demise of Bear was seen at the time as a stunning casualty of the unfolding credit crisis, but over the summer, though global equity markets sagged, many felt that the worst had passed. The housing debacle created high levels of foreclosures in the United States, and that in turn led to a rapid devaluation of trillions of dollars of derivatives that had been bought and sold by financial institutions around the world. But as bad as the ramifications were for Wall Street profits during the summer of 2008, the real world economy appeared weakened but not in critical condition. A recession had already begun, though that was not officially proclaimed until December 2008. Unemployment was rising in the United States, and exporters in China started to feel the effects of softer U.S. and European demand. Still, the summer of 2008 was notable for its relative calm. For generations that lived through World War I, especially in England, the summer of 1914 was remembered as the end of an era, a last moment when the illusion of how things used to be remained intact—until shattered by the guns of August that saw the assassination of Archduke Ferdinand of Austria and the rapid escalation to a war that would last five years, destroy three empires, kill tens of millions, and end with an untenable peace.

Because in September 2008, as everyone now knows, after the athletes had gone home and the summer holidays had ended, the global financial system came within shouting distance of completely unraveling. It began with the collapse of Lehman Brothers on September 15, and the decision by the U.S. government not to provide the company with enough capital to continue operating. But Lehman was simply the final straw. In the first weeks of September, the largest providers of mortgage bonds, Fannie Mae and Freddie Mac, were de facto nationalized by the federal government in order to prevent a massive default on the trillions of dollars of mortgage-backed securities held globally, and the insurance giant American International Group (AIG), which had of all things begun life in 1919 in post–World War I Shanghai, was also partly taken over by the government in the form of more than $100 billion of secured loans.

As the crisis unfolded throughout the spring and summer, China was atypically critical of the American system. Having listened to the hectoring of Washington to revalue the currency, open the economy, and reform the banking system, Chinese officials took some pleasure in the plight of the U.S. They blamed the issues on America's "warped conception" of the balance between the free market and government regulation, and chided Wall Street and Washington for having become so absorbed in soaring home and asset prices that they lost sight of anything resembling risk controls.[8] Internally, some of those who had been advocating for more direct investments in American businesses and closer integration with Wall Street were discredited. The troubles of the financial system in the United States and Western Europe, combined with China's hosting the Olympics, initially boosted the confidence of the Chinese leadership. It seemed to validate their hybrid approach to the market and their adamant belief that stability could be maintained only by strong state control and intervention. But as the crisis morphed into something deeper in September, gloating gave way to concern, and concern soon gave way to a sense of urgency that unless something was done, the United States and its failing banking system could pull down China in its wake.

For years, economists and analysts had warned of structural weaknesses in China's banking sector. That perception was primarily based on the belief that after decades of experience as well as trial and error, Western financial institutions had learned to price risk and to integrate considerations of risk into complicated quantitative computer models. As it turned out, however, the banking system on the verge of collapse because of structural defects wasn't China's, it was America's.

China's banks, however, were not completely separate from the financial institutions of the West. Not only had the major ones gone public on foreign exchanges and raised new capital from the outside world, but institutions such as the Bank of China had invested heavily in the same derivatives and bonds that were at the heart of the credit meltdown. That was bad enough. Even worse was that the central bank had used some of its rapidly increasing reserves to become the largest foreign purchaser of mortgage-backed bonds issued by none other than Fannie Mae and Freddie Mac—more than Japan and more than the many hedge funds incorporated in the Cayman Islands. In fact, China may have held as much as $376 billion of securities issued by the two American mortgage companies, and when those companies teetered on the brink of solvency in the late summer of 2008, the problems of the United States quite suddenly became the problems of China.

That also meant that the actions of the United States government quite suddenly took on a rather different dimension. It was one thing to allow Bear Stearns or Lehman Brothers, large Wall Street investment firms though they were, to fail or be absorbed. But Fannie Mae and Freddie Mac were integral to the way that the United States funded its housing market, supported mortgage lending, and provided foreign investors with higher-yielding alternatives to U.S. Treasuries. They were viewed by most buyers as being backed by the full faith and credit of the U.S. government and therefore not at risk of default, and they were highly rated by agencies such as Standard & Poor's and Moody's. So when China was confronted with the real possibility that one-sixth of its reserves just might become worthless if those institutions became insolvent, what had been an example of American foolishness and hubris became a Chinese problem. And what had been for the U.S. government a domestic issue of a crumbling credit system, a plummeting housing market, and an escalating wave of defaults transmogrified into an international crisis.

It's often been said that when a bank lends you a million dollars, it's your problem, but when it loans you a hundred million dollars, it's their problem. By 2008, China had become the largest creditor to the United States. It was the primary foreign buyer of everything from U.S. Treasuries to highly rated mortgage-backed securities. It made those investments because the United States was the largest market for China's exports and something had to be done with the dollars that were piling up due to the trade surplus with the United States. And because China's currency was pegged against the dollar, the investment focus of China's central bank was on American assets. Creditors and debtors have an intimate relationship, and given the trillions of dollars involved in the case of China and the United States, that intimacy began to yield some rather odd results.

Though no one has ever admitted so publicly, at some point during the late summer of 2008, one of the many conversations Secretary of the Treasury Henry Paulson had was with Wen Jiabao. Paulson, after all, had spearheaded the regular dialogue with China's leaders, and he was familiar with them and they with him. As it seemed that Fannie Mae and Freddie Mac might fail, China's leaders must have conveyed their displeasure that there was a chance that hundreds of billions of their investments might lose significant value. Jiabao must have also suggested that if the United States was so unable to manage risk and make its foreign creditors whole, then China would have to carefully consider its long-standing policy of investing so heavily in the United States in the future. The head of the People's Bank of China floated the possibility of allowing the yuan to appreciate and even become less linked to the dollar because soaring energy and commodity costs priced in dollars were beginning to place strains on China's growth. Paulson, well aware that America desperately needed credit and liquidity, recognized that loans from China were essential. In mid-September, therefore, the Treasury Department placed Fannie Mae and Freddie Mac into a government-run conservatorship and all but promised that the outstanding obligations on the securities it had issued would be honored in full.

Of course, had the decision been different, China would have been in a terrible bind. If it no longer purchased U.S. debt, what would the country do with its vast dollar-denominated holdings? And if the U.S. economy truly collapsed, what would happen to those parts of the Chinese economy that depended on exports to the United States? Having lent the United States so much money, what happened on Wall Street was now Beijing's problem just as it was Washington's albatross. And having borrowed so much from China, and with the bulk of American companies depending on China for growth, the fortunes of the United States were now linked to Beijing.

The economic turmoil was profoundly unsettling. It shook the United States to the core, and ushered in a stunning electoral victory for Barack Obama. But it also forced China to reassess its self-image of being a poor nation trying to move forward in a world dominated by the United States. Americans took their growing dependence on China as a sign of just how bad things were, while vulnerability to the United States was taken by the Chinese as a wake-up call that the model of relying on foreign capital and expertise for domestic development needed serious reconsideration.

What neither side recognized was that as bad as things were, they would have been much, much worse were it not for what had happened over the past 20 years. The events of 2008 did not highlight the perils of the superfusion of China and America; it proved how invaluable the relationship had become. The near meltdown didn't show how tenuous the global system was; it demonstrated that even in a worst-case scenario, the system had become remarkably stable, and the fusion of the world's two most dynamic economies was the reason.

CHAPTER 14

An Idea Whose Time Has Come

WE ARE NOW FACING the worst crisis since the Great Depression." Those words became a familiar refrain in the autumn of 2008, both in the United States and throughout the world. The collapse of Lehman Brothers was the final straw. By early October, the global credit system had essentially ceased to function, and credit and liquidity are to the wheels of commerce what water is to the body. The system can limp along if buying slows, just as the body can live for weeks without food. But shut off the spigot of short-term credit and money flows between private and national banks, and you can count the minutes until everything just stops. A world where credit doesn't flow is as inert as one where the power has gone out. That is what governments from Washington to London, Dubai to Beijing, confronted.

For years, the apostles of Wall Street finance had preached a new paradigm for risk. The innovations and financial models made possible by information technologies of the 1990s led to a proliferation of new products, many of which were backed by the flimsiest of real-world collateral. The subdivisions of Nevada, Florida, and central California were odd choices for the foundation of the new global economy, and not what the home builders and mortgage brokers who made them possible had intended. But between 2005 and 2008, those homes supported more than middle-class families. They became the building blocks for trillions of dollars of derivatives and contracts that were supposed to spread risk and dilute it. Instead they concentrated risk and magnified it.

While the decline in U.S. housing prices was the proximate cause of the recession, housing alone would never have caused the global credit crisis of 2008. There is still debate on that issue, with some arguing that housing was indeed the culprit. But even if five million homes went into foreclosure in the United States and an equivalent percentage in Western Europe, that would have dented economic activity—even pushed the developed nations into recession—but it would not have brought the financial system to the brink. Only because the mortgages on those homes were used as the raw material for credit worldwide did things deteriorate as rapidly and severely as they did.

After 1989, China tied its fortunes to the United States, and U.S. companies tied theirs to China. That then led the balance sheet of the U.S. government to become more reliant on China. It also led China to become more vulnerable to the global economic system than Chinese authorities either intended or fully realized. In the United States, there was complacency that risk had been banished. In China, there was complacency that the domestic economy was still insulated from the global. The insolvency of Fannie Mae and Freddie Mac combined with the evisceration of stock and bond markets worldwide exposed the fallacy of all of these assumptions.

And yet, grim though things were, they would have been much grimmer without the bonds that had previously been forged. It is impossible to prove that assertion. Yes, without trillions of dollars invested by China in the United States, the ability of the U.S. government to spend its way out of the crisis would have been much more limited. And the injections of liquidity into the global financial system by central banks everywhere were also dependent on countries with huge surpluses—China being the largest—and were all that prevented implosion in October 2008. Still, we cannot replay the tape of the past few years as if the China factor were not there and as if the integration of China and the United States had not occurred. There are no controlled experiments in the real world, and that is why for all the desires of economists to achieve the discipline of science, in the end, predicting outcomes based on past patterns is a fool's errand. The variables are constantly changing and constantly altering the trajectory of other variables. The present may echo the past, but in most respects, it is different in ways that make historical comparisons incomplete and misleading. That doesn't mean that past experience is uninformative, simply that it isn't determinant. How would the present have looked had the past been different? Would the credit crisis have been deeper and sharper in the absence of continued Chinese lending to the U.S. and growing Chinese consumption domestically? Though there's good reason to believe that the answer is yes, it's important to acknowledge the caveat that we have only the world we have—not the hypothetical ones we might like.

Some have argued that the crisis was actually caused by an unhealthy economic relationship between China and the United States. Years of relying on lower-cost goods exported by China allowed for higher levels of consumer spending in the United States than incomes alone might have justified, and years of depending on China's purchases of American debt kept the system more liquid than it would have been otherwise. That is why many experts, from Wall Street to the World Bank, concluded that the global system had become untenable and too reliant on Chinese production and U.S. consumption.

As these pages have shown, however, Chinese consumption has been a more important factor than most acknowledge, as has U.S. and foreign investment in the China market. China's growth was never as export dependent as many economists claimed and as Wall Street believed. Contrary to claims that a third or even more of China's growth was due to exports, the actual figure was closer to 15 percent and perhaps much lower. Given that some Chinese factories produced for both the domestic market and for exports, precise calculations are impossible—hence the heated debates.[1] Without question, parts of the Chinese economy existed solely to make things for sale in the developed world, and those were precisely the ones that suffered most in the economic downturn that began in 2008 and continued into 2009. Factories that were largely dependent on orders from abroad took a sharp hit, and millions of workers saw reduced hours or job loss. But that shortfall was offset by massive state spending on infrastructure, well in excess of the $600 billion that was announced in November 2008. The ability of the Chinese government to spend owed much to the manufacturing prowess of Chinese businesses, but growth had begun with the state and remains grounded in state spending. Until the events of the recent past, state-driven capitalism was disdained by the United States; because of recent events, it has been embraced. China's model is proving more stable, and whether intentionally or not, it is being partly emulated by the United States under President Obama.

Had the global system still been as dependent on the United States in 2008 as it was for the second half of the twentieth century, then the housing and credit crisis that originated in America would almost certainly have brought down the rest of the world. That did not happen. While bond markets panicked and equity suffered extreme declines of more than 50 percent, economic activity took a sharp hit but did not crater in those parts of the world that had accumulated large cash reserves and had developed their own domestic markets. Rather than turning to Washington and to the capitals of Europe for answers, they began to take their own initiative. Brazil's President Lula da Silva, India's Premier Manmohan Singh, and, of course, China's President Hu were shocked by what happened, but they were resilient. Their systems relied more on the state than on global capital markets, and more on spending by the state than on credit creation by banks. These countries and their leaders also recognized that in spite of new strength, their continued health depended on a stable United States. That is one reason why they remained so committed to working with the United States even as the American economy plunged.

In this, however, the relationship between China and the United States stands apart. It is every bit the special relationship that once existed between the United States and Great Britain before World War II. The challenge today is whether the new entity of Chimerica will be allowed to grow and evolve or whether it will be stifled. As strong as the movement toward fusion has been, the fact that it has taken place beneath the collective radar has been beneficial. The more aware people have become in both China and the United States, the more uncomfortable many of them have been, as the Olympics demonstrated.

For China, what is required is a fundamental shift in attitude. As it has developed over the past 20 years, Chinese officials have repeated the mantra of "We are a poor country still emerging from decades of bad policy and struggling to maintain our own growth." Or as one official said not long ago, "China can only save herself because the scale of China is still rather small."[2] That self-conception is increasingly at odds with reality. No doubt, China is poor at a per capita level. That is because hundreds of millions of people are still mired in an agrarian dead end, and millions more live on the fringes of urban economies. But as many as 300 million people are middle class or upper middle class by any definition, and that number is equivalent to the population of the United States and of the European Union. On a purchasing power basis, hundreds of millions of Chinese have more than $7,000 a year in income. That may be a fraction of the United States per capita income of nearly $40,000, but unlike the United States—where incomes are stagnant and costs are rising—middle-class income in China is growing 10 percent a year. The global recession of 2008 and 2009 certainly slowed that rate of growth in China, but not enough to derail it. That is one reason why the National Intelligence Council, in its 2008 predictions for the world in 2025, said that China will shortly be the world's second largest economy and will surpass the United States as the world's largest sometime after 2030.

"The unprecedented shift in relative wealth and economic power from West to East now under way will continue," the NIC report predicted. That means not just the transfer to China but also to resource-rich countries like the United Arab Emirates, Saudi Arabia, Brazil, and Russia. While the meltdown of 2008 led to a steep decline in commodity prices, as India, China, and other emerging nations reenergize their economies, raw materials will return to their upward trajectory. Already, as a result of China's massive stimulus spending, the price of commodities such as copper rose sharply in the spring of 2009 and into the summer. And China, whatever bumps it encountered in the aftermath of the credit crisis, is likely to lead the global recovery. "Few countries," the report concluded, "are poised to have more impact on the world over the next 15 to 20 years than China." How the United States—and the rest of the world—manages that reality will determine the shape of the world in the years to come.[3]

Yet even though U.S. intelligence agencies correctly identify China as the most important change factor, the analysis remains locked in the nation-state framework. The idea that national economies will become even more enmeshed, with capital flows increasing and a common market emerging, is not considered. And the degree to which the economies of China and America have already merged into a sui generis system is not discussed. While there is an acknowledgment that the power of nonstate actors, including corporations, is on the rise, there is little consideration of anything resembling Chimerica. The nation-state, with its capitals, bureaucracies, and armies, remains the dominant framework, even as other realities are intruding.

Clearly the nation-state is not in immediate danger of being supplanted. Even in the European Union, which is gradually becoming a superstate, the individual countries remain, and they retain the loyalties of the various populations. In both China and America, the reaction to the trauma of 2008 has been to reinforce national identity rather than to erode it. The governments of both countries turned inward to focus on shoring up domestic economic activity. But as we have seen, there is an inverse relationship between the allegiance to the nation-state and its ability unilaterally to solve its problems and manage economic systems that are not only much more complex than ever but much less rooted in any one physical place. Governments—particularly powerful governments of major powers such as China and America—crave sovereignty, but increasingly, their reach exceeds their grasp.

Over the past few years, there has been a good deal of speculation about the future of the United States and its position in the world. Few argue that the first decade of the twenty-first century has been anything but grim. The millennium began for Americans with a popping of the tech bubble and steep declines in equities followed by a recession and then the attacks of 9/11. The year following, 2002, brought the scandals of Enron and WorldCom and legislation designed to prevent their recurrence, combined with the buildup to an invasion of Iraq that took place early in 2003. After a brief moment of triumphalism,

Iraq turned sour, with mounting casualties and increasing chaos. While the next years saw a housing bubble that tempered the effects of a generally anemic economy, the only real bright spot was the strength of economic activity outside the United States and in China above all. By 2007, though many U.S. companies remained hugely profitable, that wasn't trickling down to millions of workers, and then, of course, came the fall of 2008 and its aftermath.

Not surprisingly, much of the commentary about the future of the United States has focused on the changing nature of American power relative to the rest of the world. Some have seen the glass half full and emphasized the "rise of the rest" as Fareed Zakaria put it, while others have painted a bleaker picture of an America in retreat and in decline.[4] The election of Barack Obama as president in many ways represented a collective acknowledgment that the relative status of the United States in the world has shifted. Unlike the Bush administration, Obama has explicitly acknowledged that the United States can neither manage the problems of the world unilaterally nor solve its own issues in a vacuum. The rising influence and affluence of China, India, Russia, Brazil, and various petro-states has altered the landscape. So too did the singularly bad decisions of Wall Street institutions, regulatory agencies, and millions of individual Americans who pursued desires and fulfilled needs beyond their actual ability to finance them. Regardless of who was at fault—and there is blame to go around—the result was a marked decrease in the financial and cultural strength of the United States in the world at large.

There is little reason to think that these changes are anything but permanent. While some may cling to the belief that once the excesses and weaknesses of the financial system have been addressed, America will return to a status quo that has the United States dominant and the rest of the world revolving around an

American axis, that is not going to happen. The American military in conventional terms looks to remain unchallenged for decades, but the utility of military force as a coercive tool is more limited today than at any point in human history. Unless the United States is willing to destroy adversaries regardless of cost, loss of life, and loss of moral standing, its military prowess can enhance its power only if used in a way that a majority of the international community accepts. As for the other pillar of American dominance, no matter how robust the American economy is in the future, it will share space with new centers of global capital and capitalism.

Furthermore, the events of the past two years have only deepened the interdependence between China and the United States. The preponderance of the largest U.S.-listed companies are now immersed in the domestic Chinese market. While the U.S. government bailed out Fannie Mae and Freddie Mac in no small measure to satisfy Chinese interests, China continued buying U.S. Treasuries during the heart of the crisis not because the yields were good (they weren't) or because there was any reason to believe that U.S. economic activity would accelerate anytime soon (there wasn't) but simply because China could not afford for the U.S. to fail. It was placed in the unfamiliar position of being able to float the U.S. balance sheet and de facto bail out the world's largest economy. That flew in the face of decades of seeing America as both a senior partner in the free market and a powerful, threatening adversary. The Chinese leadership, wedded though it was to its sense of China being a poor, emerging nation, was able to recognize that its previous path of tending to its own affairs and leaving global governance to others was no longer feasible.

The question now is whether the United States will be able to make similar adjustments. To be fair, it has been easier for the Chinese to roll with changing circumstances. They have been less vested in the old order, and they have had the advantage of designing policies since 1989 at a slight remove from the rest of the world. While the changing global balance forced them to modify their strategies and reassess their policies, it did not require them to give up an illusion of omniscience.

For much of the latter half of the twentieth century, Americans advocated a global market anchored by free trade and capitalism. They did so in the belief that the more economic activity there is, the more there will be, and that commerce begets commerce. In that view, more centers of activity were better than a few, and only one was the least optimal situation. Markets thrive when there is competition and access, and starve when there isn't room to grow. That at least was the mantra of creating open markets and trying to construct open societies around the world.

By the beginning of the new millennium, that vision had been adopted by almost every country in the world. The last major holdout was Communist China. As we have seen, China ceased to be Communist in all but name after 1989 and embraced capitalism and many of the rules of international commerce. True, it also rejected some, at least in the short term, and refused to make its currency convertible while maintaining a closed banking system that insulated its finances from global capital flows. Nonetheless, its leadership committed China to long-term integration and openness, and enacted reforms in order to move in that direction. The slant of the reforms has been to evolve ever closer to the mores and rules of a capitalist system created not by them but by the Western world in general and by the United States in particular.

Yet success did not breed American contentment but fear and anxiety. Even before the meltdown in the credit markets, Americans had become more ambivalent about free trade, more insecure about their place in the world, and more antagonistic toward China. Some of that was a response to the excesses of free-market ideologies that privileged capital at the expense of labor and saw a powerful concentration of wealth in corporations and in the hands of an elite. Some of that anxiety was the result of the continued shift away from an economy that rested on manufacturing toward one that rests on commerce, services, and ideas. And some was simply a response to the emergence of China on the one hand and the symbiosis between China and the United States on the other, both of which represent a loss of sovereignty.

There's an inherent tension between what is best for markets and what is best for states. Much of modern history, in fact, has been the story of that tension. States have usually attempted to control commerce for their own self-interest. The United States is no exception. One reason that it was a passionate advocate for free trade and open markets in the twentieth century was because its interests were well served by a world that was more open to its capital and its companies, given that both its capital and its companies were in a dominant position and usually had the upper hand wherever they had free reign. That is why many on the left drew little distinction between U.S. military power and U.S. economic power—both served to enhance the dominance of the United States globally.

But the very success of open markets undermined that power, and now America faces a new challenge: can it adjust to a world of greater affluence in which it is one of several important pillars, or will it judge any permanent change in relative status as something negative that should be reversed? Can Americans define power differently and accept a world where they can no longer coerce others by force, whether militarily or economically? And can Americans accept the possibility that a decrease of sovereignty can also be the path to greater affluence in the future?

That is the test of Chimerica. China has its own challenge:

namely, to recognize that its size and scale mean that it cannot simply be on the receiving end of global commerce. It can no longer afford to focus predominantly on itself and its immediate neighbors and must instead assume a more active role in the world. To some extent, it already has. Not just Hu but other officials have traveled far and wide over the past few years, more than any set of Chinese leaders ever, but much of that has been to foster better relations between China and various countries that its leaders deem of strategic interest because of natural resources. Chinese leaders need to understand that the viability of the international economic system now depends in part on what China does and that it must take an active role in shaping that system going forward. Like the United States, it faces a decrease in sovereignty and more constraints on what it can unilaterally do. Unlike the United States, however, it seems more able to adjust to the world as it now is.

The Obama administration has approached these new realities with equanimity and maturity. That is one positive, and an improvement over what preceded it. There are, however, still troubling signs that many Americans do not accept either the rise of China or the symbiotic relationship that has evolved. The U.S.-China Economic and Security Review Commission, an official government body that reports annually to Congress, continues to treat China as a hostile power, inimical to American interests and intent on undermining the security of the United States. In its report at the end of 2008, the commission stated baldly that "China relies on heavy-handed government control over its economy to maintain an export advantage over other countries. The result: China has amassed nearly $2 trillion in foreign exchange and has increasingly used its hoard to manipulate currency trading and diplomatic relations with other nations." The facts are indisputable: China's government does have a strong hand in steering the economy and seeks to maintain an edge in exports, and it has amassed $2 trillion in reserves. But the adjectives belie more than the facts, and say volumes about American anxiety.

The problems the commission documents, including the efforts of Chinese intelligence agencies to gain access to sensitive technology and the myriad hidden tariffs that benefit Chinese products and companies at the expense of foreign entities, are undoubtedly real. But even staunch allies of the United States such as Israel have been guilty of espionage and attempts to obtain military secrets, while other allies such as Japan, Korea, and many European nations maintain food subsidies and duties that violate the spirit or the letter of one clause or another of the World Trade Organization. The growth of common rules and fewer barriers to trade does not mean that everyone agrees on the extent or limits or that the playing field is level. The United States has its own areas of protectionism, whether for its cotton and soybean farmers or certain industries at certain times. Trade may be increasingly free, but it is a myth that it is everywhere fair.

Many also view the increased dependence on China as a critical weakness and dangerous vulnerability. They are alarmed by the steep erosion of the U.S. manufacturing base and the stagnation of wages, as well as the ability of corporations doing business globally and in China to eliminate benefits ranging from pensions to health care. Many unions vehemently disagree that American jobs, purchasing power, and incomes are positively impacted by China, and instead see the synergy as one that helps only large corporations and harms not just most Americans but the long-term viability of American prosperity. Those voices dominated the debates over whether CNOOC could purchase Unocal, and they remain a prominent part of the national chorus.

Many in China are also uncomfortable. Some decry the rush

to market capitalism as a soulless path that will soon undermine whatever tenuous legitimacy the Communist Party retains. Others believe that the world continues to look down on China and will take advantage whenever there is an opportunity. They view the losses that Chinese state-run funds have incurred in their investments in U.S. financial institutions as proof that the West in particular still takes China for a fool. And there remain strong currents of nationalism and xenophobia in the Chinese military establishment, which views the Pacific Rim as destined to be a Chinese lake and sees the continued independence of Taiwan as well as a strong Japan as challenges to be confronted as China grows more economically powerful and confident in the years ahead.

What these voices don't recognize is that it's too late. Whether or not Chimerica is a good thing or a bad thing, it has become so embedded that undoing it would be hugely destructive and disruptive. That is more true after 2008 than it was before. They need us; we need them. The two economies have fused in the past 20 years, and not just in terms of China producing and the U.S. consuming. In fact, now and in the years ahead, the dominant feature will be China consuming and providing finance to the U.S. government and growth to U.S. companies. The only thing that can prevent that is concerted action on the part of either government to stand in the way, and the costs of that are so prohibitive that it is hard to see how that could happen.

Yes, if the economy of the United States were to deteriorate further in the years to come, there could be a wave of isolationism and protectionism. If American self-conception doesn't adapt to a changed world, if Americans cling to outdated notions of their own power and self-importance, that too could create serious obstacles to the forward progress of Chimerica in particular and to global commerce in general. And if the benefits of these trends accrue only to the few, then it is inevitable that the many will object and do what they can to arrest these developments.

For simple reasons, more obstacles are likely to come from the United States. America is now acutely aware of its vulnerabilities and still searching for new strengths. It has seen its model of deregulated capitalism nearly break under the weight of its excesses, though it is slowly digging itself out from under a mountain of leverage. Substantial stimulus spending has helped, but many still expect that once balance is restored, the United States will again assume a preeminent status. Those who argue for a more confrontational policy toward less friendly regimes have been muted, but they have hardly disappeared.

But for almost anyone over the age of 20 in China, the world today offers opportunities and freedoms that were unimaginable before 1989. That isn't about being able to walk into a KFC, or put on an Avon lipstick, or wash at night with Oil of Olay. It's about being able to travel freely, buy an apartment, move to another city, get a new job, and have some reasonable hope that with hard work and focus, you can improve your own lot and that of your family without the threat of sudden and unpredictable action by the state to take that away or make that impossible.

As for the negatives, environmental degradation is a serious and troubling development, but at least the central government recognizes that and has begun to take steps to address it, however slow progress may be. And while the lack of political freedoms and open democracy disturbs many, the true test will come when the generation of children today become adults 10 to 20 years from now. They will grow up in relative affluence and will have taken the economic openness for granted. Will they be as willing as their parents to accept Deng's trade-off? Will they make do with economic openness without political voice? Or is the notion of liberal participatory democracy a Western value system that has less resonance elsewhere? Are elections the only way people can feel free? And what of the intractable issue of Tibet and its desire for autonomy? Those are questions that only time will resolve, but to assume that the only answer is the one provided by Locke, Rousseau, and Thomas Jefferson is presumptuous, to say the least.

As for those who believe that China's growth has been built on a flimsy foundation, with too much state intervention, too much spending on big projects, too little entrepreneurial activity, insufficient innovation, and inadequate individual consumption, the fact is that no one knows the secret formula for economic success. The Washington mantra of open markets and less state activity was the orthodoxy until it proved to have some critical flaws, but no other system has proven better. If there were a clear road map to prosperity, everyone would use it. Add to the mix incomplete data and anachronistic models, and you are left with the recognition that anyone who claims certainty about the outcome of China's unique path is at best fooling himself.

As Chimerica evolves, it will almost certainly encounter other obstacles. How much sovereignty can countries lose before they try to stem the tide? Even in the European Union, which unlike the China-U.S. fusion was formed with intent and planning by the major states that created it, publics and governments have been wary about explicitly granting more power to bureaucrats in Brussels. The publics of Europe support the union and have been willing to give up some autonomy in the interests of the greater good. But even so, they have resisted the loss of national identity. For China and the United States, whose publics have never endorsed the de facto merger of the financial and economic systems, the road ahead might be much more complicated.

On top of that, there is the larger issue of whether China—not to mention India and billions of people in the emerging world—can continue on the path of rapid industrialization, consuming natural resources at a rapid clip and emitting more greenhouse gases with each passing month. It is hard to see how that growth is sustainable. What if every Chinese family and every Indian family and every Brazilian family wants a car, and appliances, and a few thousand square feet of living space, and all the bells and whistles? Where will the resources come from? The growth imperative of Western-style capitalism demands more every year, but is there a limit? Or will technology and innovation once again solve the problems that seemed so impossible to one generation and so negligible to the next? At the turn of the nineteenth century, few imagined that the world could support a population of a billion people let alone six, seven, eight, or more. There would be no way to feed them all, so the thinking went. But then came the steam engine, and then modern fertilizers and new strains of seeds, and producing enough food was no longer an issue.

These are longer-term questions for the United States, for China, and for the world. What is certain is that China has arrived, and it has done so care of a unique fusion with the world's largest economy and most dynamic source of growth, the United States. While the American century lasted less than a century, there is nothing either surprising or unusual about the emergence of China. The one constant in history is that things change, nations rise and fall, and new ones take the place of the old. That script is familiar, so familiar that it makes one wonder why the emergence of China should have been greeted with such disbelief by so many. Whatever the shape of the future, China will be a central part of it, and attempting to prevent that, derail it, or curtail it is to make tilting at windmills seem sane and reasonable. No one can stand athwart history and arrest change, though that hasn't prevented people from trying.

As for the immediate present, for all the soul-searching and wrenching disruptions caused by the first decade of the twenty-first century, we have all been living in a more stable, secure time than rhetoric or public attitudes would suggest. There is more material affluence than at any time in human history and less risk of disease or death by hunger and war than at most times in the past. China has had brief periods of stability and prosperity, but today's version trumps them all. Yes, parts of the world are plagued by violence and poverty, to be sure, but the material conditions of life are incomparably better for most.

In short, even a United States and a developed world mired in slow growth or no growth are better off than they were a hundred years ago. What has been lost in the United States is a sense that the future is what we make of it; that spirit is everywhere evident in China. It is the single most important ingredient to a thriving society, and it has been the spark that made the fusion of China and America possible. It is what led Deng to renounce the path his country was on and choose another, even though the means were at times brutal. It is what led U.S. corporations to seek opportunities in China long before the odds of success outweighed the likelihood of failure. And it is what allowed Americans for generations to reinvent themselves in the wake of their mistakes. In the end, Chimerica is an idea, a vision of the future no more or less fraught with ambiguity, uncertainty, and complications than any other idea for how the world might look. It is also an idea whose time has come, and as Victor Hugo wrote, such ideas are "greater than the tread of mighty armies." We can try to turn back the tide. Or we can embrace the world as it is, and work to fashion a future that satisfies our collective yearning for peace and prosperity.

Coda

T HE WAR WAS OVER, and the enemy had been vanquished. It had taken six years and millions of lives. It had required everything, but they never surrendered. In 1945, Nazi Germany could no longer menace the skies and threaten an invasion, and the emperor of Japan had surrendered to the Americans. The imperial outposts of Hong Kong and Singapore were once again in the fold, and the empire was intact. Great Britain had won, but the country was broke.

In order to pay for the war, Britain had spent nearly 25 percent of its national income and taken on nearly $15 billion in debt, which at the time was an extraordinary amount of money. Having managed to fund World War I with receipts from its global empire, Britain had remained a creditor nation throughout the Great Depression. The Second World War changed that forever. Global exports were severely disrupted during the war and that led to a sharp decline in income. In order to pay for the armies and air force and fleet, Britain had relied on its closest ally, which just happened to be one of the few solvent countries in the world. The United States provided not just money but materials and men, and together the two allies were able to triumph.

With its finances in tatters and infrastructure in cities such as London and Liverpool severely damaged by bombings, Britain needed cash, and it turned to the United States. It asked for an interest-free loan of $5 billion, repayable over a 50-year period. The British were certain that their friend and ally would say yes without so much as a question. Astonishingly, the Americans said no. The British responded, in so many words, that unless they received a loan, they would be unable to honor their debts and unable to import sufficient food to feed the populace. The British government was nearly insolvent, and the world's one remaining empire was in danger of default.

After heated negotiations, the United States agreed to extend Britain a loan of $3.7 billion at 2 percent interest. The fact that the British had to beg for the money and then be charged interest was galling enough. The conditions were worse. Under the terms of the agreement, the British had to terminate any tariffs and duties that privileged its colonies. It had to abide by the outlines of the Bretton Woods Agreement of 1944, which made the dollar the reference point for global exchange rates rather than the English pound sterling, and it had to allow the pound to be freely convertible against the dollar. What these conditions meant in practice was that the entire edifice of the British Empire was about to be dismantled.

That empire had relied on two things: the British navy and a closed system of trade and commerce. Britain could export to India and know that it had a market because it did not allow India to import freely from other parts of the world. By demanding that Britain open its colonies to American trade, and by forcing the British to allow exchange between dollars and pounds, the United States effectively forced Britain to end its empire. That didn't happen immediately, but it did happen swiftly. India became independent in 1947, and decolonization of the rest of the empire followed over the next decade. One British official, remarking on the dramatic change in the balance between Britain and the United States, said bluntly, "It was impossible not to be conscious that we were playing second fiddle."[1]

That was precisely what the United States government desired. While the relationship between the wartime prime minister, Winston Churchill, and the wartime president, Franklin Roosevelt, could not have been warmer, powerful advocates in the U.S. government both during and after the war wanted to see an end to imperialism and an end to the British Empire. Some of that drive was based on principle and some on power, but as much affection as there was between the countries, the United States wanted its own place on a world stage that had been dominated by Britain. With its position strengthened by the war and the British severely weakened, the United States was able to force the British to take a backseat.

By 2030 and perhaps sooner, China will have a larger economy than the United States, though it will probably be poorer on a per-person basis. Trying to guess whether the United States is a creditor or debtor more than three decades in the future would be foolish, but it is certainly possible that well before then, the United States will find that its need for foreign capital is so great that it will be forced to abide by conditions that it will find as onerous and humiliating as the British did in 1946. Just as Britain maintained an imperial system that slowly led to stagnant growth, the United States could adhere to a particular form of market capitalism that will lead to diminishing returns—and perhaps already has. That could place China in the enviable position of being able to dictate conditions, and those conditions are likely to suit China's sense of how the world should be rather than America's.

It does not have to be an either-or. China may find that its need of the United States in particular and of the world in general, for raw materials, for markets, and for things not yet known, will trump its interests as a nation-state to acquire more power at the expense of others. Even if by some unexpected twist China manages to evolve over the next three decades without losing more of its autonomy and sovereignty in a world of open markets, that doesn't mean that it will then become an enemy or that the relationship with the United States will become antagonistic. And slipping behind China will not necessarily spell the end of the United States as a viable, energetic society. In truth, as lost as Britain was for several decades after 1945, it managed to remain a prosperous country with considerable standing in the world, even if it was no longer the most powerful nation. There are worse fates than to be Britain after 1945.

But there are better fates as well. The United States still has vast resources of capital and culture, and China still has a ways to go before it has the wealth and confidence to match that. The two together are stronger than either is alone, and it will take more than the events of 2008 and 2009 to end the long march of prosperity that the United States has helped generate.

It is also true that the relationship between China and America may encounter unexpected wrinkles. If the past years have taught anything, it's to expect the unexpected. The sudden collapse of the Soviet Union came as a profound shock, as did the events of 9/11, to name just two of the black swans that took the world by surprise. While the emergence of China seems relatively certain now, the future may hold some dramatic twists. And while the fusion of the two economies is central to grasping the world today, it may of course wane or succumb to pressures in the years ahead. Other factors, whether environmental or geopolitical, may also alter the trajectory in ways that are impossible to predict but should at least be considered.

To preserve this fusion, and ensure that it provides stability and enhances global prosperity in the future, both societies will need to consider radical innovations. The United States currently deploys part of the 7th Fleet in the Pacific Rim to keep the peace and shield Taiwan. That raises the question of whether Taiwan needs shielding from China, especially given the degree to which both have been moving closer as economic ties deepen. While close financial bonds in no way preclude armed conflict, the price of that for both Taiwan and China has become much higher. As for formerly antagonistic neighbors such as Japan and China, Japan's fortunes increasingly depend on Chinese demand for its high-end equipment, and while neither bears the other much affection, they too have been drawn into a tighter embrace. In that light, the continued presence of the American fleet may be as anachronistic—and unnecessarily provocative—as the divisions once stationed in post-1945 Germany.

Both the Chinese and American governments continue to set economic policy within their borders, and while they consult one another, they treat things like interest rates, currency values, and budgets as sovereign rights that no one can or should infringe upon. But in a world where much of China's reserves are held in American assets, and where U.S. budgets are facilitated by Chinese credit, and in a world where capital flows between the two shape the domestic balances of each, it might make more sense if policy were decided in tandem. Yes, there is now an ongoing dialogue, but that is different than officials of the Federal Reserve and the People's Bank of China sitting down and deciding jointly on interest rates. As unthinkable as that is now, the fusion of the two systems may soon demand it.

Other possible shifts are no less momentous. Rather than trying to preserve and guard intellectual property against Chinese piracy, U.S. companies and by extension Washington might focus more on innovation and on access to China's markets. Rather than trying to protect secrets from possible Chinese misuse, Americans might instead accept that technology is almost impossible to monopolize, that innovation is the only edge, and that selling China almost anything they may want to buy—with a few select exceptions of weaponry—is ultimately in everyone's interest. That includes letting Chinese acquire ailing American companies that China's increasing purchasing power will allow them to purchase, provided the United States doesn't stop them. The same, of course, is true for China, which should adopt a similar approach and not put barriers in the way of American and foreign companies buying Chinese businesses.

Finally, there is the pressing issue of the environment. China and the United States are now the primary sources of greenhouse gases, and the pace of China's development ensures that this problem will become worse in the near term. Rather than engaging in a blame game of who is most responsible and who should make the most effort to curb their emissions, China and the United States need to act together, especially since a portion of China's environmental impact is the result of foreign-owned factories producing goods for American consumption. There are encouraging signs of cooperation in setting future environmental policy, but embracing the extent to which the two economies form one system would mean an even more comprehensive joint approach.

Whether these and other changes are ones that either society will adopt willingly or unwillingly, and whether they will stand in the way of even greater fusion, remains to be seen. For the United States, however, the story of how the British Empire came to end is sobering. Its demise came not at the hands of an enemy but of a supposed friend, and it happened without drama and without fanfare but with no less permanence. It suggests that the challenge for the United States in the years ahead may not be the enemies abroad, the conventional threats of aggressive, hostile states or the unconventional ones of terrorism, but instead things that the state is ill equipped to confront. Climate change is one such challenge, but changing global commerce is another. China may well drive both. The U.S. government is structured to meet all sorts of contingencies, but economic competition from rivals that it cannot coerce is not one of them.

If the United States is to avoid the fate of Great Britain, if it even can, it must reorient itself away from the military and security challenges of the twentieth century and to the economic challenges of the twenty-first. That will require not just a shift in how Americans think about the world but in how they interact with it, which will in turn demand a fundamental rethinking of the shape of the government and the national security state that emerged to meet the challenge of a Cold War and a Soviet Union that ceased to exist at precisely the same time that China began its steady rise.

Since 1989, the Chinese have had two decades to reshape their economy and their government. In those 20 years, the U.S. government changed hardly at all, until the breakdown of the financial system led to intervention in the economy on a scale unknown since the 1930s. But even the bailout of the financial system was managed with the tools of an earlier era, and by bureaucracies that were never designed to handle today's issues. And so there is a choice: try to regenerate our system with archaic tools, outmoded concepts, and government agencies from an earlier era, or channel our wellsprings of innovation and ingenuity to recasting our institutions and our thinking to fit the world we are now in. It's either that, or prepare for long evenings watching the sun set and wistfully yearning for a time that lives only in our memories. Let's hope we choose well.

Acknowledgments

My interest in the relationship between China and the United States was sparked in the aftermath of 2001, when I was working for Fred Alger Management and thinking about what investment opportunities were underappreciated at that time. Urged by Fred Alger to explore the possibility of creating a fund that would allow American and European investors to participate in the remarkable story of China's economic emergence, I began going to China and eventually helped set up a fund in the fall of 2003. My education was helped by many, including investment professionals working for Jardine Fleming Investment Management in Hong Kong, especially Man Wing Chung who later became the co-portfolio manager for the fund. I also spent valuable time with Scobie Ward and Blair Pickerell, both old hands in the somewhat complicated world of investing in China. In addition, I benefited greatly from working with Dan Chung, my comanager on the fund and now CEO of Alger, whose experience and discipline pushed me and taught me. Later on, I gained further insight from the interaction with the investment professionals at Martin Currie, especially James Chong. And during those years, I also was helped by many at Alger, including Christina Halpern and Charles Bonello.

As the idea for the book took form, I found in Scott Moyers of the Wylie Agency the ideal agent: engaged, intimately skilled in the arcane arts of book publishing, hard-nosed about business and content, and passionate. My thanks to him, and to many others at Wylie, including James Pullen in London who has worked tirelessly to see that the book has a life in Asia and the rest of the world.

Several people devoted time and energy to reading drafts at various stages—never a rewarding task, especially given my tendencies toward unusual and confounding typos, which is quite a feat in our age of spell-checking. My wife, Nicole Alger, who would likely not have read this type of book were it not for her husband, was once again a crucial guide, helping me clarify and making sure that the pace didn't lag. My father, David Karabell, was once again a perfect first hurdle; if it works for him, it has a chance of working with all lawyers. And Eric Olson gave me vital tips as someone who has been working in the trenches of business. Orville Schell and Minxin Pei both provided detailed critiques of fact and argument, and while I'm sure I managed to make mistakes in spite of their acute readings, they steered me away from the more egregious ones.

At Simon & Schuster, I have had the privilege of working with Alice Mayhew, whom I admired for years as she published author after author whose works have made an indelible impact on the world. I'm honored that she saw in this project a book she'd be willing to add to her list. David Rosenthal not only blessed the book, but was key to its title. And without the daily exertions of Karen Thompson and Roger Labrie, this would never have assumed its final form. Also at S&S, Victoria Meyer and Kelly Lynch were essential to bringing the finished product to public attention and have done so with a level of enthusiasm that any author would find gratifying. And at Greater Talent Network, Don Epstein has continued to promote the topic and helped create a wider audience.

I also owe a debt to Niall Ferguson for popularizing the term "Chimerica," which is the perfect neologism for a unique relationship. While I see that hybrid as more multifaceted and lasting than he may, he was among the earliest to identify that the interaction between the two was not a run-of-the-mill close relationship between two countries.

Finally, my wife, Nicole, and my boys, Griffin and Jasper. The boys still don't quite know what their father does, and I plan to tell them as soon as I know, but they provide a delightful and infinite excuse not to write. Nicole has never wavered in her faith in me, and in her unequivocal support. Never. She cares that her husband is following his own path infinitely more than she does about whether the world reacts well or not. And for that, I am and will forever be grateful.

Notes

INTRODUCTION: SUPERFUSION

1 The term has been used before, most notably by Niall Ferguson in his recent book, *The Ascent of Money* (Penguin Press, 2008). I use the term repeatedly throughout the book as a shorthand for the fusion of the two economies, but owe Ferguson a debt for coining the term.

CHAPTER 1: BLACK CAT, WHITE CAT

1 Quotations from various party officials in John Gittings, *The Changing Face of China: From Mao to Market* (Oxford University Press, 2006), pp. 215–216. Also, Merle Goodman, *Sowing the Seeds of Democracy in China: Political Reform in the Deng Xiaoping Era* (Harvard University Press, 1994).
2 Quoted in Joseph Fewsmith, *China Since Tiananmen: The Politics of Transition* (Cambridge University Press, 2001), p. 35.
3 On State Owned Enterprises, see James Reidel, Jing Jin, and Jian Gai, *How China Grows: Investment, Finance, and Reform* (Princeton University Press, 2007), pp. 7ff; Barry Naughton, *The Chinese Economy: Transitions and Growth* (MIT Press, 2007), pp. 297–328; Georges Desvaux, Michael Wang, and David Xu, "Spurring Performance in China's State-Owned Enterprises," *McKinsey Quarterly* (2004 Special Edition, "China Today").
4 "From Rags to Cigarette Lighters (and Dildos and Property too)— Wenzhou," *Economist* (June 4, 2005).
5 Laurence Brahm, *Zhu Rongji: The Transformation of Modern China* (Wiley, 2002); Bruce Gilley, *Tiger on the Brink: Jiang Zemin and China's New Elite* (University of California Press, 1998).

6 Yang Guohua and Cheng Jin, "The Process of China's Accession to the WTO," *Journal of International Economic Law* (June 2001), pp. 297ff; Joseph Fewsmith, "The Political and Social Implication of China's Accession to the WTO," *China Quarterly* (2001), pp. 573ff.

CHAPTER 2: THE NEW ECONOMY AND THE
NOT-SO-NEW ECONOMY

1 One of the best articulations of these changes was penned by the CEO of IBM. Samuel J. Palmisano, "The Globally Integrated Enterprise," *Foreign Affairs* (May 2006).

2 M. Corey Goldman, "Brave New Economy," CNNfn.com (May 22, 2000).

3 For a sharp, left-leaning critique of the economy of the 1990s, see Robert Kuttner, *The Squandering of America* (Knopf, 2008). Also, Kevin Phillips, *Wealth and Democracy: A Political History of the American Rich* (Broadway Books, 2002), and, of course, Joseph Stiglitz, *Globalization and Its Discontents* (Norton, 2002).

4 Transition memos to the secretary of state from December 1996, cited in the superb account of the 1990s by two former staffers. Derek Chollet and James Goldgeier, *America Between the Wars: From 11/9 to 9/11—The Misunderstood Years Between the Fall of the Berlin Wall and the Start of the War on Terror* (Public Affairs, 2008), pp. 150-151.

CHAPTER 3: SO GOOD, YOU SUCK YOUR FINGERS

1 David Schweisberg, "So Good You Suck Your Fingers," United Press International (November 13, 1987); David Halley, "At Seat of Communist Power, Kentucky Fried Chicken 'Finger-Lickin' Good' Comes to Beijing," *Los Angeles Times* (November 13, 1987); "Chicken for China," editorial, *Boston Globe* (November 15, 1987); Carlye Adler, "Colonel Sanders' March on China," *Time* (November 17, 2003).

2 For the history of KFC in China, see the in-depth case study: Paul Beamish and Allen Morrison, "Kentucky Fried Chicken in China," *Ivey Business Journal* (November 2000). Also, Eriberto Lozada, "Globalized Childhood: Kentucky Fried Chicken in Beijing," in James Watson, et al., eds., *The Cultural Politics of Food and Eating*

(Blackwell, 2005). There is also considerable discussion of KFC in James Watson, ed., *Golden Arches East: McDonald's in East Asia* (Stanford University Press, 2006). And, of course, hundreds of newspaper articles throughout the 1990s.

3 Leo Paul Dana, "Kentucky Fried Chicken," *British Food Journal* (Vol. 101, No. 5/6, 1999), pp. 493–495.
4 Alan Kirschembaum, "The 'Original Recipe' for International Success," *Lane Report* (May 1, 1992).
5 Joseph Kahn, "Decision to Delink Trade, Human Rights Relieves U.S. Firms, Chinese Officials," *Wall Street Journal* (May 31, 1994), p. A12; Amy Borrus, et al., "China Gates Swing Open—U.S. Companies May Well Become Key Partners," *BusinessWeek* (June 13, 1994); Mark O'Neill, "KFC Announces $200 Million Investment in China," Reuters News (May 28, 1994).
6 Joe Studwell, *The China Dream: The Quest for the Last Great Untapped Market on Earth* (Grove Press, 2002), argues that China today is still a trap for Western businesses. An alternate view is James McGregor, *One Billion Customers: Lessons from the Front Lines of Doing Business in China* (Free Press/Wall Street Journal Books, 2005).

CHAPTER 4: AVON COMES CALLING

1 Andrew Tanzer, "Ding-Dong, Capitalism Calling," *Forbes* (October 14, 1991). The quotation at the beginning of the chapter comes from George White, "Avon Will Go Calling on China Despite Political Controversy," *Los Angeles Times* (June 18, 1990), p. 3.
2 Kathy Chenault, "Avon Calling, This Time to Populous China," Associated Press (November 22, 1990); Drew Wilson, "Avon Ladies Calling in China Provinces," *Crain's New York Business* (September 13, 1993).
3 Preston quoted in Laura Klepacki, *Avon: Building the World's Premier Company for Women* (Wiley, 2005), p. 135.
4 Catherine Sampson, "Chinese Women Become a Big Market for Beauty in a Jar," *International Herald Tribune* (May 6, 1994).
5 "Firms Find How to Negotiate Mainland Maze," *South China Morning Post* (November 10, 1994).
6 "China Slams the Door on the Avon Lady," Reuters (April 24, 1998); "China Halts Honeymoon," *Cosmetics Insiders' Report* (May 18, 1998).

7 Elizabeth Croll, *China's New Consumers: Social Development and Domestic Demand* (Routledge, 2006); Jonathan Garner, *The Rise of the Chinese Consumer: Theory and Evidence* (Wiley, 2005).

8 These reforms began in earnest in the 1980s. See Nicholas Lardy, *Foreign Trade and Economic Reform in China 1978–1990* (Cambridge University Press, 1992).

9 See Wang Hui, *China's New Order*, Theodore Huters, ed. (Harvard University Press, 2003).

CHAPTER 5: UP, UP, AND AWAY

1 Fred Smith interview conducted by the Academy of Achievement, May 23, 1998, at www.achievement.org/autodoc/page/smi0int-1. Fred Smith interview with Charles Fishman, *Fast Money* (Issue 47, May 2001); online interview with Fred Smith, *BusinessWeek* (September 20, 2004), at www.businessweek.com/magazine/content/04_38/b3900032_mz072.htm. Also see Fred Smith testimony to Congress, July 9, 1998. For a glowing insider account, see Roger Frock, *Changing How the World Does Business: FedEx's Incredible Journey to Success* (Berrett-Koehler Publishers, 2006).

2 Lardy, *Foreign Trade and Economic Reform in China, 1978–1990*.

3 For the comparison between UPS and FedEx, see Douglas Blackmon and Diane Brady, "Focus on the U.S.: FedEx and UPS Take Different Routes in Campaign to Capture Chinese Market," *Wall Street Journal Europe* (April 9, 1998).

4 Data on foreign direct investment in the 1990s from Jonathan Story, *China: The Race to Market* (Prentice Hall, 2003), chapter 8.

5 Janet Matthews, "Express Delivery—DHL Delivers the Goods," *China Economic Review* (September 1, 1996).

6 Details on roads from the World Bank, see info.worldbank.org/etools/reducingpoverty/docs/newpdfs/case-summ-China-ICT.pdf. Also, the entertaining Jim Rogers brings the contrast between China roads in the late 1980s in Jim Rogers, *A Bull in China* (Random House, 2007), pp. 104ff.

CHAPTER 6: FREE TRADE AND ITS DISCONTENTS

1 Interview with China's Zhu Rongji, *Wall Street Journal* (April 6, 1999), p. A23. Also see Lawrence Brahm, *Zhu Rongji and the Transformation of Modern China*, passim. Zhu also had several constructive meetings with the influential chairman of the Federal Reserve, Alan Greenspan, briefly alluded to in Alan Greenspan, *The Age of Turbulence* (Penguin Press, 2007), pp. 294ff.

2 Bruce Einhorn, "China: After the Rage: Damage to U.S. Ties May Last for Years," *BusinessWeek* (May 24, 1999).

3 Helene Cooper, "China's Bid to Join WTO Would Face Bipartisan Opposition in U.S. Senate," *Wall Street Journal* (March 15, 1999), p. A20; Helene Cooper, "No Deal," *Wall Street Journal* (April 9, 1999), p. A1; Maurice Meisner, "China-U.S. Relations: A Habit of Distrust, Mutual Racism, and Arrogance Undermine Ties," *Los Angeles Times* (May 30, 1999); Carlota Gall, "Crisis in the Balkans: Belgrade; Embassy Attack Followed by Defiance Toward NATO," *New York Times* (May 10, 1999).

4 From Ian Cuthbertson, "Chasing the Chimera: Securing the Peace," *World Policy Journal* (July 1, 1999); Johanna McGeary, "The Cox Report/The Fallout," *Time* (June 7, 1999).

5 Quoted in Dele Olojede, "Resentment on the Rise," *Newsday* (May 16, 1999).

6 Dexter Roberts, "Welcome to the Club," *BusinessWeek* (November 29, 1999); Yang Guohua and Cheng Jin, "The Process of China's Accession to the WTO," *Journal of International Economic Law*, Vol. 4, Issue 2 (June 2001); Jonathan Story, *China: The Race to Market*, pp. 140–160.

7 "Labor Unions Ready to Fight Hard to Keep China Out of WTO," *Seattle Post-Intelligencer* (December 9, 1999); Maria La Ganga, "WTO Summit: Protest in Seattle Infiltrates Campaign 2000 Politics," *Los Angeles Times* (December 2, 1999).

CHAPTER 7: DATA DUPED

1 See these marvelous books: Eric Beinhocker, *The Origin of Wealth: Evolution, Complexity, and the Radical Remaking of Economics* (Harvard University Press, 2006); David Warsh, *Knowledge and the Wealth*

of Nations: A Story of Economic Discovery (Norton, 2006); Nassim Nicholas Taleb, *The Black Swan: The Impact of the Highly Improbable* (Random House, 2007).

CHAPTER 8: STILL WATERS, RUNNING DEEP

1 See Pietra Rivoli, *The Travels of a T-shirt in the Global Economy* (Wiley, 2005).
2 Many of the trade figures for China and the United States as well as China and the world can be found on the World Trade Organization Web site, at www.wto.org/english/thewto_e/countries_e/china_e.htm. Also see the Web site of the U.S.-China Business Council, which compiles the trade data from the U.S. Census Bureau and the Department of Commerce, among other sources, at www.uschina.org/statistics/tradetable.html. Also, various essays in David Shambaugh, ed., *Power Shift: China and Asia's New Dynamic* (University of California Press, 2005).
3 Amy Gardner, "Layoffs Prime Election Issue," *News & Observer* (October 22, 2002).
4 David Lampton, *The Three Faces of Chinese Power: Might, Money and Minds* (University of California Press, 2008), p. 96. Also see official data from the U.S. Treasury Department at www.treas.gov/tic.
5 Wang Hui, *China's New Order*, edited by Theodore Huters (Harvard University Press, 2003); also, Joseph Fewsmith, pp. 110ff.
6 Jack Perkowski, *Managing the Dragon: How I'm Building a Billion Dollar Business in China* (Crown Business, 2008); Tim Clissold, *Mr. China* (HarperBusiness, 2004).

CHAPTER 9: WOW, YAO

1 "China's Telco Titan Grows," Red Herring.com (February 18, 2006).
2 Doug Young, "Piracy Disputes Still Tough to Resolve in China Courts," *USA Today* (March 5, 2004); Chris Buckley, "Rapid Growth of China's Huawei Has Its High-Tech Rivals on Guard," *New York Times* (October 6, 2003); William Mellor, "A Chinese Challenger Takes On Cisco in Networking Equipment," *International Herald Tribune* (November 5, 2003).
3 Gabriel Kahn, "Factory Fight," *Wall Street Journal* (December 19,

2002). Clyde Prestowitz, *Three Billion New Capitalists: The Great Shift of Wealth and Power to the East* (Basic Books, 2005), pp. 62–64.

4 Philip Pan, "Yao Holding Court in China," *Washington Post* (December 13, 2002); Brook Larmer, *Operation Yao Ming* (Gotham Books, 2005). Also, Philip Pan, *Out of Mao's Shadow* (Simon & Schuster, 2008).

5 Hung Huang Hung, "Safety in Shopping," *Newsweek* (October 28, 2002); Elisabeth Croll, *China's New Consumers*, pp. 204ff.; Jonathan Garner, *The Rise of the Chinese Consumer*, passim; research reports prepared by CLSA, under the direction of Melissa Cook, "Brands in China," November 2007; "Mr. & Mrs. Asian Consumer," November 2007; Louis Uchitelle, "When the Chinese Consumer Is King," *New York Times* (December 14, 2003).

CHAPTER 10: THE GREAT WALL AND THE GOLD RUSH

1 Keith Bradsher, "China Anxiously Seeks Soft Landing," *New York Times* (May 7, 2004); Andy Xie, Morgan Stanley Chief Asia Economist note to clients August 10, 2004; Mark Gongloff, "China: When Hot Turns Sour," CnnMoney.com (May 19, 2004); Brian Bremner, Dexter Roberts, and Frederik Balfour, "Headed for a Crisis?" *BusinessWeek* (May 3, 2004).

2 Robert Buderi and Gregory Huang, *Guanxi (The Art of Relationships): Microsoft, China, and Bill Gates's Plan to Win the Road Ahead* (Simon & Schuster, 2006); James McGregor, *One Billion Customers: Lessons from the Front Lines of Doing Business in China* (Free Press/Wall Street Journal Books, 2005); *Harvard Business Review on Doing Business in China* (HBR Press, 2004).

3 Franklin Allen, Jun Qian, and Meijun Qian, "China's Financial System: Past, Present, and Future," in Loren Brandt and Thomas Rawski, eds., *China's Great Economic Transformation* (Cambridge University Press, 2008), pp. 506–569. For a much more negative view, see Minxin Pei, *China's Trapped Transition*, passim. Another interesting overview is Yasheng Huang, *Capitalism with Chinese Characteristics* (Cambridge University Press, 2008). Also, Kenneth DeWoskin and Kenneth Chung, "What's Ahead for China's Financial Markets," *PricewaterhouseCoopers Journal* (December 2002).

4 Thomas Deng, "China Financial Monitor" (Report of Credit Suisse, January 6, 2004). Also, see "Non-performing," *Economist*

(March 20, 2004). Stephen Harner, "Privatizing China's Banks," *Asian Wall Street Journal* (November 25, 2002).

5 Clay Chandler, "Wall Street's War for China," *Fortune* (May 17, 2006); Bei Hu, "Morgan Stanley Leading the Way in Chinese IPOs," Bloomberg News (October 3, 2007); Allen Wan, "Interest in China Stocks on the Rise," CBSMarketwatch (February 2, 2004); "A Warning on China: Interview with Rudolph-Raid Younes," *Money* (June 2004); Mark Clifford and Frederik Balfour, "Open Season for Banks," *BusinessWeek* (September 9, 2002); Burton Malkiel and Patricia Taylor, *From Wall Street to the Great Wall: How Investors Can Profit from China's Booming Economy* (Norton, 2008).

6 For the Tony Soprano comment, see David Smick, *The World Is Curved: Hidden Dangers to the Global Economy* (Portfolio, 2008); also see Niall Ferguson, *The Ascent of Money* (2008).

CHAPTER 11: BENEDICT ARNOLD GOES TO MISSISSIPPI

1 Pete Engardio and Dexter Roberts, "The China Price," *Business-Week* (December 6, 2004); Alexandra Harney, *The China Price: The True Cost of Chinese Competitive Advantage* (Penguin Press, 2008). On job loss in America, see Louis Uchitelle, *The Disposable American* (Knopf, 2006); Martin Baily and Diana Farrell, "Is Your Job Headed for Bangalore?" *Milken Institute Review* (Fourth Quarter 2004). Also, Andrew Ross, *Fast Boat to China: Corporate Flight and the Consequences of Free Trade* (Pantheon, 2006).

2 Frederick Balfour, "Another Big Reason China Won't Revalue," *BusinessWeek* (October 6, 2003); David Hale and Lyric Hughes Hale, "China Takes Off," *Foreign Affairs* (November/December 2003).

3 Eduardo Porter, "Looking for a Villain and Finding One in China," *New York Times* (April 18, 2004); Matt Forney, "Tug-of-War over Trade," *Time* (December 22, 2003).

4 John Hood, "Bush's Boudoir Tax," *National Review* (November 21, 2003); David Lynch, "As Quotas End, China Stands Ready to Be Clothing Giant," *USA Today* (December 22, 2004).

5 Matthew Forney, "How Nike Figured Out China," *Time* (October 17, 2004); Ryan Levesque, "Nike in China: Strategic Planning," *Harvard Business School Case Study Analysis* (December 2003).

6 Weiner Development, "China Field Trip," *Weiner Report* (Spring

2005); Charles Fishman, *The Wal-Mart Effect* (Penguin Books, 2006); Clay Chandler, "The Great Wal-Mart of China," *Fortune* (July 25, 2005); Dorinda Elliott, "Wal-Mart Nation," *Time* (July 19, 2005); Jonathan Watts, "Wal-Mart Leads Charge in Race to Grab a Slice of China," *Guardian* (March 25, 2006); Eruck Basker and Pham Hoang Van, "Wal-Mart as Catalyst to U.S.-China Trade" (April 2008), academic paper online at ssrn.com/abstract =987583.

7 Robert Scott, "The Wal-Mart Effect: Its Chinese Imports Have Displaced Nearly 200,000 U.S. Jobs," *Economic Policy Institute Issue Brief #235* (June 2007).

8 Interview with Caterpillar group president Stu Levenick, *China People's Daily* (December 21, 2007); Oril Gadiesh, Philip Leung, and Till Vestring, "The Battle for China's Good-Enough Market," *Harvard Business Review* (September 2007).

9 Ilan Brat, "Rebuilding After a Catastrophe," *Wall Street Journal* (May 19, 2008).

CHAPTER 12: A NOT-SO-HARMONIOUS RISE

1 "China's CNOOC Drops Bid for Unocal," *Associated Press* (August 2, 2005); Edmund Andrews, "China's Oil Setback: The Politics," *New York Times* (August 3, 2005).

2 "China's Peaceful Rise," *Economist* (June 24, 2004); Evan Medeiros, "China Debates Its 'Peaceful Rise' Strategy," *YaleGlobal* (June 22, 2004).

3 Ling Zhijun, *The Lenovo Affair: The Growth of China's Computer Giant and Its Takeover of IBM-PC*, trans. Martha Avery (Wiley, 2005); John Spooner and Michael Kanellos, "IBM Sells PC Group to Lenovo," CNET (December 8, 2004).

4 Paul Reynolds, "China's 'Peaceful Rise' Running into Criticism," BBCnews.com (February 1, 2007); Jina-ye Wang and Abdoulaye Bio-Tchane, "Africa's Burgeoning Ties with China," *F&D: Finance and Development: A Quarterly Magazine of the IMF* (March 2008); Statement of Thomas Christensen, Deputy Assistant Secretary of State for U.S. Policy, Before the Subcommittee on African Affairs of the Senate Foreign Relations Committee, June 5, 2008 (www.state.gov/p/eap/rls/rm/2008/06/105556.htm). Indicative of a more paranoid take are Andrew Malone, "How China's Taking

Over Africa, and Why the West Should Be Very, Very Worried," *Daily Mail* (July 18, 2008); Peter Navarro, *The Coming China Wars* (FT Press, 2008); Stephanie Kleine-Ahlbrandt and Andrew Small, "China's New Dictatorship Diplomacy," *Foreign Affairs* (January/ February 2008).

5 See research reports prepared by Calyon/CLSA Securities: Melissa Cook, et al. "Capital Goods: Beyond Elbow Grease: Lifting the Chinese Economy" (October 17, 2007); Melissa Cook, et al. "China Consumer: An American Diet: U.S. Products on Chinese Shelves" (July 16, 2007); Andy Rothman, "Harmonious Society: China's Economic and Political Future," (Summer 2007). On GE and intellectual property, see James Kynge, *China Shakes the World* (Houghton Mifflin, 2006), pp. 118–119.

6 Tian Yang, "Toyota Tops GM China Car Sales, May Take Global Title," Bloomberg (October 21, 2008); James MacKintosh and Richard McGregor, "A Leap Over the Cliff: Are the Big Profits to Be Made in China Blinding Foreign Carmakers to the Risks Ahead?" *Financial Times* (August 25, 2003); Joseph Kahn, "Made in China, Bought in China," *New York Times* (January 5, 2003).

CHAPTER 13: THE (IN)GLORIOUS OLYMPICS

1 "What the Games Will Do for China," *BusinessWeek* (July 30, 2001).

2 For an insightful examination of the crisis, see Richard Baum, "Beijing Recoils Under the Global Spotlight," *Far Eastern Economic Review* (April 2008).

3 Ambassador Sha Zukang, "Poverty Alleviation Remains Priority of Human Rights," *Xinhua News* (March 19, 2004).

4 Andrew Jacobs, "China Eases Internet Restrictions for Foreign Journalists," *International Herald Tribune* (August 1, 2008). For the best expose of China's self-defeating Internet policies, see James Fallows, "Their Own Worst Enemy," *Atlantic* (November 2008).

5 See Elizabeth Economy, *The River Runs Black* (Cornell University Press, 2004).

6 See Pew findings released in July 2008 at pewglobal.org/ reports/display.php?ReportID=261. See Chicago Council from the summer of 2008 at www.thechicagocouncil.org/UserFiles/ File/POS_Topline%20Reports/POS%202008/2008%20POS_ Chinas%20Rise.pdf.

7 For Eurobarometer surveys conducted under the official auspices of the European Commission, see ec.europa.eu/publications/booklets/eu_documentation/05/txt_en.pdf.

8 Edward Wong, "Booming, China Faults the U.S. Policy on the Economy," *New York Times* (June 17, 2008).

CHAPTER 14: AN IDEA WHOSE TIME HAS COME

1 Various Wall Street firms tried to estimate the impact. See Casandra Choi, "Withstanding the U.S. Slowdown," Citibank research, January 29, 2008; Timothy Bond, "Measuring Impact of U.S. Slowdown on China," Merrill Lynch research, January 25, 2008; Hong Liang, "China: Recoupling, Rebalancing, and Recharging," Goldman Sachs research, November 29, 2007.

2 Remarks of Lou Jiwei, chief executive of the China Investment Corporation, at the Clinton Global Initiative in Hong Kong, December 3, 2008, reported by Keith Bradshser, *New York Times* (December 4, 2008).

3 *Global Trends 2025: A World Transformed*, published by the National Intelligence Council (November 2008), at www.dni.gov/nic/NIC_2025_project.html.

4 Fareed Zakaria, *The Post American World* (Norton, 2008); Andrew Bacevich, *The Limits of Power* (Metropolitan Books, 2008); Parag Khanna, *The Second World* (Random House, 2008).

CODA

1 Evelyn Shuckburgh quoted in Lawrence James, *The Rise and Fall of the British Empire* (St. Martin's Press, 1994), p. 521.

Index

Dollar, U.S., 204, 215, 246, 280, 302
Dorgan, Byron, 237
Dot-com businesses, 45, 47

Eastern Europe, 152, 160
Eaton, 247
Economic decline. *See also* Financial crisis of 2008–09; Recession
  in Asia, 92–93, 116, 119
  in China, 168
  in Japan, 164, 184–85, 198, 199
  in Russia, 35, 92, 120
  in U.S., 12, 160–61
Economic growth
  in China, 109, 164, 228, 286
  in Japan, 48
  in U.S., 37–38, 39, 161
Economic reform (China), 17–36
  acceleration of, 93–95
  agricultural, 17
  under Deng, 17–23, 25–26, 29–30, 31, 101, 111
  domestic companies and, 23–24
  internal debate over, 19–20
  magnitude and speed of, 25–26
  market-state relationship in, 18–19, 23
  regional variations in effects of, 18
Economics, 137–52
  emergence as a profession, 142–43
  equilibrium notion in, 145–46
  financial institutions and, 146–47
  government institutions and, 147–48
  "laws" of, 146
  macro, 142, 145

nation-state in, 141, 142, 144–45, 146, 151, 288–89
  outmoded indicators in, 141–53
  radical change and, 150–51
  regional variations and, 140–41
  as a science, 143–44
Economic Strategy Institute, 218
Economist, 189
Economy. *See* Economic decline; Economic growth; Economic reform (China); Economics; Inflation; Interest rates; New Economy
Embassy bombing, Chinese, 46–47, 124–26, 166
Emerson Electric, 189
Employment. *See* Labor; Outsourcing; Unemployment; Wages
Enron, 167, 289
Entitlement spending, 148
Environmental issues, 10, 250–51, 269–71, 297, 306
Ericsson, 173, 248
Estée Lauder, 82, 249
Eurobarometer surveys, 274
Europe, 160, 168
  Eastern, 152, 160
  mercantilism in, 158
  trade with China, 155
European Union (EU), 3, 24, 36, 42, 47, 120, 131, 133, 134, 199, 228, 242, 298
  CNOOC and, 237
  discontent with, 274
  nation-state principle in, 256–57, 289
  Olympics and, 262
  per capita income in, 183
  trade with China, 216
  Turkey entry into, 152

About the Author

Zachary Karabell is president of River Twice Research, where he analyzes economic and political trends, and is a senior adviser for Business for Social Responsibility. He received a Ph.D. from Harvard University and was formerly chief economist, portfolio manager, and president of a New York–based investment firm. He is the author of *Parting the Desert*, *The Last Campaign*, and *Peace Be Upon You*. He is a regular commentator on CNBC and a contributor to *Newsweek*, *The Wall Street Journal*, the *Los Angeles Times*, *The New York Times*, *Foreign Affairs*, and *The Washington Post*.